# Glorious Causes

# Glorious Causes

The Grand Theatre of
Political Change, 1789 to 1833

JULIA SWINDELLS

OXFORD

UNIVERSITY PRESS

# OXFORD
## UNIVERSITY PRESS

Great Clarendon Street, Oxford OX2 6DP
Oxford University Press is a department of the University of Oxford.
It furthers the University's objective of excellence in research, scholarship,
and education by publishing worldwide in

Oxford New York

Athens Auckland Bangkok Bogotá Buenos Aires Calcutta
Cape Town Chennai Dar es Salaam Delhi Florence Hong Kong Istanbul
Karachi Kuala Lumpur Madrid Melbourne Mexico City Mumbai
Nairobi Paris São Paulo Shanghai Singapore Taipei Tokyo Toronto Warsaw
and associated companies in Berlin Ibadan

Oxford is a registered trade mark of Oxford University Press
in the UK and in certain other countries

Published in the United States
by Oxford University Press Inc., New York

British Library Cataloguing in Publication Data
Data available

Library of Congress Cataloging in Publication Data
Data available
ISBN 0-19-818729-7

1 3 5 7 9 10 8 6 4 2

Typeset in Times by
Cambrian Typesetters, Frimley, Surrey
Printed in Great Britain
on acid-free paper by
T.J. International Ltd,
Padstow, Cornwall

# *Acknowledgements*

I thank Brian Ridgers for invaluable assistance with research and with discussion, particularly of the 1832 Select Committee on Dramatic Literature and of George Colman the Younger's *Inkle and Yarico*. In relation to the latter, I extend thanks to all those involved in the 1997 production of the play at Cambridge Festival Theatre, particularly to Simon Godwin, Emma Stenning, and Peter Raby. I am grateful to Ben Bradnack, Jacky Bratton, John Gray, Sue McPherson, Joan Swindells, and Belinda Baker, Matthew Hollis, and Sophie Goldsworthy at Oxford University Press, together with four advisers to the Press, for comment, variously, on the structure and content of the book.

Discussions of illustrations with Ben Heasman have been exhilarating and illuminating; his ideas have been influential, particularly on the cover design, which derives from an original motif by him. Cas Bulmer has been generous in the personal loan of exciting illustrative material, particularly of *Melodrama* (1981), edited by Louis James and Stephen Lutman, Faculty of Humanities, University of Kent, and *Print and the People 1819–1851* (1976) edited with an introduction and commentary by Louis James (Penguin, Harmondsworth).

The following items are reprinted by permission of the British Library: frontispiece illustration from Moncrieff's *Reform* (shelf mark: 643a15) (Pl. 1); frontispiece illustration from *Obi; Or, Three-Fingered Jack* (shelfmark: 11770bbb4) (Pl. 8). The following items are reprinted by permission of the Syndics of Cambridge University Library: frontispiece illustration from Colman's *John Bull* (Pl. 5); David Wilkie's *The Rent Day* and *Distraining for Rent* from *The Wilkie Gallery* (George Virtue, London) (Pls. 11 and 12); *Florizel* and *Perdita* from memoirs of Mary Robinson (1894 edition) (Pl. 13); *Am I not a woman and a sister?* from Robin Blackburn, *The Overthrow of Colonial Slavery* (Verso, London, 1988) (Pl. 14); *Political Showman* (Pl. 4); *The Reformers' Attack on the Old Rotten Tree* (Pl. 3); *A Factory* Victim (Pl. 9); *The Riot* (Pl. 2). Géricault's *La traite des nègres*, (Pl. 6) is reprinted by permission of the École Nationale Supérieure des Beaux–Arts, Paris. *Am I not a man and a brother?* (Pl. 7) is reprinted by courtesy of Wisbech and Fenland Museum. De Loutherbourg's *Coalbrookdale by Night*, 1801 (Pl. 10), is reprinted by permission of the Science and Society Picture Library. *The OP Spectacles* and *The NP Spectacles* (Pls. 15 and 16) are reprinted by permission of the Victoria and Albert Museum Picture Library.

Photographers and librarians have proved to be extremely helpful and congenial people, and I thank them for strenuous efforts put into meeting deadlines; not all names are known to me, but I include Ruth Long and Tony Harper at Cambridge University Library, Janice Burr at the British Library, Martin Durrant and Mike Bergin at the Victoria and Albert Museum, Clare Newman at the Science Museum, Robert Bell at Wisbech and Fenland Museum, and Françoise Portelance at The École Nationale Supérieure des Beaux-Arts.

# Contents

# List of Plates

# Setting the Scene

In 1812, Hannah Smith, 54 years old and from Manchester, was sent to the gallows for her leading role in rioting against the prices of potatoes, milk, and butter—products which she had also been selling off cheaply in the streets. She had apparently prided herself for a number of years on her managerial skills in producing a crowd and staging such demonstrations. Food riots were one of the few means by which women had been able to express resistance publicly for over two hundred years. Hanging was not the most customary punishment for involvement in rioting, particularly of women, who were rarely armed with any weapons. Hannah Smith was probably hung as much for her refusal of deference and for her objection to the authorities as for her involvement in riot *per se*.[1]

Unlike most of the individuals whose contributions to theatre and politics are examined in this book, Hannah Smith was not a playwright, theatre manager, politician, or prominent political radical. We do not know what her views were, or even if she had any, on the issues of parliamentary reform, the abolition of slavery, the factory movement, or the agrarian situation, although we might make a guess at what she thought of women's rights. We do not know if she was

---

[1] E. P. Thompson *Customs in Common* (Merlin Press, London, 1991) widely cited in my concluding chapter, first drew my attention to Hannah Smith, in the chapter 'Moral Economy Reviewed'. Thompson cites Malcolm I. Thomis and Jennifer Grimmett, *Women in Protest, 1800–1850* (1982), for more about Hannah Smith, including citation of the passing of judgement at Lancaster Assizes, 'You, Hannah Smith . . . were one of the most determined enemies to good order, and it is fit to be understood, that sex is not entitled to any mitigation of punishment, when the crime is of such a nature as to deserve it . . . [Let others] take warning from your example and observe that they cannot with impunity conspire to disturb the public tranquility' (*sic*) (44). Thompson substantiates the idea that Hannah Smith's 'crime' was lack of deference; such women, writes Thompson with cryptic irony, would hardly have attracted patrons who might have rallied to their defence; 'What clergyman was likely to give a character reference, what nobleman to intercede, on behalf of such viragos?' (334). See Ruth and Edmund Frow (eds.) *Political Women 1800–1850*, (Pluto Press, London, 1989), for accounts by and of more women like Hannah Smith.

literate or if she ever went to a theatre. Nevertheless, what she represents captures something very important for my account. In so far as Hannah Smith achieved notoriety, it was not for physical violence or organized militancy, but for the staging of public objection and the insistence on clamour in the refusal to suffer privately poverty, hunger, and complaint. Her crimes were those of contestation: she shouted back, incited others to do the same, and insisted on making collective objection visible to the authorities. Above all, she made a public spectacle of the subject of private suffering. In many ways, such actions constitute the defining relations between the politics and theatricality of late Georgian Britain.

I have set out to demonstrate that, from 1789, under the strong influences of the French Revolution, until the Emancipation Act in 1833, theatricality was indispensable to the attempt by various agents, groups, and movements, whether successful or not, to produce a less hierarchical social order and a more democratic form of representative government than had existed previously in Britain. Definitions of the term theatrical will surface in any given context, but can be broadly interpreted as embracing a consciousness of performance involving actor, audience, and setting in a staged event, whether rehearsed or not.

I use the language of glorious causes to prioritize the individual and collective struggles of those involved in political and theatrical action. Their commitment to social and ideological causes seems to me both manifest and of paramount significance in this history. It is also important that this is the vocabulary of the age. Speakers and commentators are many in claiming that events and struggles *were* glorious to those involved, and that they did feel themselves to be participating in one or more cause. However, I am not committed to what has been rather reductively described as a Whiggish account of historical progress as success story, of lack of achievement being overtaken by achievement, of effort leading to triumph, cause leading to glory. Nor am I committed to a mode of historical interpretation which involves a simple narrative of cause and consequence: this followed from here to there, this led from this to that.

By beginning my account with events in Britain in 1832, rather than with 1789 and the French Revolution, or 1833 and the Emancipation Act, I make deliberate play with chronology in order to establish the book's priorities and emphases. 1832 stands as an important real and symbolic moment, independently of those events which predate it, in that as a crucial year for reform legislation in relation to theatre as well as parliamentary franchise—the year of the Dramatic Literature Act and the Reform Act—it is a defining one for the relations between theatre and politics in Britain. The glorious causes of parliamentary reform, abolition of the slave trade, factory and agrarian reform, and of women's rights, are not, of course, less important, and it is possible that any single one of them could have provided a good way of focusing this particular set of concerns. What *is* more important, though, is both the significance of these causes as independent struggles and the many important interconnections between them, across the politics and theatre of this history.

In focusing primarily on the *relationship* between theatre and politics, I have inevitably prioritized the principle of interconnection over an investment in either domain distinctly. I have, however, made certain alignments in relation to genres. In the case of theatre, I have offered commentary on some playtexts the existence or political content of which may have been unknown to some readers.[2] In the case of political movements, I have looked at the autobiographical writings of some of those who could be described, in theatrical language, as protagonists and central players. My interest is specifically in the autobiographer as a political activist, an actor in a cause.[3] Autobiographical testimony is therefore explored for what it might reveal about the activist's representation of the relationship between individual political action and collective mobilization of the political movement, and the theatrical character of this representation. The playtext, by comparison, signifies the collective character of enactment itself, and I have looked to it for an illumination of the political character of performance and assembly in late

---

[2] I have also signalled possibilities for performance in relation to a range of plays, published or unpublished, which some readers may feel are ready for revival for that purpose.

[3] Jurgen Habermas 'Further Reflections on the Public Sphere', trans. Thomas Burger, in Craig Calhoun (ed.), *Habermas and the Public Sphere* (MIT, Cambridge, Mass., 1998) for theorization of the public sphere in the late 18th c. Essays in the collection particularly pertinent to the relations between the individual and the public are Michael Warner, 'The Mass Public and the Mass Subject" and Nancy Fraser, 'Rethinking the Public Sphere'. Further references to theorizing of the public and the private, and to autobiographical theory, occur in the main text, although it is not within the terms of my project for such references to be extensive.

Georgian theatre. In each case, I have attempted to demonstrate the width and scale of the spirit of reform, its theatrical characteristics, and the participation of political actors and audiences not always credited with involvement.[4]

In arriving at an emphasis on the defining relations between politics and theatre, and attempting to give parity to each category, I have inevitably had to sacrifice detailed commentary on important aspects of both domains. I have not given as much time or acquired as much expertise in relation to performance history, either theoretically or in relation to individual plays, as I might have done had I been less interested in political ideas articulated outside as well as inside theatre.[5] I have not devoted as much attention to elements of playtexts which would be crucial to performance as I might have done had I been less intent on the languages of reform and on the textual analysis of vocabulary and dialogue.[6] I have not gone into so much detail in the biographies of individual playwrights as I might have done had I been less interested in other figures, particularly political activists as autobiographers.[7]

What I have tried to do is to explore and spotlight the mutually constitutive relations of theatre and politics in the radical movements of late Georgian Britain, as evidenced primarily across playtext and autobiography. My reference to Hannah Smith forms a very slight cameo, but her struggle against the State is one small test of the success of the stage effect, demonstrating the political character of theatricality, and

[4] In so far as I am interested in individuals as distinct from movements, it is in those who have devoted or sacrificed themselves to the cause, rather than those who are mostly celebrated for it (only occasionally the same people).

[5] Julia A. Walker 'Getting to the "Point": A Proposal for Historicising Performance Form', *Nineteenth Century Theatre*, 27, 1 (Summer 1999), Department of Drama, Theatre and Media Arts, Royal Holloway College, University of London; see also Daniel Duffy and that journal issue as a whole for the most recent information and thinking about performance theory in relation to this history. Also published recently; Jeffrey D. Mason, 'Performance and Culture: Mutual Productions', *Nineteenth Century Theatre*, 26, 2 (1998).

[6] In relation to some plays, I have touched on the subject of the use of music, a fascinating area of enquiry on which some theatre critics have commented.

[7] I have given next to no attention to William Shakespeare's influence on late Georgian theatre, which is undoubtedly extremely important, but already a very rich field of enquiry. Jonathan Bate, *Shakespearean Constitutions: Politics, Theatre, Criticism 1730–1830* (Clarendon Press, Oxford, 1989) has been generative.

the theatrical character of politics. Hers is also a small example of the attempt to establish 'a new social contract' out of the interaction of actor, spectator, and assembly; demonstrating the power of staging a performance for the purpose of furthering a cause.[8]

[8] Ngugi Wa Thiong'o, in his *Penpoints, Gunpoints, and Dreams*, (Clarendon Press, Oxford, 1998), *Enactments of Power: The Politics of Performance Space*, 37–69. 'The war between art and the state is really a struggle between the power of performance in the arts and the performance of power by the state—in short, enactments of power . . . The main ingredients of performance are space, content, audience, and the goal, whose end, so to speak, could be instruction or pleasure, or a combination of both—in short, some sort of reformative effects on the audience' (38–9). Hannah Smith, we might say, conducted her own 'enactment of power'.

# *Prologue*

The Theatre engrossed the minds of men to such a degree
. . . that there existed in England a fourth estate, King, Lords and
Commons and Drury Lane Playhouse.[1]

## Reform in the Theatre, Causing a Hubbub

### The 1832 Select Committee

In 1832, the playwright, George Colman the Younger, also Examiner of
Plays to the Lord Chamberlain at that time, was asked a telling question by a member of a parliamentary committee by whom he was being
interviewed:

Question: In the exercise of your censorship at the present moment, if the word
reform should occur, you would strike it out?

In reply, Colman declared:

No; I should say, 'I think you had better omit it; I advise you to do so for your
own sakes, or you will have a hubbub.'

The context was that of giving testimony to the Select Committee on
Dramatic Literature, convened in 1832, the same year as the Reform Act,
and initiated in many ways by Mr Edward Bulwer-Lytton, to whose
views I shall return.[2] The committee's aim was to account systematically
for the state of British drama at a moment when it was no accident that
debates about extended parliamentary franchise were taking place. It is
important to remember that the state of the English law was such that,

---

[1] Arthur Murphy, 'The Life of David Garrick' (1801) cited in *The Georgian Playhouse*:
*Actors, Artists, Audiences and Architecture 1730–1830*, Catalogue of the exhibition devised
by Iain Mackintosh assisted by Geoffrey Ashton, Hayward Gallery, London, 21 Aug.–12
Oct. 1975, Arts Council of Great Britain.

[2] Testimonies recorded in Report from the Select Committee on Dramatic Literature, in *Reports from the Committees 1831–2*, vol. vii, 6 Dec. 1831–16 Aug. 1832, ordered,
by the House of Commons to be printed, 2 Aug. 1832, pp. 1–252. George Colman's testimony features on pp. 59–70, questions 840–1061. For a dramatized version of part of
Colman's testimony, see Epilogue. For more on Edward Bulwer-Lytton, see Ch. 6.

although many of its edicts were ferocious in their proposed penalties, the practical application of the law was arbitrary and erratic.[3] The same combination of theoretical stringency and mismatched practice characterized theatre legislation, where practice was much more volatile than censorship laws might suggest.

Censorship of the stage had existed since the sixteenth century, embodied in the figure of the Master of the Revels and later reinforced by Robert Walpole's Stage Licensing Bill of 1737, which consolidated the powers of the Lord Chamberlain, a royal appointment unaccountable to Parliament. The state of the legislation had remained unchanged for a hundred years, so that when the Select Committee met in June 1832, Walpole's Stage Licensing Act still empowered the Lord Chamberlain to solicit a 'true copy' of every play to be acted 'for hire, gain or reward' fourteen days before a projected performance. The Lord Chamberlain, through the office of the Examiner of Plays, had unlimited powers of veto over any material deemed unsuitable.

The 1737 Act had also perpetuated the patent theatre monopoly, the so-called Killigrew and Davenant patents created by Charles II at the Restoration.[4] These were the patents conferred upon Drury Lane and Covent Garden. Consequently, along with the Haymarket Theatre (operating under Royal patent from 1766) and the King's Theatre, licensed only for opera, Covent Garden and Drury Lane were the only theatres allowed to stage what passed as serious drama. For minor theatres, the constrictions of the patent system reduced their performances to 'entertainments', their licence stating that they could only perform burlettas unassisted by the spoken word and accompanied by music.[5]

---

[3] Eric J. Evans, B*ritain before the Reform Act: Politics and Society 1815–1832* (Longman, London and New York, 1989), ch. 11, 'the legal code, in theory extremely severe but in practice enforced haphazardly'.

[4] John Russell Stephens, *The Censorship of English Drama 1824–1901* (Cambridge University Press, Cambridge, 1980), chs. 1 and 2; L. W. Conolly, *The Censorship of English Drama 1737–1824* (Huntington Library, San Marino, Calif., 1976); F. Fowell and F. Palmer, *Censorship in England* (London, 1913). See Watson Nicholson, *The Struggle for a Free Stage in London* (Constable, London, 1906) for a detailed account of the 1737 Act and the theatre patents.

[5] Theatre managers were supposed to include at least five songs into the three-act structure. Many theatres attempted to escape the patent system by submitting a manuscript to the Lord Chamberlain with five songs present for the sake of official sanction and then either dropping some of the material or changing the words to include material previously censored.

So, what Bulwer-Lytton and the Select Committee faced as they convened was a scenario in which the official space of the London stage was severely limited and its dramatic material carefully controlled, in theory, at least. Testimony to the Select Committee appears to reveal, however, that the practice, as with other areas of the law, defied or ignored the legislature not insubstantially, and that members of the Lord Chamberlain's office may well have exploited or connived in these practices.[6] George Colman Esquire, Examiner of Plays, shared something of Bulwer-Lytton's position in being both an officer of the State and a playwright, the author of several comedies highly popular with London audiences.[7]

On the occasion when Colman was called to give testimony to the Select Committee, the chair was taken by Mr Thomas Slingsby Duncombe, a Whig and radical, as many members of the committee appear to have been. Although reports do not record who else was present on the particular date of Colman's appearance before the committee, it is clear that it was constituted from a body of notable figures.[8] It is significant that Colman's first move after he was called to give his response was to offer 'a paper', supposedly containing all

[6] John Brewer, *The Pleasures of the Imagination: English Culture in the Eighteenth Century* (HarperCollins, London, 1997), ch. 10, also records that there had been recognition by Parliament, in 1788, that there were anomalies in the laws relating to dramatic literature, and some attempt to ease restrictions. The Enabling Act gave magistrates some control over licensing in the provinces.

[7] George Colman the Younger (1762–1836) held the position of Examiner of Plays for the Lord Chamberlain from 1824 until his death. As well as holding office he was also an extremely popular playwright of the late 18th and early 19th c. *Inkle and Yarico* (first performed at the Haymarket Theatre, 11 Aug. 1787, and referred to in Ch. 2) was Colman's first great success. Until 1800, it was performed 164 times and became the fourth most-produced play of all plays produced between 1776 and 1800. Colman's greatest success was *John Bull* (1803), upon which I comment later in this chapter. His other plays include *The Surrender of Calais* (1791), *The Iron Chest* (1796), and *The Blue Beard* (1798). Many of his contemporary playwrights underwent a process of disillusionment as his strictures as Examiner not only failed to maintain the spirit of his plays, but he also became increasingly stringent as he progressed in office. Most of the theatre managers in London were at odds with him at some stage.

[8] One member of the Select Committee was Alderman Waithman, self-taught man of letters, successful linen draper and one-time Lord Mayor of London. E. P. Thompson, *The Making of the English Working Class* (Penguin, Harmondsworth, 1963), ch. 13, comments on his radicalism in relation to the City of London. Another was Lord John Russell, notable for his controversial speech supporting extension of the suffrage, later Home Secretary and then Prime Minister. See Epilogue for further details of Select Committee membership.

possible answers to his interrogators and designed to 'save the committee a vast deal of trouble'.

Colman's strategy (one which, by all appearances, conspicuously failed either to impress or succeed) was presumably designed to circumvent difficult questions, not least ones which might invite him to account for the relationship between his role as censor and the liberties he had taken in his former career as playwright. The committee, in an appropriately stern but respectful tone, required him to answer their searching questions, most of which focused precisely on how he could reconcile his style of playwriting with his role as the official censor, albeit as the Examiner of Plays rather than the Lord Chamberlain himself. One consequence of this rigorous line of enquiry is that Colman's testimony illuminates many of the key confusions and contradictions confronting legislators in relation to dramatic literature and performance.

It is significant that, in the exchange about reform which heads this chapter, George Colman insists that he would take a more circumspect course than simply deleting the word 'reform' from a script. His assertion that he would merely advise about the possible consequences of the use of the word, and that that advice would be given in the plural form ('for your own sakes'), appears to suggest that he has already moved beyond the script itself, and beyond the prescriptions of his literal task as Examiner, to negotiations with playwrights and theatre managers themselves. In other words, Colman's role as Examiner has been redirected away from that of giving advice to the Lord Chamberlain exclusively on the basis of scrutinizing a script, in order that the latter should make a recommendation on the basis of that information, to the much more interventionist and potentially compromised activity of dealing with theatre managers and their authors directly. Certainly, there is evidence to suggest that managers might well have been thoroughly complicit in this, thinking themselves above the law, and exercising far more power over what was performed in their theatres than the state of the legislature might imply.[9]

When asked by committee members to give a definition of the role of the Examiner, Colman responds: 'The Examiner of plays takes care that nothing should be introduced into plays which is profane or

---

[9] Ellen Donkin, *Getting into the Act, Women Playwrights in London 1776–1829* (Routledge, London and New York, 1995) documents the power of theatre managers.

indecent, or morally or politically improper.'[10] At the same time, he is at pains to point out to his interviewers that he, as Examiner, is a 'subordinate person', and has 'no power over the theatres', that being the sole jurisdiction of the Lord Chamberlain. As his testimony develops, however, it appears, quite apart from questions of accountability, that both those definitions of impropriety which committee members attempt to elicit, and the mechanisms by which it is possible to 'take care' that nothing profane or indecent appears on the stage, are rather shaky. When asked at one moment if he would interfere in a script, Colman responds: 'It must be very palpable to everybody before I should interfere. I allude to political and personal allusions, downright grossness and indecency, or anything that would be profane, which any candid man could not but say was improper, about which there could be two opinions.'[11] The invoking of the 'candid man' is in keeping with the practices of English law, and anticipates the later development of 'the man on the Clapham omnibus' as a touchstone for common-sense judgements. However, when committee members press Colman for particular instances, they begin to find themselves drawn into a moral and legal maze. Making reference to the paper which Colman had announced himself ready to offer as an alternative to subjecting himself to the rigours of interview, a committee member cites Colman's objections to plays representing 'adultery, murder, and parricide', asking whether the Examiner would take steps to limit the production of *Macbeth*. The ease and familiarity with which his interviewers invoke Shakespeare as a common reference-point in formulating their questions is a significant comment on their knowledge of theatre, and the popularity of the playwright in the period.[12] Colman casually dismisses the possibility with the response that that play represents history, not contemporary matters. His interviewer takes the question further, arguing that adultery, murder, and parricide might be taken to result from those 'passions upon which the interest of great dramatic performance is founded'.[13] In response, Colman appears to prevaricate, hedging over the question of whether he might interfere in such matters, or whether

---

[10] Report from the Select Committee on Dramatic Literature (1832), answer to question 844.

[11] Ibid., answer to question 851.

[12] Performance of Shakespeare in the late Georgian context remains a fascinating issue, beyond the scope of my project, but widely researched.

[13] Report from the Select Committee on Dramatic Literature, question 963.

he might not. Central issues about morality, about the endorsements of history, and about the universal qualities of the drama are thereby traduced in an evasive pragmatism, by which knowledgeable interviewers remain unimpressed.

The discussion subsequently shifts ground on to two significant legislative matters, the question of whether or not the powers of the Examiner are only enshrined in law in so far as they are set by precedent, and the attempt to clarify whether the taking of fees from authors and theatre managers by the Examiner is a legal practice or not. Colman offers much verbiage, but little illumination on both issues, showing most clarity, and certainly most passion, over the case of an oratorio and one Mr Hawes, who not only refused to pay the fee having been granted a licence, but also, 'placarded' Colman in his publicity. Colman declares that, 'he played it and chuckled at his triumph, and sung and roared away. His oratorio went on, he had his licence and I had not my two guineas.' Thus, a moment of unashamed personal pique displaces any account which might lend itself to an interpretation of the legalities or illegalities of the fee-taking practice.

What must have bewildered and bemused committee members most of all, though, is the transparency of Colman's volte-face from immoral playwright to moral Examiner, his failure even to attempt any coherent account of the relationship between the two roles from his own experience, his utter lack of interest in the integrity of autobiography. When asked how he reconciles his censorious opinions about immoral oaths with the success of such language in his own theatre productions, he replies: 'If I had been the examiner I should have scratched them out, and would do so now; I was in a different position at that time, I was a careless immoral author, I am now the examiner of plays. I did my business as an author at that time, and I do my business as an examiner now.'[14] Asked about the language, the oaths and scriptural allusions, in his play *John Bull*, he concedes that he should have removed some 'bad plums' from the pudding, and regrets that he did not do so. Indeed, he appears ultimately to frustrate the committee (and could it have been Bulwer-Lytton posing some of the more trenchant questions?) not only by refusing them any coherent account, from his own experience, of the relationship between playwright and Examiner, but by appearing to

---

[14] Report from the Select Committee on Dramatic Literature, answer to question 860.

make a virtue of incoherence. In becoming the moral Examiner as against the immoral playwright, he turns critic not only of his own plays, but of autobiographical integrity itself.

[*Question*] Do you suppose that those plays of yours (which were so pleasing to the public, and are acted still with great success, for which you have the power of erasing those small oaths) have done much mischief to the morals of the town?
[*Answer*] They have certainly done no good, and I am sorry I inserted the oaths. As a moral man, one gets a little wiser as one goes on, and I should be very happy to relieve my mind from the recollection of having written those oaths.
[*Question*] In that play also you talk of Eve, there is a very good joke about Eve; one of the characters has no more idea of something, than Eve had of pin-money. Do you call that improper?
[*Answer*] Yes, that had better be omitted.[15]

I have dwelt at some length on Colman's testimony, not only because he is an influential figure at this time, but also because his testimony amounts to a classic, if parodic commentary on the issues of responsibility and accountability raised by the Select Committee in relation to the condition of the drama in a democratizing society. Committee members are searching, in one sense modestly, for an informed account of legislative practices in relation to contemporary theatre, instead of which they find themselves confronted with a random and somewhat farcical failure to account for any coherence, even over one lifetime, in relation to the drama.

Colman's account is supposed to be crucial, in that he is supposedly the representative of the official view from the Lord Chamberlain's office, as well as a successful playwright with power accruing from popularity with audiences. He is also involved in theatre management.[16] For members of the committee, an account of the relationship between Colman's various roles could, in theory, have both clarified the Examiner's official functions and made sense of them in relation to the state of the legislature in relation to the works of playwrights and the dramatic interpretation of scripts in the context of theatre performance and management. Instead, Colman appears intent on producing a separation between theatrical productivity and accountability, which

---

[15] Ibid., questions 861 and 864.
[16] See Jeremy F. Bagster-Collins, *George Colman the Younger (1762–1836)*, 2 vols. (Bentley, London, 1946) for biographical detail.

amounts to denying any coherence to his own values and in such a way as to make nonsense of any understanding of contemporary legislation.

It was not that Colman was alone, though, in giving responses to the Select Committee which reveal contradictions and confusions of an extensive kind, particularly that between the supposedly legal and ideological requirements of the State, on the one side, and the practices of theatre managers, especially in relation to the popularity of playwrights on the other. Aspects of Colman's testimony suggest that popular dramatists, such as himself, were quite able to out-manœuvre that legislation which was clear to them, where complicity with admiring audiences could be relied upon to carry their influence. Successful playwrights and theatre managers together were able to exploit and manipulate confusion in theatrical legislation at the end of the eighteenth century.[17]

Although Colman's testimony is probably unique in its particular ability to obfuscate, other interviewees are also unclear about what is legal in the theatre's practices.[18] In order even to begin to consider the issue of reform of the drama, committee members were under inevitable pressure to account for the existing state of the legislation in relation to current practices. The obstacle in relation to the drama was that many practices appeared to operate beyond the law, and that interpretations of the law were, to put it euphemistically, inconsistent and erratic. Perhaps the sheer difficulty of accumulating any kind of coherent account of the legislative practices surrounding the drama was what prevented the committee from making radical proposals on the basis of its findings. Certainly, their recommendations did not stretch to an abandonment of the patent system, which was to come later, in the Victorian period.[19]

However, the very pressure that Colman is under to produce some kind of accountability, particularly in relation to the term reform, is an indication of the interconnections of the public forms of drama and politics at this moment of history. In addition to attempting to gather reliable information on the basis of which they can document theatrical activity coherently and comprehensively, committee members are also leaning on the drama to act as alibi for political reform more generally.

---

[17] See Nicholson, *The Struggle for a Free Stage*, 124–40, for a summary of conflicting theatrical legislation in England at the close of the 18th c.

[18] David Osbaldiston of the Surrey Theatre is a notable example.

[19] See Nicholson, *The Struggle for a Free Stage*, 1–19, for more on this subject. It was not until 1843 that the patent monopoly was broken.

It is as if they see the importance of the committee's work not primarily in terms of reforming the drama, or even, conversely, as a pretext for tighter legislative controls, but as a litmus test for how reform is regarded and treated in the theatrical world, particularly in the city of London, where its political effects are potent. Amongst all the confusion, there are moments of real significance in the testimonies to the Select Committee, even that of George Colman. One such moment, out of the few genuinely informative contributions made by Colman in his testimony, is about London itself, indicating a thriving London theatre, much of it illegal, and the rest of it treading a very fine line between legality and illegality. In bemoaning the state of the theatres on the 'wrong' side of the Thames, Colman somewhat inadvertently reveals the full extent of illegal practice.

> As to those theatres over the water, they are perfectly lawless; they only act under the London magistrates' licence, which is to license music and dancing; for the legislature when it passed the Act of 1737, did not contemplate that the town would get so overgrown as it is,—they never thought of those people that have since struck up, who get the common magistrate's licence for music and dancing, and abuse it to the extent you have seen.[20]

The city of London, like the big cities of the north of England, had grown beyond what the national government could imagine or could control. In this sense, the impulse for 'radical Westminster' to reform both the franchise and the drama came at least in part from the need to establish order on a potentially or literally anarchic populace. This feeling that London needed to be governed more substantially may well have also emerged from the conditions of monarchical power in the period. One argument is that the Court was no longer able to sustain its own theatre and therefore regarded London as its theatrical playground.[21] A small indication of this relationship between London theatre and the Hanoverians is the enormous increase in London theatres, during the decades after 1781, of performances of what was, by the early nineteenth century, to be called the national anthem.[22] If the monarchy were increasingly sharing leisure facilities with the London

---

[20] Report from the Select Committee on Dramatic Literature, answer to question 949.

[21] Linda Colley, *Britons, Forging the Nation 1707–1837* (Yale University Press, New Haven and London, 1992), ch. 5 on the subject of Majesty.

[22] Colley (ibid.), records more than ninety performances between 1781 and 1801, compared with only four formal performances between 1760 and 1781.

population at large, then the anxiety of legislators and their desire to introduce controls would have been so much the greater. At the same time, any controls might paradoxically have operated at the cost of those whose interests they were intended to serve. The monarchy, with its increasing attachment to royal procession and spectacle, was coming under the influence of popular theatre's performance values and methods, and would not wish to suppress that in which it had an investment.

It is significant that when Colman does invoke censorious judgements, it is in the by now relatively safe territory of gestural defence of the monarchy rather than in relation to reform politics *per se*. One such instance is his response to Mary Russell Mitford's controversial play, *Charles the First*.[23] Mitford's play was submitted for licence by the theatre manager, John Kemble, who described it as 'admirable but somewhat dangerous'. For Colman, however, the very title of the play 'brings instantly to mind the violent commotion, and catastrophes of that unhappy monarch's reign'. The terms of his letter to the Duke of Montrose, as current Lord Chamberlain, do reveal a preoccupation with blasphemous language and an anxiety about democracy, but Colman's central concern is with the by then somewhat spurious defence of monarchy:

The Piece abounds (blasphemously, I think) with Scriptural allusions, and quotations, and the name of the Almighty is introduced, and invoked over and over again, by hypocrites, and regicides. If it be *in keeping* thus to delineate the morals and religion of the Cromwell party, the political part of their dialogue is, by the same rule, democratical, most insulting to Charles, in particular, and to the Monarchy in general.[24]

He objects to the play on the grounds that it is in favour of the democratic tendency and because of its religious allusions (simply because it has them, rather than for the character of that use), but above all because it is anti-monarchist. He also makes it clear that it is the sensitivity of the play in relation to the current monarchy which is at issue; it represents *recent* history whereas *Macbeth*, also about the death of

[23] Mary Russell Mitford, *Charles the First* (1825) in *The Dramatic Works of Mary Russell Mitford*, (Hurst and Blackett, London, 1854) vol. i. Mitford was more famous for her genteel pastoral verse, e.g. *Our Village*, than for her plays.

[24] George Colman to the Duke of Montrose, 29 Sept. 1825. British Library Add MS 42, 873, vol. ix.

kings, is apparently neutralized by its historical distance. Under the pressure of Colman's advice, the Duke of Montrose could wish to do no other than reject the play, which indeed he did. Far from making any attempt to appease Kemble, Colman cursorily dismisses the latter's ambitions for the play, noting that 'where there could have been little hope of permission, there can be little disappointment in a refusal', rather betraying that he could afford to be somewhat dismissive of a theatre manager who was not having particular success at the time.[25]

As has been argued, the history of theatrical legislation since 1737 had set up 'the possibilities of conflicting authority' not only between theatres of different status, according to how far they were protected by royal patents, monopolies, magistrates' licences, or not at all, but also between the various representatives of the apparatus of theatrical management; managers, playwrights, actors and audiences themselves, Parliament and the Lord Chamberlain's office, had competing as well as relative interests, arising as much from the powerful influences of the market as legal injunction.[26] It appears frequently to be the case that the Lord Chamberlain, rather than implementing specific legislation was in the position of arbiter, responding to and negotiating with theatre managers and playwrights, particularly those who had been successful in generating audiences. What is significant about the mission of the 1832 Select Committee, whose proceedings drew on a wide range of testimonies from performers and theatre managers as well as officials of the State, is not so much its success or failure in clarifying or enacting legislation as the recognition of its members that there was much at stake in understanding and indeed sustaining the relationship between contemporary theatre and politics.

As well as taking the opportunity to discover more about the theatre world's attitude to reform, Select Committee members appear to demonstrate, in the particular character of their questioning, both a wide understanding, amongst themselves, of the theatrical experience, and often a sympathetic appreciation of theatrical radicalism, under the influence of Enlightenment ideas. As members of the Whig reforming government, they appear, for instance, as mistrustful of Colman's establishment

[25] Ibid.
[26] Nicholson, *The Struggle for a Free Stage*, 141–74; 'the possibilities of conflicting authority . . . had lurked in the theatrical monopoly, and especially since 1737'.

conservatism as they are of the possibility of his being engaged in potentially shady practices over the taking of fees. Whatever their legislative
concerns *vis-à-vis* government control of the theatres, they appear to
represent, at least in part and however unwittingly, that aspiration to a
new condition for the drama in a democratizing State. Perhaps they
were seeing what it has taken historians some time to credit about the
character of political radicalism at this time, that theatrical energy and
vitality were essential to the reform project, both inside and outside the
theatres.

What historians are coming to understand . . . is the extent to which radical
leaders and organizers were able not only to create an attractive radical platform
but also to produce compelling radical theatre. Radical leaders played upon the
rich traditions of popular culture to make elaborate appeals to the people
through the careful utilization of civic and national celebrations, through
dinners and toasts, through the dazzling deployment of light and colour and
the accompanying recitation of music, rhyme and stories.[27]

When asked by the Select Committee to consider what he would take
to be 'politically wrong', George Colman evades the question of
whether he would regard anything against the Tories as wrong under a
Tory administration, and under a Whig administration, anything
against the Whigs. Demonstrating his attachment to that word
'hubbub', he reiterates his primary concern, that the word 'reform' has
and will produce 'a row in your theatre'.[28] Colman's response to the
question could be seen as woefully inadequate, both in terms of party
politics and in relation to the issue of political reform in general, but it
is also curiously symptomatic in that he responds not with an informed
political knowledge or opinion, but with a dramatic utterance, captur-
ing something of the heightened dialogue of the occasion and of the
theatre of reform.

### Censorship or Franchise? The Fair Experiment of Public Support

There has been a tendency to interpret the 1832 Select Committee on
Dramatic Literature in terms of certain ideas about censorship; to

---

[27] Frank O'Gorman, *The Long Eighteenth Century* (Arnold, London and New York, 1997), ch. 9.
[28] Report from the Select Committee on Dramatic Literature (1832), questions 967–9.

suggest that here was an attempt by government to exercise firmer legislative control over the drama, particularly London theatre. The assumption of such a discussion is that the legislator's primary task was interventionist, potentially repressive. It does seem to be the case that the Lord Chamberlain's powers were exposed as arbitrary and limited, implying that his position, operating above the law by royal appointment, was insufficient in itself to secure effective policing of the stage. Such a state of affairs would appear, certainly, to give some justification for government intervention. However, there is a different set of arguments which draws the Dramatic Literature legislation alongside those other major parliamentary enactments of the period, the 1833 Emancipation Act and the 1832 Reform Act itself. In one way, the Dramatic Literature Act's failure to achieve very much—it did not even manage to bring about the abolition of the patent system—can be seen in similar terms to the Reform Act itself, which notoriously led to dissatisfaction in its failure to extend the parliamentary franchise very far at all. Each was, to some extent, an enemy of promise.

However, the Whig government, which as Linda Colley argues, has had 'a raw deal from some recent historians',[29] was humanitarian, and not repressive, in its reforming character, and it can be argued that the proceedings of the Select Committee itself, like the events and processes leading up to the Reform Act, capture the true reform character generated out of the theatrical dynamic of the plebeian–patrician continuum.[30] The Whig aristocrats presiding on the Select Committee, along with their colleagues from local government, were themselves significant, for their knowledge and interest in theatre. As we shall see, some of them, like Bulwer-Lytton, were playwrights, theatre commentators, or managers, and there is evidence from the committee's lines of enquiry and the character of the questions that were put to interviewees that they also constituted an informed and pleasure-taking theatre audience. If they had decided, on the basis of the committee's findings, that they should recommend to the government of the day that it ought to take repressive measures against the drama, this would not only have been out of keeping with the spirit of reform in general; it could also have been counter to their own interests. In other words, to police a London theatre would

---

[29] Colley, *Britons*, ch. 8, 'Victories?'
[30] Thompson, *Customs in Common*, cited widely in Ch. 6.

have been to police their own literary endeavours as playwrights and possibly to constrain their own freedoms as audience members.

When the committee members interview George Colman, and many others such as Douglas Jerrold (who denounces Colman for having deleted some 'angels' from one of his playscripts[31]) it is apparent that they do not take Colman's part, the official line as it were, but respond with amusement and sympathy, as they do to Jerrold's outrage at such petty tyranny over the script. Throughout the long proceedings of the committee, there is much evidence, as there is in the Colman interview itself, of a set of government representatives whose primary concern is to see a thriving, popular theatre. If they are concerned with insurrection and turmoil from the lower orders, they do not do very much at all to demonstrate it, appearing rather to wish to air their views about the qualities of great drama, the virtues of Shakespeare, and their own enthusiastic involvement in matters theatrical.

It has also been argued that the aristocracy increasingly signalled their desire to withdraw from popular entertainment of the period. Evidence to the Select Committee makes this appear most unlikely, except in the sense that there may have been some uncertainty and anxiety, as there was in relation to the Reform Act, about the wisdom of energetic alignments and allegiances across class.[32] The aristocracy, seeing that State control over London theatre would restrict themselves as well as the artisans, the servants, and the prostitutes, may well have felt nervous about the extent to which extending the parliamentary franchise might bring the classes closer to each other, ultimately threatening the power of landed interests. However, such concerns seem to me to apply as realities only to a later era, and not primarily to what the Select Committee was signalling.

The Dramatic Literature Act tacitly acknowledged, in response to

---

[31] Douglas Jerrold, referred to in Chs. 3 and 4, and occasionally elsewhere. Colman had argued to the Select Committee that the problem with 'angels' was that of scriptural allusion.

[32] Brewer, *The Pleasures of the Imagination*, documents attempts, largely by the aristocracy, to establish a music world distinct from the theatre. It is possible that they were seeking a separate space, distinct from that occupied by what Brewer chooses to call the *hoi polloi*, for their own élite versions of culture for an upper-class audience. It could be argued, however, that this sort of strategy was as much about the diminished significance of the Court as it was about distaste for other members of theatre audiences. There is no particular suggestion that aristocratic membership of theatre audiences diminished in this period.

the Select Committee's proceedings, that the Lord Chamberlain's office, far from being an active and systematic vehicle for suppression, was an anachronism and a shambles, no longer able, if it had ever been, to implement effective censorship over the theatre.[33] As the regions, whatever their differences, were united in their pursuit of reform, so theatres in Leeds and Manchester, Bristol and Birmingham shared in the generation of a theatre which the authorities had failed to repress. London theatre, as we have seen, was way beyond the imposition of systematic controls. However, whatever the inadequacies of the Lord Chamberlain's office, the alternative was not going to be governmental intervention in the form of repression (particularly at a moment when monarchs were enjoying the delights of London theatre in more ways than one[34]), outside of their own remit of the Court, and when members of the aristocracy might thereby have subjected themselves to their own censorship edicts.

I would argue, then, that the Lord Chamberlain's powers were left in place not to testify to his authority, let alone to strengthen it, but as an alternative to the introduction of a more systematic or forceful regime. In other words, to leave in place a token figurehead (whose office was made up of a bunch of mavericks and 'loose cannon') was preferable to any acknowledgement that Parliament should take upon itself the more rigorous and systematic approach represented by legislative control. The Lord Chamberlain continued, it is true, to be an irritant into the late nineteenth century, as we see in some wonderful polemic from George Bernard Shaw, and up to the 1960s, as we see in some splendid vitriol from Kenneth Tynan, but he (and there never was a woman in the role) was little more than that.[35]

By 1832, government ministers and legislators were no more interested in repressing British political theatre than they were in silencing the heirs of Thomas Hardy and Olaudah Equiano in pressing for State

---

[33] The persistence of the Lord Chamberlain's office into the second half of the 20th c. seems to me merely to show that the anachronism continued, as a token gesture towards authority.

[34] More on the subject of these delights in Ch. 5.

[35] This is not, however, to underestimate the power of the Lord Chamberlain's office to block or delay the production of a play. It is, though, to suggest that playwrights were well up to engaging with such strategies, and even derived a certain intellectual energy from doing so. The Lord Chamberlain's edicts may have inhibited some playwrights, but only as much as they charged others with opposition!

reform (matters to be dealt with in later chapters) Indeed, they were doing their very best to relinquish judgements about theatre and leave these to 'the fair experiment of Public support'.[36] Lord John Russell, member of the Select Committee on Dramatic Literature, later to become Home Secretary and then Prime Minister, was one of the most 'dramatic' speakers on the Reform Act itself, arguing for further extension of the franchise than was eventually implemented. Such parliamentary languages borrowed, learned from, and interacted with the modes and forms of the theatrical domain. Whatever their eventual failures of nerve in Parliament itself, ministers and members were too caught up in the spirit of change and the radical energies of reform to be arguing for repression and censorship. They were also energetically involved in the pleasure of theatregoing and, often, in theatrical creation. Where they were not playwrights, they were audiences and critics. In short, they were much too immersed in theatre either to wish or will the stage to be throttled by the State,[37] and much too immersed in the drama of reform to put in jeopardy powerful new developments in the symbiotic relationship between theatre and politics. The exhilaration of that relationship is captured in an account, by Thomas Macaulay, of the impact of the parliamentary debate of the Reform Bill itself:

Such a scene as the division of last Tuesday I never saw, and never expect to see again. If I should live fifty years the impression of it will be as fresh and sharp in my mind as if it had just taken place. It was like seeing Caesar stabbed in the Senate House, or seeing Oliver taking the mace from the table, a sight to be seen only once and never to be forgotten. The crowd overflowed the House in every part. When the doors were locked we had six hundred and eight members present, more than fifty five than were ever in a division before . . . When Charles Wood who stood near the door jumped up on a bench and cried out, 'They are only three hundred and one.' We set up a shout that you might have heard to Charing Cross—waving our hats—stamping against the floor and clapping our hands. The tellers scarcely got through the crowd. But you might

---

[36] Report from the Select Committee on Dramatic Literature (1832), pp. 5–6. Regulations and amendments proposed by the committee included that of 'more general exhibition of the regular Drama', which would 'afford new schools and opportunities for the art'.

[37] Neither did they believe that the activities of the stage and the State could be untouched by each other.

have heard a pin drop as Duncannon read the numbers. Then again the shouts broke out—and many of us shed tears—I could scarcely refrain. And the jaw of Peel fell; and the face of Twiss was the face of a damned soul. We shook hands and clapped each other on the back, and went out laughing, crying, and huzzaing into the lobby.[38]

---

[38] Thomas Macaulay, letter to Thomas Flower Ellis on the vote in the House of Commons on the Reform Act (30 Mar. 1831). http://www.spartacus.schoolnet. co.uk/PRI832.htm

CHAPTER ONE

# The Grand Theatre of Reform

Immediately on the words "NOT GUILTY" being pronounced by the foreman of the worthy jury, the Sessions House, where the court sat, was almost rent with loud and reiterated shouts of applause. The vast multitude that were waiting anxiously without, caught the joyful sound, and like an electric shock, or the rapidity of lightning, the glad tidings spread through the whole town, and were conveyed much quicker than the regular post could travel, to the most distant parts of the island, where all ranks of people were anxiously awaiting the result of the trial.[1]

In his memoir, Thomas Hardy, founder of the London Corresponding Society, recounts the story of his acquittal, after the Treason Trials of 1794, and the moment in which he is released from prison to cheering crowds. Britain, the whole of the island, becomes the audience to the spectacle of innocent men acquitted, whose only crime had been to maintain the principle 'of every rational being', the desire to pursue liberty. The crowd, containing all ranks of people, pays testimony to the heroes who have suffered for the cause of reform, not only witnessing the event of Hardy's release, but also endorsing the politics of his stand.

The accusations which led to the trial for high treason of Hardy himself, together with other members of the Society, are dramatized in the memoir, in such a way as to re-create moral and political topography via theatrical vocabulary. Reform activists, previously vilified as traitors, become the heroes of the hour, and members of governments, previously the accusers, become the villains of the piece: 'These virtuous men have been since falsely represented by successive governments and their hirelings, as traitors and enemies to their country; a dark and shameful blot on the annals of this civilized land, that its destinies

---

[1] *Memoir of Thomas Hardy*, in *Testaments of Radicalism, Memoirs of Working Class Politicians 1790–1885*, pp. 25–103, ed. and introduced by David Vincent (Europa Publications Limited, London, 1997), 71–2.

should be confided to the management of men, either so ignorant or so wicked!'[2] Drawing on the vocabulary of melodrama and tragedy, Hardy also recounts the extremely harrowing events from earlier in his life as a reformer, including the consequences for his wife and children of attacks on their home and of his incarceration in the Tower of London. The poet who commemorates Mrs Hardy's death, which took place during her husband's imprisonment, appeals to his audience to 'BEHOLD THE SCENE, the piercing scene appears!'[3] Written accounts thus dramatize the protagonists and the scene, but also, with Hardy's release from the Tower, a crucial extension has occurred, from dramatic characterization of protagonists to a palpable sense of audience.

It is salutary to be reminded by Thomas Hardy of how few British subjects participated in the parliamentary franchise when the Society was established in the 1790s. The growing cities of Leeds, Manchester, and Birmingham did not have a single vote between them. Significantly, these were some of the populations which were subscribing in huge numbers to anti-slavery and reform petitions. It was this type of audience, disfranchised, but with a growing commitment to participating, at some level, in resistance to political injustice, that was swelling the ranks of those 'anxiously awaiting the result of the trial'.

Hardy's memoir is, in some senses, a reform manifesto of its own. He disowns the individualism of the first-person pronoun (he writes that he wishes 'to obviate the necessity of calling the great *I* so repeatedly to my assistance'), and uses a language drawn largely from popular melodrama in his representation of reform politics.[4] Virtuous and villainous protagonists, fighters in the cause and their opponents, are substituted for the autobiographical persona and reflective narrative mode of the more typical memoir. The acts of those in power are cast in terms of the dark and shameful deeds of the melodramatic scenario. Release from prison

---

[2] Ibid. 49. Judith Pascoe, *Romantic Theatricality: Gender, Poetry, and Spectatorship* (Cornell University Press, Ithaca, NY, and London, 1997), ch. 2, documents the 'courtroom theatre of the 1794 Treason Trials', pointing out that E. P. Thompson and John Barrell before her have highlighted 'the theatrical nature of the trials' (33)

[3] Citizen Lee, a friend to the distressed patriots, in *Memoir of Thomas Hardy*, 62–3. See Pascoe, *Romantic Theatricality*, for more on the subject of Mrs Hardy.

[4] See Elaine Hadley, *Melodramatic Tactics: Theatricalized Dissent in the English Marketplace, 1800–1885* (Stanford University Press, Stanford, Calif., 1995) and Ch. 6 for more on melodrama as a politicizing force. Hadley argues that melodramas 'mythologize the centrality of all moral beings within a hierarchical society' (75). By doing so, they challenge the inevitability of that hierarchy.

is described in terms not of the personal impact of a momentous event for the individual, but of audience reception of a set of political ideas. Such language and techniques create a strong relationship between a dramatic lexicon and the polemic of the period, and appeal to individual readers of the memoir to embrace both sympathy for the reform heroes and a sense of themselves as part of a righteous and participating audience. The drama of reform is thus performed across the political and theatrical domains, as the activist becomes the hero, as the crowd becomes the audience, determined to judge and respond to the action, to applaud heroes whilst signalling commitment to the cause.

## 1789, French Revolutionary Connections

'Kings are no longer destinies'[5]

Thomas Hardy is far from being the only commentator on reform politics in Britain to use theatrical language and to register the significance of the properties of theatre in the political cause. Arguments between three central eighteenth-century protagonists within the classic British tradition of polemic, certain of whose writings are positioned very significantly in relation to the emergence of the London Corresponding Society, draw strongly on theatrical language and techniques in making different interpretations of French Revolutionary events for their significance in Britain. Edmund Burke's *Reflections on the Revolution in France* (1790) argues against an anti-monarchist revolution in the process of advocating constitutional reform; Tom Paine's *The Rights of Man* (1791), written as a response to Burke, supports the revolutionary movement; and Mary Wollstonecraft's *The Rights of Men* (1790) and *The Origin and Progress of the French Revolution* (1794), engage directly with Burke, whilst offering her own very distinctive account of this history.[6]

---

[5] Edward Bulwer-Lytton, *England and the English* (University of Chicago Press, Chicago, 1970); for further comment, see Ch. 6.

[6] Edmund Burke, *Reflections on the Revolution in France* (Dodsley, London, 1790) (Penguin edn., 1969, used here, based on Pelican edn., 1968) Thomas Paine (1791) *The Rights of Man* (J. Johnson, London, 1790; Oxford University Press, Oxford, 1995) Mary Wollstonecraft, *A Vindication of the Rights of Men* (J. Johnson, London, 1790); and *An Historical and Moral View of the Origin and Progress of the French Revolution and the Effect it has Produced in Europe*, in *The Works of Mary Wollstonecraft*, ed. Janet Todd and Marilyn Butler vol. vi (William Pickering, London, 1989). This text was part of a larger project for a history of the Revolution that was never written. In comparison to the constant reprinting of both Burke and Paine's books, Wollstonecraft's work had only one edition.

What is in dispute between the commentators is the character of constitutional reform in Britain, and an important issue is how far the existence of a monarchy (and the death of the French king) is relevant to that discussion. The power of the *British* monarchy declined at the end of the eighteenth century, and although the monarch was still influential over the appointment of prime ministers, responsibilities for government were increasingly in the hands of ministers themselves.[7] However, in the iconography of State power, and its embodiment in theatricality and dramatic conventions, monarchy remained a central area of contestation, and reform languages played across French Revolutionary models of regal power and public performance. For Burke, the French monarchy stood for certain values which Britain would abandon at her peril, but for Wollstonecraft and Paine, the French king and queen were icons of despotism, no better than British slavers and more guilty of abusing their absolute power.[8]

Revolutionary France had yielded evidence that the discourses and the public forms of the drama and the body politic were inextricably related.[9] France and the *ancien régime* continue to be invoked, both in discussions of civil and constitutional rights in Britain and in relation to the condition of British drama, at least a generation after the Revolution itself. Much commentary on the state of the drama is pioneering and idealistic in its exhortations on behalf of theatre as a potential force for democracy in Britain, invoking what its authors describe as the intellectual spirit of the time, often in overtly political terms and in very direct references to the legacy of the Revolution—'The mind of the age has been . . . shaken up by the revival of noble doctrines . . . and by the glorious example of the second French revolution.'[10]

The rhetoric deployed by Burke to describe the French Revolution

---

[7] It is likely that, in Britain, the 'Tory' administration led by Lord Liverpool was more concerned with opposition to French concepts of citizenship and to the French version of representative government than with implications for the British monarchy itself of events in France.

[8] Jane Moore, in Carl Plasa and Betty Ring (eds.), *The Discourse of Slavery* (Routledge, London, 1994), argues for the universality of Wollstonecraft's version of rights, as against the nationalism of Burke's programme.

[9] Paul Hindson and Tim Gray, *Burke's Dramatic Theory of Politics* (Avebury, Aldershot, 1988) posit, interestingly, that theatre is an organizing principle of French society at this time; ch. 6, 'Tragedy', 'French society was being organised under the concept of the total theatre which emphasised the power of the collective will.'

[10] Leigh Hunt, *Selected Dramatic Criticism 1808–1831*, ed. by Lawrence H. Houtchens (Columbia University Press, NY, 1949), 257.

itself is, as Tom Paine later argues, highly charged with theatrical vocabulary.[11] Burke constructs an analogy between the Revolution and the stage, depicting them both as 'spectacle', and contrasting the different emotions invoked in terms of a moral topography, in which the impulse to respond to the atrocities which occur to 'principal actors' in real life should be held in common with an individual's response to a play as a member of its audience. In delineating this reaction, Burke draws attention to what he assumes is the appropriate theatrical sensibility:

Some tears might be drawn from me, if such a spectacle (the arrest of the French king and queen) were exhibited on the stage. I should be truly ashamed of finding in myself that superficial, theatric sense of painted distress, whilst I could exult over it in real life. With such a perverted mind, I could never venture to shew my face at a tragedy. People would think the tears that Garrick formerly, or that Siddons not long since, have extorted from me, were the tears of hypocrisy; I should know them to be the tears of folly.

    Indeed the theatre is a better school of moral sentiments than churches, where the feelings of humanity are thus outraged.[12]

Burke would be 'ashamed' if his reactions to political events could not demonstrate coherence and consistency with responses in a theatre, whose dramatic conventions he takes to be fundamentally moral in their intolerance of such tragedy and trauma as the death of kings (not for nothing did eighteenth-century theatre adapt *King Lear* to a happy ending). It is not that he is concerned with being accused of artificial and contrived responses as a member of a theatre audience—hypocrisy is an issue, but not the primary one—but he *is* concerned to invoke the conventions of audience response as the arena in which appropriate reactions to political events can be determined.

    However, Burke's conflation of theatrical and political judgements

---

[11] See Hindson and Gray, *Burke's Dramatic Theory*, for an account of the relationship between theatricality and politics in Burke's writing; 'Burke's political theory is best conceived as a *dramatic* understanding of the moral and political organisation of society', introduction (their emphasis); 'Drama was Burke's way of viewing and understanding the order of the political world', conclusion. See also, Steven Blakemore, *Burke and the Fall of Language* (University Press of New England, Hanover, NH, and London, 1988) for an analysis of the French Revolution as 'linguistic event'.

[12] Burke, *Reflections on the* Revolution, 175–6. Sarah Siddons, née Kemble (1755–1830) was thought by many to be the greatest actress of her generation, frequently playing the role of tragic heroine. Her Shakespearean tragic heroines of the 1782 season at Drury Lane led to the coining of the term 'Siddonsmania' by the popular press. Burke regularly attended her performances in the years before *Reflections on the Revolution in France* was written.

overloads the discussion with expressive feeling and emotive significa-
tion, implying that analysis of political events can be reduced to questions of appropriate aesthetic, dramatic sensibility, as individualized in
the reaction of the privileged onlooker. Part of Tom Paine's project in
responding critically to Burke is to expose this reduction. Paine rounds
on the entirety of Burke's text as 'a dramatic performance', in which 'the
whole machinery bends to produce a stage effect'. Paine reminds Burke
that he is supposed to be writing history, 'not Plays', and that the thesis
of *Reflections* is fatally flawed by 'the spouting rant of high-toned excla-
mation', which exhibits consequences without exploring historical and
political causes.[13]

Burke's account of Marie Antoinette gives one vivid instance of how
theatricality and the trope of sensibility pervade his conceptualization of
historical and political events:

It is now sixteen or seventeen years since I saw the Queen of France, then the
dauphiness, at Versailles, and surely never lighted on this orb, which she hardly
seemed to touch, a more delightful vision. I saw her just above the horizon,
decorating and cheering the elevated sphere she just began to move in—glittering like the morning star, full of life, and splendour, and joy. Oh! What a
revolution! and what an heart must I have, to contemplate without emotion
that elevation and that fall! Little did I dream when she added titles of venera-
tion to those of enthusiastic, distant, respectful love, that she should ever be
obliged to carry the sharp antidote against disgrace concealed in that bosom;
little did I dream that I should have lived to see such disasters fallen upon her
in a nation of gallant men, in a nation of men of honour and of cavaliers. I
thought ten thousand swords must have leaped from their scabbards to avenge
even a look that threatened her with insult.[14]

It is significant that Burke looks backwards, taking his image from the
recent past, from 'sixteen or seventeen year since'. As a member of her
audience, he has observed the young Marie Antoinette as an icon, a
'delightful vision . . . glittering like the morning star', presented to his
view from 'the elevated sphere' of the stage. This image, drawing on

---

[13] See Hindson and Gray, *Burke's Dramatic Theory*, ch. 3, 'The Language of Drama',
for a version of the exchange between Burke and Paine over theatricality; citation on p.
40, 'the essential business of drama—the imaginative interpretation of reality in terms of
figures created to embody the dramatists's (*sic*) attitudes and values—perfectly focuses
Paine's charges against Burke', from J. T. Boulton, *The Language of Politics in the Age of
Wilkes and Burke* (RKP, London, 1963).
[14] Burke, *Reflections on the Revolution*, 169–70.

both the Court and the drama, is the pivotal representation for him, in elaborating what he takes to be the appropriate sensibility in terms of audience response, and in defending the monarchy, through a gendered construction of the Queen, whom, because of historical distance, he is able to construct as virginal perfection, untouchable by any sin or criticism.[15] This sentimental recollection—'what a heart must I have to contemplate without emotion'—allows him to lead into an unproblematic association of the Queen with fine and noble feeling. This valorizes his moral certainty and allows him to substitute sensibility for historical and political analysis. It is then an easy transition to claiming that a whole society has been 'extinguished', and an excuse for Burke to go into mourning for the demise of the *ancien régime* (significant to note that this hasn't actually happened yet—it needs another five years):[16] 'Never, never more shall we behold that generous loyalty to rank and sex, that proud submission, that dignified obedience, that subordination of the heart which kept alive, even in servitude itself, the spirit of an exalted freedom.'[17]

Paine is not alone in finding problems with Burke's style of representation. Mary Wollstonecraft presents us with a very different kind of representation of Marie Antoinette from that of Burke:

Her opening faculties were poisoned in the bud; but before she came to Paris, she had already been prepared, by a corrupt, supple abbé, for the part she was to play; and, young as she was, became so firmly attached to the aggrandizement

---

[15] See Pascoe, *Romantic Theatricality*, 'Embodying Marie Antoinette: The Theatricalized Female Subject', 95–129, for more on the gender construction, and on the responses of both Burke and Mary Wollstonecraft to Marie Antoinette; also Lynn Hunt, 'The Many Bodies of Marie Antoinette: Political Pornography and the Problem of the Feminine in the French Revolution', in Lynn Hunt (ed.) *Eroticism and the Body Politic* (Johns Hopkins University Press, Baltimore, 1990) Julie A. Carlson, *In the Theatre of Romanticism: Coleridge, Nationalism, Women* (Cambridge University Press, Cambridge, 1994), ch. 4, cites Christopher Reid for the theory that Burke models Marie Antoinette on Sarah Siddons.

[16] One of the symptoms of the demise of the *ancien régime* was a number of scandals involving outrageous amounts of money, implicating Marie Antoinette. Todd and Butler, *The Works of Mary Wollstonecraft*, vi. 30 n., record: that 'In 1785 Boehmer, the court jeweller, offered Marie Antoinette a diamond necklace for 56,000 livres which she declined because of the vast expense. However, the Comtesse de la Motte forged the Queen's signature, obtained the necklace and absconded with it. She was caught, tried and sentenced in 1786, but escaped to London. At the time the French public suspected the Queen of involvement in the fraud.' Louis XIV built two pleasure palaces at Trianon; Louis XVI gave one of these, 'le petit Trianon' to Marie Antoinette.

[17] Burke *Reflections on the Revolution*, 170.

of her house, that, though plunged deep in pleasure, she never omitted send-
ing immense sums to her brother, on every occasion . . . Lost then in the most
luxurious pleasures, or managing court intrigues, the queen became a profound
dissembler; and her heart hardened by sensual enjoyments to such a degree,
that when her family and favourites stood on the brink of ruin, her little
portion of mind was employed only to preserve herself from danger. As a proof
of the justness of this assertion, it is only necessary to observe, that, in the
general wreck, not a scrap of her writing has been found to criminate her;
neither has she suffered a word to escape her to exasperate the people, even
when burning with rage, and contempt. The effect that adversity may have on
her choked understanding time will show . . . A court is the best school in the
world for actors; it was very natural then for her to become a complete actress,
and an adept in all the arts of coquetry that debauch the mind, whilst they
render the person alluring.[18]

Like Burke, but writing in France during the Terror after Marie
Antoinette's execution, Mary Wollstonecraft is put in mind of the image
of the actress in relation to Marie Antoinette. At the moment of her
youth, Marie Antoinette appears to Burke as an object of purity and
unblemished virtue.[19] By contrast, she appears to Wollstonecraft as a
subject, a key agent in the plot, who, being prepared for performance—
'the part she was to play'—is 'poisoned in the bud'. In other words, the
two commentators construe the image of performance very differently.
For Burke, her performance demonstrates that Marie Antoinette is
above reproach; for Wollstonecraft, that same performance provides
evidence of moral degeneracy and political intrigue. Marie Antoinette
is 'a profound dissembler', in other words a good actress, who utilizes
those skills for the purposes of political self-interest, to the extent that
no crack can be perceived in her faultless performance—'neither has she
suffered a word to escape her'.

For Burke, the dramatic vocabulary of the Siddonesque tragedian is
used to valorize Marie Antoinette. Wollstonecraft utilizes similar terms
of reference for the purposes of a starkly different interpretation. For
her, Marie Antoinette the actress has perfected the performance skills of

[18] Todd and Butler, *The Works of Mary Wollstonecraft*, vi. 72–4; original edn. 129–37.
Marie Antoinette was guillotined on 16 Oct. 1793—nine months after Louis.

[19] See Blakemore, *Burke and the Fall of Language*, ch. 4, 'Revolutionary Criticism and
the Fall into Knowledge', for a sympathetic account of Burke's representation of Marie
Antoinette; also, Hindson and Gray, *Burke's Dramatic Theory*, produce extended
commentary on Burke's attitude to the French Revolution and to the 'debauchery' of
Revolutionary women, in ch. 6, 'Tragedy'.

simulating emotion and virtue, and Marie Antoinette the politically influential figure becomes representative of how the entire Court comes to stand for corruption.[20] That which makes the figure of the Queen 'alluring' and 'adept in all the arts of coquetry' is precisely that which signals political degeneracy. Both Burke and Wollstonecraft invest much in Marie Antoinette as a central figure of representation of the French Court, but in their histories of the French Revolution, the Queen comes to stand for opposing rationales of that history.

It is not just a question of what the Queen represents. In the Wollstonecraft account, like that of Tom Paine, the language of the drama, far from being required to stand unproblematically for a moral topography, is critiqued for what it conceals in terms of political and historical analysis. Even more than Burke, Wollstonecraft invokes 'sensibility' as an issue, but it is not for her a question of matching appropriate sensibilities across the drama and the politics, or even of displacing one form of appropriate sensibility in the interests of discovering another. Sensibility is a problem in itself in that it leads in the direction of 'erroneous inferences', as opposed to reason, which is 'the only sure guide' in its 'beaming on the grand theatre of political changes'. What is significant here is not so much the appeal to reason as against emotion, a classic Enlightenment antithesis if ever there was one, as the acknowledgement of the extent to which theatrical vocabulary persists in the analysis of politics—'the grand *theatre* of political changes'. It is recognized that the particular character of the audience and of the individual spectator cannot simply be ignored, but that spectator response, like the character of the performance itself, can be challenged and rendered problematic in its claim to vouch for the significance of political events.[21]

In seeking to validate either the values and virtues of the *ancien*

---

[20]   Political corruption appears to run parallel with sexual intrigue, and the increasing identification of actresses as prostitutes dates from this period. For a discussion of this refer to Tracy C. Davis, *Actresses as Working Women: Their Social Identity in Victorian Culture* (Routledge, London, 1991). Wollstonecraft is drawing upon this conflation of the sexual and the political in her representation of Marie Antoinette as performer. For more information about Wollstonecraft and her relationship to discourses of sensibility see Syndy McMillen Conger, *Mary Wollstonecraft and the Language of Sensibility* (Fairleigh Dickinson University Press, London and Toronto, 1994).

[21]   See Ch. 6 for commentary on the need to distinguish performance conventions in relation to theatre and politics (and the contribution of Diderot to the discussion); also, for further exploration of the meanings of sensibility.

*régime* (Burke), or the move towards greater democracy (Woll-stonecraft), it is as if theatre, as if *performance* (I use the term inclusively to cover spectator response as well as dramatic enactment) is the centrally contested area. For Burke, a particular performance style had vouched for virtue and quality in the body politic. For Wollstonecraft, that same performance forms the evidence of political corruption. As the Court comes increasingly under criticism, its principal actors are exposed as dissemblers; they are no longer stars decorating the elevated sphere.[22] Burke and Wollstonecraft are placed at that intriguing moment when both the drama and the body politic are under pressure and under scrutiny through the lens of 'performance' values—as if those confident eighteenth-century notions of appropriate sensibility are under challenge in a very public way, not only in relation to the state of theatre, but over the whole question of how to govern.

### The Plays Risk a Hubbub, and John Bull Grows Radical

Released from his imprisonment, Thomas Hardy finds himself delightfully surprised to perceive that the rioters who had gathered earlier to break the windows of his home (possibly hirelings of the government) have been displaced by sympathetic supporters, who are anti-Establishment and object to those who have punished him and deprived him of his rights. The 1790s was the era in which 'the mob' underwent a change from riot-ing or demonstrating *with* the Establishment, as in the Gordon riots, to congregating in order to object *to* the Establishment.[23] This change in political attitude, together with the momentum set in motion in terms of audience reception of radical ideas, finds its parallel in dramatic possibili-ties within the theatre. Part of the challenge for the drama was to develop the process of discovering new systems of representation, in which kings,

---

[22] Blakemore, *Burke and the Fall of Language*, in ch. 4, 'Revolutionary Criticism and the Fall into Knowledge', outlines an argument about 'the philosophic wardrobe of old Europe' which is pertinent here. The French Revolutionaries were about freeing 'man' from 'society's repressive social wardrobe', but for Burke, this was only to dispense with 'the decent drapery of life'. The theatrical language of costume is, of course, significant.

[23] Evans, *Britain before the Reform Act*, 13–20, 'Rioting was endemic in eighteenth-century society and, when it had a political rather than an economic basis, its motiva-tion was likely to be conservative if not atavistic. The anti-Catholic Gordon riots of 1780 and the anti-Dissenting and anti-reformist Priestley riots of 1791 are prime examples. [para.] By the early nineteenth century . . . pro-establishment rioting and crowd activ-ity all but disappeared.'

queens, and courts, would no longer be central to the action, and audiences would be interested in the destinies of individuals coming from other classes of society than the aristocracy.

It was George Colman's play *John Bull*,[24] the very piece that he claimed to the Select Committee he should have approached with a more searching eye to censorship, which played a key part in the radical disturbances of the Old Price riots, known as the OP riots, in the autumn of 1809. The riots took place over sixty-seven nights, and consisted of violent demonstrations by theatregoers on the reopening of the new Covent Garden Theatre (after its rebuilding because of fire). The rioting was against higher prices of admission, levelled upwards to pay for the new building.[25] Significantly, Francis Place and other members of the London Corresponding Society are held to have played a part, if not in orchestrating the riots, at least in supporting them.[26]

Colman's *John Bull or the Englishman's Fireside* (see Plate 5), the story of the honest brazier, Job Thornberry, pitted against the landed gentry, who include the Earl of Fitz Balaam and Lady Caroline Braymore, played twice uninterrupted, an event rarely enjoyed during the riots, although it is notable, particularly given Colman's later expressed fears to the Select Committee about riotous assembly, that the disturbances themselves never once invaded the stage space itself. Critics from the Tory Walter Scott to the Whig Leigh Hunt agreed that the play exhibited a powerful influence on those who saw it.[27] The attitudes of the rioters were reflected and even celebrated in the play's final lines, which point criticism in the direction of John Kemble, the theatre manager

---

[24] George Colman the Younger, *John Bull; or, The Englishman's Fireside*, a comedy in five acts, first performed at the Theatre Royal, Covent Garden, in 1803 (Longman, London, 1806), with remarks by Mrs Inchbald.

[25] See Marc Baer, *Theatre and Disorder in late Georgian London* (Clarendon Press, Oxford, 1992) for an account of the OP riots; also, Hadley, *Melodramatic Tactics* particularly ch. 2, 'The Old Price Wars'.

[26] Baer, *Theatre and Disorder*, ch. 6. Francis Place also gives testimony to the Select Committee, questions 3689–3740, arguing strongly against censorship. When asked whether there would be *political* plays if monopolies on theatres were removed, he replies, 'Yes; and there ought to be.' He also argues that there is no need to censor plays as, 'There is a sufficient safeguard in the deference they (performers) are compelled to pay to the audience.' When asked to reiterate—'Do you mean to state that, in your opinion, there ought to be no limit to any political allusions in a play, or any indecency or immorality, which might be produced at a theatre, other than the limit which would be imposed upon it by the judgment of the audience?'—he replies confidently, 'Yes, I think no other restriction is necessary.'

[27] Baer, *Theatre and Disorder*.

who had tried to introduce the price rises: 'no one deserves forgiveness, who refuses to make amends, when he has disturbed the happiness of an Englishman's fireside.'[28] Such sentiments appear to have been influential in persuading John Kemble to 'make amends' in the form of an eventual capitulation on the question of ticket prices.[29] The quotation from Hume's *Essays* on the title-page of the 1805 edition of the play gives some indication that it has broad political aspirations: 'The English Government is a mixture of monarchy, aristocracy, and democracy;— and the great liberty and independency, which every man enjoys, allows him to display the manners peculiar to himself.'

As Mr T. Dibdin announces in his prologue, John Bull does not figure as a character in the play, but he represents, as Dibdin puts it, a particular version of the free-born Englishman found wherever 'you mark a wight revering law, yet resolute for right'.[30] There is some play made of the idea that Job Thornberry is a freeholder, and therefore has voting rights. His support at the polling station is an issue for Sir Simon Rochdale's son, Frank, who, it is mentioned in passing, will be standing in the next election. On hearing that Job is a freeholder, Sir Simon comments, 'Zounds! one of Frank's voters, perhaps, and of consequence at his election.'[31] Similarly, there is a glancing reference to the Earl of Fitz Balaam's thirty-year history in the Upper House, the cryptic note being that he has only ever spoken in the House for a minute.

However, Colman's *John Bull* is no reform play as such. The central dynamic of the play, very much as in the work of the women playwrights (especially Elizabeth Inchbald's comedies), derives from sexual mores, particularly the concept of men offering protection to women, rather than more explicit political challenges.[32] Job Thornberry's grudge against the aristocratic Rochdales derives from the son, Frank, having seduced Job's daughter, Mary, and then apparently abandoned her for a richer woman. However, this is not an attack on aristocratic habits *per se*, for what the audience shortly discovers is that Frank Rochdale is himself a potential victim of his father's aspirations for an arranged

---

[28] Colman, *John Bull*.

[29] See Baer *Theatre and Disorder*, and Hadley, *Melodramatic Tactics*, for more on Kemble's position; also, Linda Kelly, *The Kemble Era: John Philip Kemble, Sarah Siddons, and the London Stage* (Random House, New York, 1980).

[30] Colman, *John Bull*, 1805 edn.

[31] Ibid., Act 5.

[32] Ibid.; Mrs Inchbald writes the remarks which form the preface to the 1806 edition. For more on women playwrights and the issue of protection see Ch. 5.

marriage which will, the hope is, enhance family finances. Colman plays off various notions of protection, as a practice open to abuse, but unlike the women playwrights, he does not challenge the basic concept. He elides the idea of the free-born Englishman with the ethical protector, in the notion of benign condescension summed up in the sentiment that 'no Englishman should neglect justice and humanity to his inferiors'.[33] Moreover, the character to utter such sentiments is not Job, the honest brazier, but Peregrine, Mary's mysterious elderly protector, newly returned from India to Penzance, where the play is set. It is only in the play's denouement that the audience discovers Peregrine's identity—he is the elder brother of Sir Simon Rochdale; in other words, he is every bit as aristocratic as the Earl of Fitz Balaam. The implication is that it is from the mouth of the *honourable* gentry that we discover the play's true ethics, not from Job who is, throughout the play, inclined to beat people about the head rather than to administer that justice, which as Peregrine tells him, 'is the only proper weapon for the injured', the English law. Colman's ideal John Bull, it begins to seem, is more a Peregrine than a Job Thornberry.

J. B. Buckstone's *The Forgery! or the Reading of the Will*, performed on the eve of reform after the Bristol riots in 1832, shares aspects of this interest in 'the ordinary man', if with a similarly compromised resolution in the direction of the trope of the upwardly mobile retreat to the gentleman protector.[34] Like Colman, Buckstone tends to displace his interest in the radical servant, Jack Spratt, onto a woman character, in this case the somewhat sentimentalized middle-class mother, whose struggle for the rights over her son, William, increasingly dominates the action. Jack Spratt's organization of the paupers in the market square, in order to protest their rights, is reported, the action occurring offstage, while the domestic scenario of mother, son, and fond cousin, Ellen, claims the audience's view.

However, the focus on the rights of mothers is interesting in itself and connects with issues raised by women playwrights.[35] Before the will's forgery is exposed, William's mother has been led to believe that she must needs part with her son to a public school. She has threatened to go to any lengths, including emigration to America, to keep him with her. The scenario rather supports the theory that women of the time were prepared to claim more rights in practice than they had under the law.[36] The male protector, Thornhill, does make the crucial financial interventions, exposing the forgery of the will, but these events happen ritualistically at a very late moment and for the purposes of rapid denouement. It is the mother's declaration of her rights to her child, *her* ability to act as protector, which carries the momentum of the action.

The play is also somewhat unusual in taking the public house as its primary setting and confining much of the action to villagers and servants. Jack Spratt, as his name suggests, is clearly intended as a caricature of the radical, literate ordinary man. He reads tomes demonstrating how the non-producer is a tax on the producer, and describes himself as a leveller, as well as demanding an increase in relief for paupers. He is significantly pitted against both the Church, satirized in the greedy and self-serving Grub, the churchwarden, and the army, again graphically lampooned in the figure of Lieutenant Lizzard, infamous as a threat to the ladies and centrally implicated in the forging of the will of the title.[37]

The play abounds in musical interludes and is described as a domestic burletta, but discourses of radicalism and reform are clearly there, represented at the level of local government, with Grub preaching about the threat posed by the likes of Jack Spratt to his own position and 'the political power of the parish'. Like Douglas Jerrold in some of his plays, as we shall see, Buckstone makes use of a painting by David Wilkie, in this instance *Village Politicians*.[38] This is the very painting which John Barrell dismisses as politically reactionary.[39] However, Buckstone, like Jerrold, attempts to invoke the painter in support of Jack Spratt and the radical politics of the villagers, as part of what Martin Meisel describes as a 'revolution in social sympathy'.[40]

---

[36] Colley, *Britons*, ch. 6, 'separate sexual spheres were being increasingly prescribed in theory, yet increasingly broken through in practice'.

[37] The play is rare in attacking the avaricious Church. Grub objects to paupers waiting for relief at the counting house, arguing that they will deter other customers.

[38] Ch. 4 analyses some aspects of the relationship between Jerrold's plays and Wilkie's paintings.

[39] See Ch. 4 for reference to Barrell's analysis.

[40] Meisel, *Realizations*, ch. 8; the politics of Wilkie's genre painting served the purpose of the drama, 'to enlarge the classes and categories perceived as fully human and deserving of justice and respect'.

It is W. T. Moncrieff's *Reform* (see Plate 1), which like Colman uses the John Bull idea, that moves firmly into the radicalism of reform, seeming unashamed, despite the Lord Chamberlain and his Examiner, of signalling its content very explicitly, *and* on the eve of the Reform Act.[41] In Moncrieff's own introductory remarks to the play, he also appears unstinting in his appeal for both political and theatre reform.[42] Just as the abolitionists write of their glorious cause in attempting to abolish the slave trade, so Moncrieff uses the same vocabulary to describe the movement for parliamentary reform.

With regard to the subject of this piece, "Reform", it is one in which every true-born Englishman—every well-wisher of his country, must heartily exult; and the author feels a proud satisfaction in reflecting that his anticipation of the success of the glorious cause he has attempted to advocate in it, promises to be fully realized.[43]

He goes on to describe 'the host of evils' which will disappear once the 'wise measure . . . of a fair and equal representation' has been introduced. Then Moncrieff calls specifically for a reform of the drama, aiming to abolish 'odious distinctions' between major and minor theatres and 'absurd regulations' in all theatres. He opposes the pirating of authors' scripts by theatre managers, describing the latter as vampires, and exhorts authors to co-operate with each other, instead of competing like 'feudal tyrants'. The drama should be 'one free and equal arena'. Without wishing to diminish the significance of Moncrieff's pioneering spirit on behalf of his play, it appears that the moment was right, whatever the supposed requirements of the Lord Chamberlain's office, for such utterances. Moncrieff himself writes of the Whigs as an 'enlightened and loyal ministry' who are ready to respond favourably to the wishes and struggles of a 'suffering people'. In the passage of nearly thirty years between George Colman's play, *John Bull*, and Moncrieff's play, political conditions have clearly changed in such a way as to render the reform spirit acceptable in terms of staged material (even though George Colman, still worried about a hubbub in the theatres, was the Examiner at the time of Moncrieff's *Reform*).

Nevertheless, *Reform* itself is not direct in its representation of the

---

[41]    W. T. Moncrieff, *Reform; or, John Bull Triumphant*, a patriotic drama in one act (Thomas Richardson, London, 1831), in *Richardson's New Minor Drama*, vol. iv.

[42]    Ibid., 'remarks biographical and critical'.

[43]    Ibid.

Houses of Parliament, but draws on allegory, together with comic parody, to achieve its effects. John Bull's 'great house' has been taken over by his opportunistic servants, whose names tell all: Lickspit the cook, Smugport the butler, Rottenstone the footman, Perquisite the housekeeper, and more. The master trusts them to look after the interests of his tenants, but the servants are more enthusiastic about their 'capital places' within the household and they enjoy the *status quo*: 'OMNES: No, No,—No change!—Things can't be going on better than they are!', and a little later, 'OMNES: No, No, No alteration—no alteration, not by any means.' The tenants, meanwhile, are dissatisfied, living in poverty and unable to pay their rents, but the servants of the great household, who are supposed to represent the interests of the tenants to the master, dismiss their claims, arguing, tellingly, that their discontentment is all the fault of the tenants having learned to read and write.[44]

It is not difficult to see a correspondence between the household servants and Members of Parliament as the supposed servants of the people who are actually more interested in 'feathering their own nests'; Thomas Hardy and William Cobbett, as well as Moncrieff, would have seen it this way. Mr Felix Prosper, the voice of the free-born Englishman in the play, comments tellingly that John Bull has 'a capital estate' and 'devoted tenantry'. The problem is only the want of 'proper management'. Scene 2 sees the classic trio of George Briton, Patrick Murphy, and Sandy Glaskey, representatives of England, Ireland, and Scotland respectively, uniting in struggle, deploring the fact that they have no one to speak for them up at the big house. Their common cause is more important than their differences.[45] In scene 3 of the play, in a recognizable dramatic convention, and after much prompting, John Bull disguises himself as a 'distressed agriculturalist', in order to discover the truth about his stewards.[46] Members of his household mock him when

---

[44] Extension of education was coterminous with the movement for reform. The London Corresponding Society wished to promote political education as well as reform of Parliament, 'diffusing useful knowledge among the people of Great Britain and Ireland', cited in *Memoir of Thomas Hardy* .

[45] Colley, *Britons*, ch. 8, makes this observation about common cause between England, Wales, and Scotland, in relation to reform agitation.

[46] I am thinking particularly of Shakespeare's *Measure for Measure*, in which the Duke disguises himself in order to find out various truths about his subjects. Of course, the convention does rather derive from the idea that those in power are dangerously removed from true knowledge of their subjects in the first instance. This is not an issue which Moncrieff confronts.

he requests employment, pleading the destitution of his family. Enraged, John Bull swears at them, vowing that their corrupt regime is over and that all will be reformed. The play concludes with a singing of the national anthem, and a tableau, out of which John Bull's daughter Albina steps, to sing 'Rule Britannia'. Britain's unity is foregrounded, as soldiers and sailors flank tenants in the front row, and members of the great household, evil and virtuous, form the back row in support.

*Reform* was originally performed, to popular acclaim, in the Royal Coburg Theatre, and appears to have escaped censorship, but it is possible that, even if the reform spirit had not been at its height, the very crudeness of its caricature would have protected it against any complaint of serious criticism of the Establishment. It also leaves the landed gentry largely unscathed, in a recognizable sentimentalizing of John Bull, the owner of the great household. This dimension of the play is reinforced through his daughter, Albina, the sentimental and suggestively named heroine of the piece, who enjoys the 'sweet task' of ministering to the poor of her guardian's estate, whilst deploring 'our wasteful establishment'.[47] At the same time, the play does identify a problem, as John Bull repeatedly puns on his constitution, which is in a terribly 'bad way', and on the decline of his greatness. The implied criticism comes from his readiness to escape to his pipe and his tankard, ignoring the condition of his tenants and Albina's pleas to manage his household properly. Significantly, too, Albina, representative of Britain, rejects her father's language of national supremacy. She professes herself uninterested in being 'a match for any one in the world', declaring: 'Nay, I have no ambition to make conquests, sir;—Albina would rather have domestic peace—would rather win the love of all! than own one heart by power or fear!'[48] At one level, this is rather an extraordinary little speech to hear on a stage which fifteen years earlier was, in some respects, celebrating the achievements of a war-mongering, colonial, and trading nation. In another way, though, support for war and nationalism had never been completely coterminous, and some sections of the population, particularly women, had always lobbied for peace.[49] Also, as we shall see in the case of Douglas Jerrold's *The Rent Day*, the play does leave its mark in pleading the cause of distressed tenants, abused and

---

[47] Albina is dressed in breast-plate and helmet, 'to personify Britannia'.
[48] Moncrieff, *Reform*, scene 1.
[49] Colley, *Britons*, ch. 6.

exploited by those whose duty it is supposed to be to represent their interests.[50] It is an allegory, albeit a brief one, for defending the people and raising objections to the behaviour of the people's representatives. As such, it makes its own small intervention in the argument for reforming the household of the landed estate and the nation.

One cannot help wondering, too, whether Moncrieff's choice of the John Bull idea as central to his reform play might have been intended, in part, as a witty provocation to George Colman, not only for his own play of that name, but in his role as Examiner. If members of the Select Committee were at all familiar with recent productions, and they give some evidence of being so, they may well have been bemused by Colman's reply when he was asked his response to the word 'reform' being uttered on the stage. Moncrieff's John Bull relishes the word, reiterating it *ad infinitum* in the final act. Colman could have been quietly cursing not only his own earlier career as a playwright, and such unhappy scriptural allusions as that to Eve and pin-money, but also the ubiquitous Moncrieff, whose script clearly survived any treatment Colman the Examiner might have attempted to bring to bear on it for its pervasive use of both the spirit and letter of reform.[51]

### Oiling the Engine of Reform

It is arguable that the change of emphasis over the 1790s from pro-Establishment mob to an audience of radical sympathizers had come about precisely because of reform activism itself, that embracing and inclusive quality of the reform spirit generated by the capacity of the London Corresponding Society and later reform societies, such as the Hampden Clubs, to provide a widespread political educational programme, formal and informal.[52] As Thomas Hardy would have it:

[50] Douglas Jerrold, *The Rent Day, A domestic drama in two acts* (Chapple, London, 1832), analysed in ch. 4.

[51] My phrase, 'the ubiquitous Moncrieff', is purloined from Professor J. S. Bratton, coined by her at the conference, 'Theatre and Politics in the Age of Reform', 1997, April, Cambridge.

[52] The section heading is derived from Hindson and Gray, *Burke's Dramatic Theory*, ch. 5, 'Political Characterisation', who cite Burke on an occasion when he attempts to distinguish between political process and the paraphernalia surrounding it: 'They must be singularly unfortunate who seek to govern by dinners and bows, and who mistake the oil which facilitates the motion, for the machine itself' (104). Burke attempts to create an interesting distinction, although perhaps he underestimates the significance of dinners and bows (as set and costume), as well as the indispensability of oil!

The London Corresponding Society did more in the eight or nine years of its existence, to diffuse political knowledge among the people of Great Britain and Ireland than all that had ever been done before . . . Its members *devoted* themselves to the cause of justice and humanity . . . in order to promote the happiness of their fellow citizens.[53]

With the revival of political activism in 1815, the growth of popular journalism had lent aid to this project. Whilst William Cobbett's *Weekly Political Register*, with its influential attacks on misgovernment and 'Old Corruption', had been founded in the earlier year of 1802, three major radical journals, T. J. Wooler's *Black Dwarf*, William Hone's *Reformists' Register* and Thomas Sherwin's *Political Register*, began their lives in the years immediately following the end of the war with France. Contemporaneously, new societies emerged to capitalize on and foster the reform spirit. In 1818, a year in which the government is reputed to have received 1,500 reform petitions, the Union for the Promotion of Human Happiness was formed.[54] Like the London Corresponding Society, it was committed to education in the objectives of parliamentary reform as well as to reform itself. Significantly, it was organized on the basis of co-operation 'between skilled workers and the lower middle classes', indicating that the reform movement operated across class boundaries.[55] Significantly, too, female unions flourished.[56]

However, there is some disagreement about the continuities and discontinuities of British political radical consciousness at this time, and historians tend to identify two important phases of popular agitation for reform of the constitution and of the franchise. Specific agitation for reform of the British constitution, together with demands for liberty and rights in the educational and social domains, took fire with the circulation of the manifesto of the London Corresponding Society, burning most brightly in the 1790s, and resurfacing again in 1815 after the Napoleonic Wars, which had inevitably focused attention on external conflict.

---

[53] *Memoir of Thomas Hardy*, preface.
[54] Evans, *Britain before the Reform Act*, 21–7.
[55] Ibid.
[56] Although women in these organizations came under greater attack than their male counterparts, bearing out feminist concerns, to which we shall return in a later chapter, about responses to women's involvement in the public sphere, particularly in political activism and overt agitation for access to education.

Despite the insistence in the manifesto of the Society on peaceful solutions, and on a reform of the franchise which would leave the monarchy untouched, the very suggestion of constitutional reform seems to have provoked the judiciary to extreme measures in the 1790s.[57] The suppression of the activities of the Society is one of the factors that makes it difficult to trace obvious continuities of radical activism. It is also significant that, throughout this history and up until 1830, with the exception of a very short period, Britain experienced continual Tory government.[58]

It is not the case, though, that reforming zeal was confined to isolated moments of activism, nor was it absent at a time of Tory rule. The momentum and cohesion of reform in terms of social and political consciousness, whatever the constraints imposed on theatre itself via the Lord Chamberlain's office, came importantly from theatrical activity.[59] It was not accidental that the London Corresponding Society had generated new energies out of the Old Price riots at Covent Garden Theatre and that, earlier, the growth of popular support for the Society and its activities had occurred over the 1790s, despite the imprisonment of Thomas Hardy and other prominent members.[60]

Reform is at one and the same time the most diverse and probably the most complex movement of late Georgian Britain, as well as the most crucial in its implications for the drama. It is also the most elliptically explained, in terms of a manifesto for constitutional and parliamentary change, whilst being also the most elusive, because of all the social and educational implications that go with agitation for a proposed extension of the suffrage. Reform is, as its name suggests, a question of form as well as content, and this has its implications for dramatic genre and theatrical method. In one sense, theatrical activity can be regarded as the oil supplied to the machinery of reform:

---

[57] Hardy was by no means alone in being persecuted for his beliefs and for his activities in the London Corresponding Society. Other reform societies also had their victims, sentenced to imprisonment and to transportation. Thompson, *The Making of the English Working Class*, ch. 5, records the extent of persecution of reformers.

[58] Evans, *Britain before the Reform Act*, comments in the first chapter that Lord Liverpool was the first Prime Minister of the period, holding office from 1812, to acknowledge the description 'Tory'.

[59] See my Prologue and Epilogue for more on the Lord Chamberlain's office.

[60] There is further commentary in Ch. 6 on analyses of the OP riots by Elaine Hadley and Marc Baer respectively.

'Political action is seen as a negotiated process relying on the skills of the theatre to achieve spontaneous cooperation between human actors.'[61]

Debates and transforming practices on and off the stage, in the plays themselves and in the polemical exchanges outlined here, bear witness to the part played by theatricality in the movement for fair representation of the people, and in the strenuous attempts to hold those responsible for government to account for their performance to and behalf of the people. Hardy had criticized Parliament directly in the manifesto of the London Corresponding Society, asserting that the 'evils' of government should be resisted and that: 'The few with whom the right of election and representation remains, abuse it, and the strong temptations held out to electors, sufficiently prove that the representatives of this country seldom procure a seat in Parliament, from the unbought suffrages of a free people.'[62]

Theatre itself was undergoing a change in its own commitments and priorities, with attempts to constitute a more democratic model of actors and audiences, in a performance space which would help to give the people their liberty—the freedom that, in Hardy's view, should be their birthright. Theatre thus supported the project of the London Corresponding Society manifesto in finding a means of representing a people struggling to be free individuals, prepared to yield up their individual interests in the cause of that which 'was necessary for the common good', whilst insisting on 'a right of sharing in the government of the country'. This was a process which was not to be reversed, however far reform societies themselves were successfully suppressed.[63]

Here emerges a new relationship between the political activist and

[61] Hindson and Gray, *Burke's Dramatic Theory*, introduction.

[62] *Memoir of Thomas Hardy*, 48. Hardy actually italicizes 'unbought' for obvious emphasis.

[63] Carlson, *In the Theatre of Romanticism:* 'When push comes to shove, English theatre spectators become actors who demand their rights to hear and be heard. Similarly, theatrical assemblies are viewed as national bodies in the minds of the audience and theatre reviewers. The permeability of these two houses of representation is particularly visible in the significance of 1832 as a date in the history of London theatre as well as parliamentary reform' (12). Carlson's primary concern is with the theatre of the canonical romantic poets, arguing that 'Not simply their plays but their writings on drama and theatre reveal the indispensability of theatre for becoming acknowledged legislators in this age' (2). Carlson also points out in her introduction that in the view of some critics, there was too much suffrage talk in the theatres.

the spectator of political events, between reformer and crowd, between actor and audience. Assembling for the purpose of articulating popular support for reform changes the terms of theatricality and political representation. It is thus in theatrical exchange as well as political activism that the transformation of the consciousness of the people takes place, reconstituting the relationship between theatre, politics, and polemic. As the character of audience changes (with audiences unwilling to condone limitless persecution of reformers by the State) so does the character of the reformer, erstwhile villain turned popular hero, who emerges out of a changing conception of appropriate dramatic action and scene. This same transformation of the audience and the actor, signalling mutual commitment to creating a participating democracy, is also happening *within* the theatres, with audiences, performers, and managers ready to engage with reform ideas and to take up the associated causes of anti-slavery, factory, and agrarian reform, and last but not at all least, women's rights.[64]

In carrying the freight of these questions of theatricality in addition to the literal application of the term to the movement for the extension of the franchise, reform emerges as the central principle or symbol representing interconnection and cohesion between the different political movements which are of concern in this book. This is at its most explicit in the relationship between the reform and abolition movements, but is also there in the connections between the reform movement and feminism, and in the contexts of agrarian and factory movements. The interplay between movements occurs at the level of activism, with many women and working men across Britain engaged, say, not only with the politics of anti-slavery, but also with those of reform more generally, whether as activists or signatories to petitions.

The age which, as we shall see, was to produce mass mobilization and petitioning as forms of resistance to the perpetuation of social and political inequalities, was also developing audiences and actors increasingly educated in the spirit of hope for emancipation, and intolerant of inhumane acts, both inside and outside the theatre; theatricality and

---

[64] Raymond Williams, *The Long Revolution* (Chatto & Windus, London, 1961), for the now widely used terms of 'participating democracy'. It is also significant, as we shall see in Ch. 5, that reform audiences are ready to object to the lampooning of women playwrights by some male writers.

performance values were central to the process of contestation and political change. In terms of a spirit uniting several political movements, and in terms of theatre itself, we can thus observe continuities of the reform spirit from 1789 until the 1833 Emancipation Act, peaking in 1832 with the twin measures of the Dramatic Literature legislation and the Reform Act itself.[65]

[65] See Thompson, *The Making of the English Working Class*, for an account of Thomas Hardy and English reform: 'the agitation of the 1790s, although it lasted only five years (1792–6) was extraordinarily intensive and far-reaching . . . It was an English agitation, of impressive dimensions, for an English democracy.' *Memoir of Thomas Hardy* went so far as to claim that the British government had deliberately contrived to block the reform movement with the declaration of war on France.

# CHAPTER TWO

# Slavery, Removing the Cloak from the Truth

## Reform, Zealous Friend of Abolition?

The interconnection between reform and abolition has perhaps been the most graphically documented of the relationships between the political movements referred to in my account, with some of the leading and most controversial figures of the abolition movement, notably Olaudah Equiano and Robert Wedderburn, also involved in challenging the terms of parliamentary franchise.[1] I turn to this relationship, before focusing more exclusively on the abolition movement itself, to give some indication of a shared frame of reference in relation to the people involved as political activists, as well as to highlight the discourse of theatricality which crosses the movements.

In Thomas Hardy's view, it was out of the contact between himself and Gustavus Vassa, as Olaudah Equiano was known to him, that the founding moment of the London Corresponding Society occurred. In his *Memoir*, Hardy records how the first letter that he ever wrote in the name of the Society was penned at the suggestion of Equiano, who was staying with Hardy at the time, working on an edition of his own memoirs.[2] The addressee was the Reverend Mr Bryant in Sheffield, known to Equiano as 'a zealous friend to the abolition of that cursed traffic, the Slave Trade'. As Hardy argues in his letter, he assumes from the form of Equiano's recommendation that Bryant will also be 'a zealous friend to freedom on the broad basis of the RIGHTS OF MAN'.[3]

Hardy is quite explicit about the analogy between the abolition and

---

[1] The chapter title is derived from Mary Prince, *The History of Mary Prince, A West Indian Slave* (Westley and Davis, London, 1831), who writes autobiographically of the need to remove the cloak from the truth about slavery.

[2] *Memoir of Thomas Hardy.*

[3] Ibid. 45–7.

the reform movements, refusing to recognize the two areas of activism as anything other than entirely complementary, indeed mutually dependent. To support 'the liberty of the black man' is to support the rights of the white man and 'vice versa'.[4] Forty years later, Hardy was to endorse his dual commitment in the preface to the *Memoir*, where he writes that the function of the autobiography is to illuminate for the younger generation how the activities of the London Corresponding Society 'saved them from the most absolute and deplorable slavery being entailed upon them before they were born'.[5]

A vigorous response from the Reverend Mr Bryant to Hardy's letter initiated the correspondence of the Society, and acted as the catalyst for the drawing-up of a manifesto, the primary aim of which was 'a fair, equal and impartial Representation of the people in Parliament', to be achieved peacefully and without attacks on the monarchy.[6] It would be simplistic to elide the issue of liberation from black slavery with the struggle for the rights of white Englishmen,[7] but the insistence on forging connections, reinforced through the language of melodrama—'zealous friends', 'cursed traffic'—should not be underestimated in terms of organizing and unifying forces provided via theatricality. [8]

It has been argued, in a theory which seems to me not to contradict the idea of the influential character of reform, but to take a particular emphasis, that the abolition movement was the dominant force in shaping 'socio-economic ideals' of reformers in general.[9] Certainly, it is

---

[4] Anthropos, or Mr Mathews of Histon, Cambridgeshire, *The Rights of Man. (Not Paines,) but the Rights of Man, in the West Indies* (Knight and Lacy, London, 1824), cited in Clare Midgley, *Women Against Slavery: The British Campaigns, 1780–1870* (Routledge, London and New York, 1992). Perhaps the title of Mathews's piece implies a slight reproach to Tom Paine for not having extended the claim for rights quite far enough?

[5] *Memoir of Thomas Hardy.*

[6] Ibid. 47–8.

[7] And the deliberate gender-specificity of Englishmen also implies questions about the rights of women.

[8] See Ch. 6 for more on the politics of melodrama, particularly with reference to Elaine Hadley, *Melodramatic Tactics.* Parliamentary debates in relation to reform and to abolition in particular were characterized by theatrical language and flourish. Richard Brinsley Sheridan yields the most obvious example of the relationship between theatrical and parliamentary rhetoric, as demonstrated in an excellent recent biography by Fintan O'Toole, *A Traitor's Kiss* (Granta, London, 1997). There are, of course, other examples, as membership of the Select Committee on Dramatic Literature demonstrates (most notably Bulwer-Lytton)

[9] Robin Blackburn, *The Overthrow of Colonial Slavery 1776–1848* (Verso, London and New York, 1988), ch. 11.

possible to see how the London Corresponding Society not only grew out of the direct influence of abolitionists, but also modelled its structures on those of the abolition movement, taking up the precedent set by the latter's pattern of regional organization.[10]

In one sense, patriotic attitudes towards English identity, alongside fierce opposition to racial and social injustice, were influential in bringing Equiano and his fellow black activist, Robert Wedderburn, who also befriended Thomas Hardy, into the reform movement as well as the abolition movement, leading them to support working people in their agitation for suffrage. Patriotism relates significantly, if with complexity, to both racial attitude and radicalism at this time, one instance being the way in which ostensibly radical speakers are also capable of acutely xenophobic pronouncements. E. P. Thompson has a problem with what he takes to be some such utterances from William Cobbett, framed in terms of attacks on the French. Thompson is far more comfortable with Cobbett as radical spokesperson in contexts where the latter 'leaves off' France and settles to vilifying 'Old Corruption' in *British* government.[11]

Even Thomas Hardy is careful to distance himself from approval of the French, whilst being acutely aware that comparisons between Britain and France are inescapable. Hostile attitudes to France can be explained in terms of the backlash against Jacobinism, but support of Britain as against France also plays across distinctions between the two countries in relation to the issue of representative government and, indirectly, slavery. However far Hardy argues that Britons were reduced to a state of slavery figuratively, he also admits that eighteenth-century Britain is crucially different from pre-Revolutionary France in having had a representative parliament, however limited the franchise, a monarchy that was far from absolute, and perhaps most importantly, a system of trial by jury. France, by contrast, is perceived as sullied by a legacy from the *ancien régime* of oppressing its own people as effectively a slave class, in addition to acting like Britain as an exploitative trading nation in slavery. Hardy sees that reform of the British Parliament is badly needed, but he never claims that the actual principle of parliamentary representation is anything new

---

[10]  Ibid., ch. 4.

[11]  Thompson, *The Making of the English Working Class*, 491–514, 'The logic which connected the despotism of Napoleon and of Pitt is by no means clear: Cobbett, so cogent in detailed argument, often blustered through the larger outlines.'

in Britain.[12] In these ways, those attitudes to France which may appear racist, in the interests of British patriotism, can represent a form of indirect support for abolition in the implied criticism of slave regimes. (It is also the case that, whatever British attitudes were to France and the French, reform rhetoric, drawing on a new theatrical language of rights and social transformation, was also strongly influenced by French Revolutionary sympathies and discourses, as shown in the attitudes taken up by some key British political commentators.[13])

Looking back from a modern perspective to the eighteenth century and early nineteenth century, over Victorian history, it is also difficult to accommodate the idea that political radicalism and patriotism in some of its more militaristic forms may have been held to be compatible, indeed mutually reinforcing. It was not only possible, but also normal for those of radical persuasion to support British soldiers fighting in the Napoleonic Wars, whilst embracing the idealism of post-Revolutionary France and its influence on British reform. Theatre audiences appear to have been able to do both. (We shall see in Buckstone's *Luke the Labourer* how the sailor returning from the wars takes command of audience sympathies for both his English nationalism and his combative challenges to social injustice.)

Call it patriotism or not, a sense of Englishness may have provided some element of motivation in the complementarities, largely initiated by black activists, forged between anti-slavery and reform movements.[14] Certainly, until recently, the part played by Equiano and other black activists in the *reform* movement and in making sense of intellectual and

---

[12] Evans, *Britain before the Reform Act*, ch. 4, points out that the displacement of inheritance by representation as the key radical issue originated in the English Revolution.

[13] The discussion is developed in the previous chapter.

[14] There is a fascinating debate amongst historians, with Seymour Drescher, *Capitalism and Antislavery: British Mobilization in Comparative Perspective* (Macmillan, London, 1986) and Betty Fladeland, *Abolitionists and Working-Class Problems in the Age of Industrialization* (Louisiana State University Press, Baton Rouge, La., 1984) tending to relate the anti-slavery campaign to working-class mobilization, and Thomas Bender and David Brion Davis tending to discuss the movement in terms of hegemonic strategies of the capitalist classes; Bender (ed.), *The Antislavery Debate, Capitalism and Abolitionism as a Problem in Historical Interpretation*, with essays by John Ashworth, David Brion Davis, and Thomas L. Haskell (University of California Press, Berkeley, Los Angeles, and Oxford, 1992). Betty Fladeland, epilogue, is convinced of this thesis about the mutuality of the two movements.

political connections with abolition has been vastly underestimated.[15] It does not follow, though, that either movement was free of racist attitudes in a society characterized by colonialism and racial ignorance, as witnessed in tensions and political differences between some of the leading white figures.[16]

What is certain is that between 1787 and 1792, the terms in which the institution of slavery was discussed in Britain changed dramatically, and the years which followed, until the Emancipation Act in 1833, brought a wave of campaigns, supported by an unprecedented number of British people.[17] Thomas Clarkson, said to have travelled 33,000 miles between 1787 and 1792 in the anti-slavery cause, has been reinstated as one of the movement's prime activists, having been for a long time overshadowed by the universally acclaimed William Wilberforce.[18] More important, though, is the evidence that the movement's achievements cannot be usefully summarized in terms of the commitments of one, or even two or three prominent men, but that people of every class of society and from most regions of Britain rallied to the anti-slavery cause, to the extent that the character of petitioning and mass mobilization changed for ever. [19]

Historians' disagreements about how far abolition and reform

[15] Keith A. Sandiford, *Measuring the Moment: Strategies of Protest in Eighteenth-Century Afro-English Writing* (Susquehanna University Press, Selinsgrove, Pa.; Associated University Presses, London and Toronto, 1988) redresses the balance, arguing in his introductory chapter that the literary works of Sancho, Cugoano, and Equiano 'played a significant part in the widespread awakening of the British national consciousness to the urgency of abolition and emancipation' (17).

[16] Adviser's report from Oxford University Press reads: 'The close links between key abolition leaders, most crucially Wilberforce, and Pittite repression, made the movement, at least in its overt parliamentary connections, deeply suspect for the majority of radicals. Those radical leaders of the 1790s (and they are few, primarily Hardy, Cartwright and Thelwall) who did make links between slaves and oppressed workers, constructed their own intellectual agendas for doing so outside mainstream abolition.'

[17] Drescher, *Capitalism and Antislavery*. My account owes much both to the evidence offered by Drescher and his interpretation. J. R. Oldfield, *Popular Politics and British Anti-Slavery: The Mobilisation of Public Opinion against the Slave Trade, 1787–1807* (Manchester University Press, Manchester, 1995), who tends to focus on the contribution of 'the provincial middle classes' to the abolition movement, acknowledges a more direct debt to Drescher, despite significant differences in position.

[18] Ellen Gibson Wilson, *Thomas Clarkson, A Biography* (William Sessions Ltd., York, 1989) has done much to retrieve Clarkson's reputation. She has also published a pamphlet, *The Clarksons of Wisbech and the Abolition of the Slave Trade* (Wisbech Society and Preservation Trust Ltd. (office: Wisbech and Fenland Museum), March 1992)

[19] Drescher, *Capitalism and Antislavery.*

movements complemented each other appear to have focused on prominent figures of either movement rather than on the large numbers of women and working men, white and black, who were able to render involvement in both abolition and reform movements compatible. It has been recorded that audiences of working people went 'in their thousands' to hear black American abolitionists speak during their visits to Britain.[20]

The evidence that the abolition movement in Britain crossed class boundaries, reaching considerable numbers of working people, challenges that interpretation which had previously argued that the movement for parliamentary reform in Britain and the abolition movement were in tension, and that there were always seeds of division between the two movements. Such an argument had always implied that the working people of Britain were too self-interested, or too easily threatened in relation to rights to employment, to recognize the need to address the sufferings of the slaves. The reality is, rather, that the major part of the movement's basic support came from working people, including black activists and women. Manchester, 'the most successful boom town of the 1780s', is said to have led the way, and 'the rough sons of lowest labour' in Leeds signed their names to anti-slavery petitions.[21] Alongside working people came aristocrats, Members of Parliament, churchmen, and academics, with a forceful intervention from Cambridge University, where Clarkson had first presented his paper outlining ideas for his *Essay on the Slavery and Commerce of the Human Species, Particularly the African.*[22]

Perhaps least noticed of all until recently has been evidence of vigorous support for the abolition campaign by women of all classes, who were excluded from early petitions, but gathered together the largest set of signatures ever collected for presentation to Parliament, in 1833 itself, on the eve of the Emancipation Act.[23] The boycott of West Indian sugar, designed to drive the anti-slavery message home to the plantocracy, had been aimed at women audiences to some extent. However, there is a difference between the attempt to target women as consumers

---

[20] Fladeland, *Abolitionists and Working-Class Problems*, introduction.

[21] Drescher, *Capitalism and Antislavery*, 72–5.

[22] Thomas Clarkson, *Essay on the Slavery and Commerce of the Human Species, Particularly the African*, (London, June 1786, and USA); for further reference, see Wilson, *Thomas Clarkson*, ch. 2.

[23] Drescher, *Capitalism and Antislavery*, 85.

(acting upon women), and women taking action for themselves: the scale of their involvement in petitioning and organization could not have been anticipated.

Mary Somerville, later to become the first signatory on the J. S. Mill petition of the 1860s on behalf of women's suffrage, accounts for the relationship between reform of the franchise and opposition to slavery in terms of a coherent political stand on behalf of freedom movements of all kinds. She comments wryly that participation in the sugar boycott, aimed at damaging British trade relations with the West Indian plantocracy, left her with an enduring distaste for sugar in her tea.[24] *The History of Mary Prince, A West Indian Slave, Related by Herself* brought the categories of women and slavery together inescapably in critique. As well as providing graphic evidence for the parliamentary bill against the flogging of black women, introduced by Canning in 1823, her account explodes the myth that slaves were content with their lot, upbraiding those who argue such a case with the accusation that they seek to put 'a cloak about the truth'.[25]

In addition to the actions of individuals such as Mary Prince and Mary Somerville, much of the political agitation at its most radical edge in relation to abolition was carried out by women committed to what they described as the 'immediatist' as distinct from the 'gradualist' approach to the abolition of slavery.[26] In 1831, the Birmingham Ladies Negro's Friend Society pioneered the demand for immediate emancipation of the slaves. It has been argued, further, that between 1823 and 1833 women radicals not only led the emancipation campaign, but 'transformed the cultural face of England' with their use of the anti-slavery discourse.[27] This is not to underestimate, though, the significance of the

---

[24] Mary Somerville, *Personal Recollections, from early life to old age, with selections from her correspondence by her daughter, Martha Somerville* (Murray, London, 1873).

[25] Prince, *The history of Mary Prince*; Mary Ferguson, *Subject to Others* (Routledge, New York and London, 1992) ch. 13, for an account of Mary Prince's contribution. Blackburn, *The Overthrow of Colonial Slavery*, ch. 11, 'British Slave Emancipation 1823–38', cites, 'a cloak about the truth'.

[26] Blackburn, ibid., cites the pamphlet *Immediate Not Gradual Abolition* by Elizabeth Heyricke, and other contributions by women.

[27] Ferguson, *Subject to Others*, ch. 24, 'Between 1823 and 1833, female emancipationists transformed the cultural face of England as a result of the discourse on slavery'. Also, Louis Billington and Rosamund Billington, ' "A Burning Zeal for Righteousness": Women in the British Anti-Slavery Movement, 1820–1860', in Jane Rendall (ed.), *Equal or Different, Women's Politics 1800–1914* (Blackwell, Oxford, 1987): 'Although women were excluded from power in the national organizations dominated by men, historians are increasingly recognizing that women's anti-slavery societies were not simply passive auxiliaries' (90).

writings of black activists and of tropes of theatricality, to which I now turn, in enabling women to provide 'the cement of the whole Anti-Slavery building'.[28]

## Olaudah Equiano: Almost an Englishman

In the 1780s, the African, Olaudah Equiano, or Gustavus Vassa, recorded how he felt when called upon to make representations to the British authorities on behalf of 'a very clever black man, John Annis', whom he wished to see released from enforced service to a cruel master.[29] With the help of the philanthropist, Granville Sharp, Equiano had brought a court case against John Annis's master, a Mr Kirkpatrick. The case failed spectacularly, with Equiano losing his money to a corrupt attorney and Annis being shipped to punishment and death in St Kitts. Equiano records how the whole episode brought him 'very low'.[30]

Equiano's two-volume autobiography tells how, after having been kidnapped as a child from an African village, he is forced on to a slave ship, and transported to slavery in the West Indies, one of the most brutal of all slave regimes. This is followed by naval service for the British, where he learns how to understand, read, and write English, and becomes particularly acquainted with London and Europe. After many adventures around the world, he returns to England as a freeman and commits himself to the movement for the abolition of slavery in Britain. The story goes on to a second volume, largely preoccupied with Equiano's conversion to Christianity, but I interrupt it at the moment of his sense of demoralization in relation to the abolition movement in Britain, marked on this occasion by his gesture of

[28] Billington and Billington, ibid., citing a contemporary commentator in support of the claim that it was recognized 'that women had played a major role in bringing the British abolitionist campaign to a successful conclusion' (90–1).

[29] *The Interesting Narrative of the Life of Olaudah Equiano or Gustavus Vassa, The African, written by Himself* (1789) printed for and sold by the author, Union Street, Middlesex Hospital; the edition to which I make reference here is that with a new introduction by Paul Edwards (Dawsons of Pall Mall, London, 1969). The account of Equiano's attempt to rescue John Annis is on pp. 121–4 of vol. ii. Also, Vincent Carretta, *The Interesting Narrative of the Life of Olaudah Equiano, or Gustavus Vassa, the African* (Penguin, Harmondsworth, 1995) for a recent edition and commentary on the life story. Also, a 1989 edition by Paul Edwards.

[30] Paul Edwards, 1969 edition.

attempting to encounter the British judicial process on behalf of another black man.[31]

The failure of his own intervention and of John Annis's case, which left Equiano traumatized and demoralized by British justice and with the England that in some senses he had loved, carry important symbolic meanings. The intention behind Equiano's intervention is that he wishes both to establish, on the particular terms required by the British judicial system, his own political agency; he is an actor representing a cause, that of abolition, and he declares a racial allegiance with John Annis in an anti-racist cause. Equiano's autobiography, together with testimonies from other commentators such as Hardy, demonstrates that he has acquired mastery of the English language and of the rhetoric of abolition, pre-requisites for service to the abolition cause.[32] In addition, in the particu-lar case of John Annis, he has attracted the support of a white man, the influential Granville Sharp. However, what Equiano discovers, in his attempt to act on behalf of John Annis, is that his own racial identity and identifications are inescapable disadvantages, and this recognition contributes to bringing him 'very low'. (The irony, however obvious, should not be missed that the potential risk involved in his attempt to act on behalf of John Annis and the abolition movement lies directly in his exposing himself to that which he seeks to counter—the practices perpet-uated and prejudices unleashed on slaves, and by extension on the black community, by virtue of skin colour and racial identity.)

To protect John Annis, Equiano had set out to serve a writ for habeas corpus on Annis's victimizer, by whom Equiano was known and from whose house he was barred. In order to disguise himself, he had whitened his face. This particular strategy had succeeded.[33] Although

---

[31] Angelo Costanzo, *Surprizing Narrative: Olaudah Equiano and the Beginnings of Black Autobiography*, Contributions in Afro-American and African Studies 104 (Greenwood Press, New York and London, 1987) develops ideas about spirituality in Equiano's narrative.

[32] I shall show how his autobiography and its reception treats these issues.

[33] Costanzo, *Surprizing Narrative*, ch. 4, for a succinct account of the episode. Also, James Walvin, *An African's Life: The Life and Times of Olaudah Equiano, 1745–1797* (Cassell, London, 1998), 101–3, 'It is scarcely surprising that the literate and politically alert Equiano would have been aware of the legal possibilities afforded by habeas corpus. With the writ in hand, and in the company of a law officer, he set out to confront Kirk-patrick at his home in St Paul's Churchyard. Kirkpatrick had anticipated such a visit and hired a look-out (a sure sign that he was aware of the significance of his wrong-doing) Even more remarkable, Equiano tried to disguise himself by whitening his face. After much manœuvring and many feints, Kirkpatrick was eventually given the writ and brought to court to answer the charge' (102).

Equiano himself passes quickly over the success of the strategy, the gesture itself carries symbolic force in terms of his actions on behalf of Annis. By whitening his face, Equiano had registered that his attempt to disguise his individual identity was inseparable from the need to conceal racial identity. It is significant that Equiano uses, on this occasion, a method from the drama—the making-up of the face, the production of a mask for the purposes of disguise and deception. In drawing on this particular convention from drama, the whitening of the face, Equiano signals his knowledge that the problems associated with his individual identity are inescapably racial ones. Theatricality, particularly the creation of literal and figurative masks, is used as part of the strategy by which Equiano attempts to appear 'almost an Englishman', as he puts it later, in the interests of serving the cause of the abolition movement (to attempt to circumvent those prejudices which he knows black people in England are likely to encounter for their blackness alone). The gesture demonstrates his knowledge and understanding of British society, in the context of which, on this particular occasion, the strategy of representing a racial brother successfully could not be sustained.

However, the gesture also represents an acknowledgement that performance values, the methods of the drama, play a crucial part in the anti-slavery struggle.[34] Equiano recognizes that he needs not only to know his audience, but to adopt the techniques which will persuade it to his viewpoint. The mask is symbolic of his attempt to negotiate the relationship between his African identity and its obvious association with slavery, and his Englishness, deriving from language and cultural experience, in its association with power and influence. His bitter disappointment over the case of John Annis arises not only from the failure of the court case, but also because he is being confronted aggressively with the representative failure of addressing his own cause and therefore his inability, however far he is by this time a freeman, to alleviate the oppression of a brother.

Despite the failure to represent Annis, Equiano's attempt, the very fact that he created that opportunity, that it was available to him to do so at this moment in history, is significant. In what it reveals about performers and audiences, the episode illustrates a number of issues

---

[34] Parliamentary debates on the subject of abolition were also characterized by theatricality; see J. R. Oldfield, *Popular Politics*, for more on the subject.

related to the politics and drama of the abolition movement. The issue for Equiano is how to represent the anti-slavery cause in a number of its different dimensions, as one who has suffered slavery, and as a moral actor, in the political domain and on whatever stage is required, in order to oppose it.[35] The failure of the court case, devastating in its consequences for both John Annis and Equiano, indicates how resistance to black slavery raises questions of racial identity and identification which are inescapably visual and theatrical. The extent to which skin colour is concealed or revealed, the issue of how far theatrical devices— masks and disguises—are required to cover the face, are measures which become inescapable and powerful in the abolition struggle.

Later in this chapter, I shall raise questions about contemporary theatre's relationship to the abolition movement and to the preparation of the ground for the emancipation of slaves. Did the drama, in its obvious emphasis on visual representation, fuel or circumvent those prejudices concerning skin colour and racial identity which it was part of the abolition movement's task to resist and dispel? What did theatre audiences want of performers and playwrights in relation to the abolition movement? Were theatrical performance styles influenced by the abolition movement's particular investment in showing or concealing 'the face' of racial oppression? Initially, though, I turn to the political movement and Equiano's writing on its behalf, to register attitudes to racial identity and slavery in the context of the slave autobiographer.

In 1789, Olaudah Equiano had decided to take responsibility himself for the publication of two volumes of his autobiography, conspicuously and specifically for the purpose of giving support to the abolition movement.[36] Chapter 1 of his book is prefaced by a list of subscribers, which

---

[35] See Ch. 6 for more on the issue of the moral actor.

[36] Equiano, *The Interesting Narrative* (1789). There is now an extensive literature examining Equiano's autobiographical writing and with the passage of time he has become something of a cult figure, as indicated by commitments to celebrating his life in an exhibition at the Millennium Dome in London. On the exterior wall of St Andrew's Church, Chesterton, Cambridge, England, there is a moving memorial to his daughter, Anna Maria Vassa, who died at the age of 4. However, my concern is primarily with the politics represented by Equiano's position, together with the theatricality revealed in his autobiographical writing, rather than in biography *per se*. Particularly useful in relation to the politics of slave narratives has been Costanzo, *Surprizing Narrative*. In his introductory chapter, Costanzo argues persuasively that 18th-c. slave autobiographers were more free than their 19th-c. counterparts to construct identities independently of 'the stereotypical roles accepted by their white readers' (4). In the following chapter, he cites Ronald Paulson on the subject of 18th-c. narrative structures,

includes several members of the government and even the royal family, together with an opening address on behalf of the abolitionist cause to the 'spiritual and temporal' governors of Great Britain.[37] The text quickly ran into eight editions, and gave every appearance of succeeding in precisely that task that it had set itself—to give evidence, weight, and also a representative voice to suffering slaves, in their urgent need for emancipation.

Five years later, though, Equiano was having to defend himself against fabricating his identity and giving a fraudulent account. In the preface to his 1794 edition, he writes of 'the enemies' who have put about 'an invidious falsehood', representing him as West Indian rather than African. In order to counter their 'false assertions', Equiano surrounds his narrative with copies of correspondence from several eminent people who, after the first edition of the book was published, had recommended both its content and its author to the chairman of the Committees for the Abolition of the Slave Trade, on the grounds of its power and authenticity. He also prints passages from a review which supports the narrative as that of a 'very intelligent African'. Equiano takes pains to emphasize that he cites these authorities not because he believes that the text either requires or warrants special privileges to exempt it from critical scrutiny, but because of the attacks that have been made on him.

The pressure that Equiano is under to defend his narrative against his enemies and their claims highlights a number of significant issues. At one level, the reason for having such opponents is obvious. White slavers would, no doubt, have found whatever means possible to undermine the influence of a record such as that of Equiano, which authoritatively and unquestionably showed them in a most unfavourable light.[38] Certainly, there are graphically documented accounts of all

influenced by 'the metaphor of life as a stage, in which a role-playing protagonist has to interact with other actors' (26). Later, in ch. 4, Costanzo returns to this issue of the influence on autobiography of theatricality, citing George Misch on the subject of Equiano's role-playing, in which he creates an autobiographical persona 'who wears a mask in a part they play on the stage of life' (64). See Adam Potkay and Sandra Burr (eds.), *Black Atlantic Writers of the Eighteenth Century: Living the New Exodus in England and the Americas* (Macmillan, Basingstoke, 1995) for more analysis of Equiano's autobiography.

[37] Costanzo, *Surprizing Narrative* relates how the initial publication of the autobiography occurred about six weeks before William Wilberforce formally introduced the abolition bill into Parliament (ch. 4).

[38] Equiano, *The Interesting Narrative* (1789), particularly in vol. i, ch. 2.

kinds of threats, including physical ones, being made against the abolitionists—for instance, in relation to Thomas Clarkson for his unswerv-
ing polemical attack on the slave traders, individually and collectively.[39]

Those who seek to claim that Equiano is West Indian rather than
African have a number of intentions in mind as a means of attempting
to discredit and silence him. If Equiano is West Indian, not African, his
account of early childhood in an African village and of being kidnapped
and sold into slavery, is, it might be argued, rendered incredible. The
power of his account of the beauty and harmony of the African village,
contrasting with the brutality of kidnapping and the white slavers, is
undermined. If he is West Indian, not African, his strenuous criticisms
of West Indian slavery and its methods are more suggestive of a betrayal
of his homeland than born of the shocked observations of an exile, and
a child at that, forced on to a slave ship and coerced into service thousands of miles from home. But, above all, if he is West Indian, then his
first language is English, and his claims to have mastered the English
language to the point of utmost fluency, to be capable of that extent of
learning and mastery, are bogus. This type of analysis fuels those prejudices which would entail arguing that no black African person is capable of both learning the English language, and of becoming as English
as the English, or almost so—'almost an Englishman'.

If the problems encountered in the reception of the autobiography
were only posed by white slavers, then that would be one form of rather
sharply defined political issue, based all too clearly on the economic and
racial exploitation of slaves by slavers, and the passionate resistance of
the latter to the idea that things might have to change. But even the
reviewer quoted by Equiano in the 1794 edition, who had entertained
no doubts about the text having been authored by a very intelligent
African, had conceded that it was so 'well-written' that there might be
the possibility of the hand of 'some English writer' in it.[40] The paradox,
as Equiano and others engaged in the abolition movement know, is that
the fluency of his English is what ensures a wide readership in Britain,

---

[39] Wilson, *Thomas Clarkson*, ch. 2, recounts how Clarkson wanted to bring three
ship's officers to trial for murder, and that he was warned that, 'he would be torn to
pieces and his lodgings burned down if be brought on a trial' (37).

[40] Equiano, *The Interesting Narrative* (1794), *Monthly Review* for June 1789, p. 551.
However, Costanzo (*Surprizing Narrative*) and Sandiford (*Measuring the Moment*) each
comment on the detail of contemporary reception of the autobiography, which does
appear to have been largely favourable. My reservations here are in relation to the racism
of critical nuance.

but that ultimately, that very fluency is what opens up the suspicion that he is not a proper African, which then undermines his ability to speak for black Africa. The more he reveals his knowledge of English and Englishness, together with the ease with which he speaks the rational language of the European Enlightenment, the more his claims to speak with the authenticity of an African can be held in doubt.[41]

The particular set of strategies used to discredit Equiano derive from equivalent prejudicial assumptions to those which Equiano and John Annis had encountered. They are about hostility and unease, on the grounds of race, to the authority with which Equiano speaks as an actor in the abolition cause. What is unacceptable, and not only to his enemies, is his claim both to be a member of the oppressed, and to *represent* the oppressed, together with his ability, in terms of knowledge and skill, to use the tools of the master to dismantle the master's house, particularly in his use of the English of the English.[42]

However, the delay in casting a slur on Equiano's character which occurred whilst the memoir ran into eight editions, enjoying huge popularity, is significant. Like the attempt at a strategy on behalf of John Annis, the 'whitening' of the autobiographical face could work and, in the case of autobiography, for quite some time. Autobiography masks the face and disembodies the voice of the autobiographer, whilst maintaining a very strong sense, through the first person, of direct experience.[43] Equiano's autobiographical writing lends itself to the abolition cause because it represents slavery as a first-hand experience, but does so in the English of the informed outsider rather than in the language of

---

[41] In good Enlightenment style, the appeal to reason is very common in abolition literature.

[42] The metaphor derives its force in this instance from Audre Lorde, 'The Master's Tools will Never Dismantle the Master's House', in Cherrie Moraga and Gloria Anzaldua (eds.), *This Bridge Called My Back* (Kitchen Table: Women of Color Press, New York, 1981).

[43] Laura Marcus, 'The Face of Autobiography', in Julia Swindells (ed.), *The Uses of Autobiography*, ch. 2 (Taylor & Francis, London, 1995) for more on the issue of the relationship between racial identity and autobiography: 'The ideology of race, that is, distorts the "face to face" encounter'; bell hooks, *Yearning, Race, Gender, and Cultural Politics* (Turnaround, London, 1991), *Talking Back: Thinking Feminist, Thinking Black* (Sheba, London, 1989) for searching analysis of the politics of racial identity and selfhood. Also, Alice Walker, *Living by the Word: Selected Writings 1973–1987* (The Women's Press, London, 1988). There is, of course, an extensive range of analysis of these questions by modern writers of polemic, fiction, autobiography, and poetry, including June Jordan, Toni Morrison, Maya Angelou, and many others.

the participant. His account is able to give the illusion, for a time, that he is both the participant, the slave, and the concerned and educated English liberal spokesperson. He can claim African and English identity coterminously.

By contrast, the theatrical performer (and the political representative appearing in public) cannot maintain this illusion. The mask only serves to draw attention to the visual disturbance and impact created by observing the face. However, this transparency of the drama, that which it cannot conceal, its immediacy and public aspect, is also its strength. I shall argue next that some playwrights attempted to use the drama's capacity for visual impact and disturbance in order to draw attention to the abolition movement and its purposes. Abolition's inextricable involvement with questions of racial origin and difference lent to the drama the possibility of a particular set of emphases around performance, drawing, as we shall see, on the powerful vocabulary and rhetoric of those seeking to claim freedom and rights for slaves, and exploiting the racial territory of visual disturbance, with its accompanying devices of facial make-up, the mask, and the intricacies of disguise. Making play with the faces of race could draw attention to a world which, for most English audiences, was well beyond their experience or even their observation, but with which they were in the process of articulating a common cause, the glorious cause of abolition.

### Obi; Or, Three-Fingered Jack

In contrasting an autobiography of an eighteenth-century black African with plays written by white Englishmen, there are, of course, already differences of national identity and race, and of standpoint, to take into account. Whilst Equiano has a knowledge of African, West Indian, and English cultures, as well as direct experience of the condition of slavery, the dramatists are often very distanced from the actuality of slavery, and distinguished by the perspective not of the participant, and not even in most cases of the observer, but of the witness to various *accounts*. It is also the case that the philosophies of the Enlightenment are highly questionable in relation to how far black people were to be admitted to full humanity by white people.[44] Any critical appreciation of the work

---

[44] Sandiford, *Measuring the Moment*, for detailed illumination of this problem and of the stereotype of the 'noble savage'; ch. 2: 'It was the *philosophes*, the ideologists of the

of white playwrights of the period needs to accommodate an under-standing of these cultural differences and constraints, and also to retain some scepticism about how far these writers, however radical their intent, were complicit in collaborationist attitudes with the mental universe of Britain's colonialists.[45]

Nevertheless, British dramatists were able to turn their perspective to some advantage, so that, while autobiographical narrative was crucial to the way in which the abolition movement articulated the *experiences* of slaves, the drama went someway towards bridging the gap with the *outsiderness* of British audiences, drawing attention to and possibly galvanizing and focusing popular support for abolition. Unlike George Colman the Younger's *Inkle and Yarico*, to which I shall return, *Obi; Or, Three-Fingered Jack*, written as a pantomime by John Fawcett and adapted as a two-act drama by W. H. Murrey, does not pretend to direct support for abolition (see Plate 8).[46]

French Enlightenment (principally Montesquieu, Raynal, and Rousseau), who estab-lished and popularized the validity of the common person's right to self-possession and the belief in personal perfectibility. But even among the philosophers themselves, there were those who had difficulty admitting Blacks to full human equality. Some solved the dilemma by ignoring them in their discussion, others by assigning them an inferior rank in the order of nature. Rousseau's celebration of the "noble savage" is often fallaciously construed as an expression of sympathy for the African slave . . . It is significant that both he and Voltaire held the African inferior in mental ability to the European' (46). My own concern is with attempting to foreground the black perspective, in particular that of Equiano, on attitudes to race. I leave much-needed work on deconstructing 'the noble savage' to others.

[45] Ngugi Wa Thiong'o, 'Freeing Culture from Eurocentrism, Creating Space for a Hundred Flowers to Bloom', in his *Moving the Centre: The Struggle for Cultural Freedoms* (James Currey, London; East African Educational Publishers, Nairobi; Heinemann Educational Books, Portsmouth, NH, 1993) wants to consign what he describes as 'collaborationist literature', to the dustbin. 'The collaborationist literature, mostly popu-lar literature, was downright racist. I shall not here dwell on this since it has been discred-ited enough in all serious discourse. Its very simplism speaks loudly enough about its intentions. The African was often depicted in the diametrically opposed polarities of the good and the bad, the noble and the savage. The good, the noble and the intelligent was the character who co-operated with the colonial process. The bad and the ugly was the African who opposed colonialism' (18). It is very important to bear his judgements in mind in relation to the plays which I analyse here, even though the rationale I produce about their connections with the abolition movement is one that I hope protects me in some measure against the accusation of reclaiming a popular literature which has noth-ing to say that is not 'downright racist'.

[46] W. H. Murrey, *Obi; Or, Three-Fingered Jack, the plot and principal incidents taken from the highly popular pantomime of the celebrated Mr. Fawcett, first performed at the Theatre Royal, Haymarket, July 2nd, 1800* (John Dicks, London, 1800). Many thanks to Rob Loe for drawing my attention to continuing popular reference to the character of

The play, set on a sugar plantation in Jamaica, opens with a celebration by the slaves of their 'great affection' for the master and his daughter, whose birthday it is.[47] The eponymous Jack, a 'giant' of a black man, is a murderer, who, estranged from this merry little community, continues, in ways graphically depicted in the play, to seek revenge on white people after having 'finished off' the master's wife. Other characters, from the sugar planter, Ormond, to the negro slave, Quashee, freed during the course of the play, equally judge Jack the 'villain', 'monster', 'accursed wretch'. The plot is a horror story, the play a melodrama with comic pretensions. However, throughout the opening scene, there is constant reiteration of reference to skin colour and racial origin: to 'black beauties' who speak through 'ebony pipes', to the 'fair' daughter, to the 'bukra man' to whom she is promised in wedlock, to 'poor blacks', 'pickaninies', 'black ninny-hammers', and 'poor negro man'.

Whether through the use of black performers or 'blacking up', the skin colour of the characters must, by definition, have been known to the audience, but it is as if the assertion of that vocabulary serves a number of purposes in addition to that of literally signifying some aspect of the racial identity of the character being performed. It is possible, given that the script was originally that of a pantomime, that the exchanges are for the purposes of cheap humour, possibly fuelling audience prejudice and ignorance; but it is also as if the playwright is invoking the vocabulary of race in order to make play with the relatively unexplored territory of racial difference, together with the novelty and visual disturbance it creates on the stage.

The terms of racial difference, though, are asymmetrical, as signified in the dialogue. The slaves are allocated a parodic dialect ('he save poor black much floggee, floggee') and are the victims of humour, while the white characters all speak in standard English, of a rather poetic and rhetorical turn ('The vessel is in harbour, and ere this he must have landed'), and are the perpetrators of the humour. Plot and character also have their collaborationist elements, drawing on fantasies about the innate goodness and liberalism of white supremacists. Quashee chooses to fight for his benign master, rather than join forces with Jack against

Three-Fingered Jack later in the 19th c., the particular instance being in Thomas Carlyle's influential essay on Chartism.

[47] Stuart Hall, presenter of the recent BBC television series about the Caribbean islands, *Redemption Song*, speaks of the power of the Barbadian plantocracy persisting well into the 20th c.

the oppressors. Furthermore, the playwright sets Quashee against Jack in the denouement, so that the white man does not even have to take his own revenge. Black resistance is thwarted and defused, in the interests of the supposedly civilizing influence of the benign white master and his liberal values. The implication is that the actions of nice masters will obviate the need for slave resistance, and that liberalism and harmony between the races will automatically bring about emancipation. British audiences, together with members of the British plutocracy and the West Indian plantocracy, can rest in their beds.[48]

The interest of the play, though, is in its attempt, through that libertarian style of melodrama to which I shall refer in my concluding chapter, to give some kind of moral and dramatic justification to Jack's crimes, in terms of the history of slavery. The key speech comes at a moment of epiphany towards the play's denouement:

*I* had a daughter once; did they spare her harmless infancy? Where is my wife? was *she* spared to me? No! with blood and rapine the White man swept like a hurricane o'er our native village, and blasted every hope! Can aught efface the terrible remembrance from my soul, how at their lordly feet we begged for mercy and found it not? Our women knelt, our infants shrieked in vain, as the blood-stained murderer ranged from hut to hut, dragging the husband and the father from their homes, to sell them into bondage! No more, no more! the vexed spirits of my wife and child hover o'er me like a holy curse, and claim this due revenge.

This is a familiar, melodramatic trope, invoking home and hearth hyperbolically to recall a desirable and lost past, but it is also a powerful dramatic and political appeal on behalf of a silenced history, from the African past to the Jamaican present, captured in the language of abolition—the 'bondage' of the slaves, the 'lordly feet' of their masters.[49] It draws, too, on that Christian evangelicalism to which Equiano also turns in the absence of judicial or political solutions.[50]

---

[48] David Brion Davis, in Bender (ed.), *The Antislavery Debate*, depicts the abolitionists as complicit in an ideal of the planter as 'a kindly, paternalistic master ministering to his grateful Negro "yeomen" ' (102).

[43] Christina Crosby, *The Ends of History* (Routledge, New York and London, 1991) for more on the subject of melodrama and history.

[50] Equiano, *The Interesting Narrative* (1789); much of vol. ii is devoted to Equiano's conversion to Christianity and the pursuits which follow. The dissenting minister, Robert Wedderburn, is another who draws on evangelical Christianity for his abolitionist rhetoric. *Robert Wedderburn: The Horrors of Slavery and Other Writings*, ed. Iain

Earlier in the play, Jack had also spoken of 'the memory of my broken-hearted wife, my helpless infants, and the wrongs of my poor country', and it is significant that, among the black characters, he is allocated standard English, separating him from the other slaves, but giving him a kind of parity with the white characters.

In his autobiography, Equiano had utilized similar language after his narrative had turned to the representation of his African past. He invites readers to consider the linguistic habits and practices of African villagers, such as their reverence for names and the absence in their language of an equivalent to swearing, implying that European and English readers judge wrongly if they take African villagers to be unciv-ilized. Then comes the focused polemic:

Are there not causes enough to which the apparent inferiority of an African may be ascribed, without limiting the goodness of God, and supposing he forbore to stamp understanding on certainly his own image, because 'carved in ebony'? Might it not naturally be ascribed to their situation? When they come among Europeans, they are ignorant of their language, religion, manners, and customs. Are any pains taken to teach them these? Are they treated as men? Does not slavery itself depress the mind, and extinguish all its fire and every noble sentiment? But, above all, what advantages do not a refined people possess over those who are rude and uncultivated? Let the polished and haughty European recollect that his ancestors were once, like the African, uncivilized, and even barbarous. Did Nature make *them* inferior to their sons? and should *they* too have been made slaves? Every rational mind answers, No.[51]

Jack is given, in however a limited and constraining context, something of the quality of the rational mind that answers No.

Another minor interest in *Obi* derives from the character of Tuckey, a black servant in the master's house, who knows about Old England, and whose part seems to have been performed by a girl or woman. Tuckey is clearly the witty, knowing manservant of contemporary pantomime, and as such he is allowed access to standard English and a certain amount of insight: 'Ah, we poor blacks have a weary time of it, and are as much railed at as if the darkness of our skins were a sample

McCalman (Edinburgh University Press, 1991); McCalman comments in his introduc-tion that Wedderburn's writing 'can be seen as a contribution to the genre of abolition-ist autobiography pioneered by three distinguished late eighteenth-century black Londoners, Ignatius Sancho, Ottobah Cugoano and Olaudah Equiano'.

[51] Equiano, *Interesting Narrative* (1789), i. 42–3.

of the colour of our hearts.'[52] At the same time, he carries with him some of that vitality which must have informed the working-class movement in England, and manifests itself in an unwillingness to accept class or racial difference as a reason for discriminatory treatment.

In terms of the abolition movement, the play fails to confront two key questions, first about the ferocity of white supremacy in the West Indies in this period, and second about the struggle entailed in the move from slavery to freedom. The sugar planter's sudden and rousing offer of freedom to his slaves, though a successful dramatic moment, is a travesty of socio-historical context. In reality, there was a long gap between the abolition of the British slave trade in 1807, bitterly resisted by the West Indian planters, and emancipation in 1833. In the interim, there was a succession of campaigns, not only within Britain, as referred to above, but at sea and in the colonies themselves. However creditable the motives of British working people in joining the cause, there was undoubtedly a more cynical strategy in play after 1807, manifested in the desire, particularly implemented by the British navy, to prevent other countries from trading in slaves once this had been made illegal for the British.[53]

Equiano himself is something of a victim of this strategy, but independently of that, he records not only the long struggle for freedom, the betrayals along the way, and the euphoric moment of its acquisition, but also the problem of identity for a freeman who has been a slave. The model of what constitutes the identity of a freeman is that preferred by the master, the member of the colonial power; in this instance, the Englishman. Equiano's craving for freedom is therefore articulated in part in terms of his identification with Englishmen. He writes of this in relation to his own development:

I now not only felt myself quite easy with these new countrymen [Englishmen], but relished their society and manners. I no longer looked upon them as spirits,

[52] There is more to be said about black servants in plays of the period, and about the particularities of their circumstances, including sometimes having standard English conferred on them, and frequently being educated. William McReady, *The Irishman in London; or, the happy African* (Longman, London, 1793), features a black womanservant called Cubba, who describes her father as a prince in the Gold Coast. Earlier, Isaac Bickerstaff, *The Padlock* (Garrick's Head, London, 1768) puts Mungo, a negro slave and house servant, at the centre of his comic opera. Mungo protests about his subservient lot, and rebels against ill treatment.

[53] See Drescher, *Capitalism and Antislavery*, with particular reference to ch. 5, for discussion of abolition of the British slave trade in 1807.

but as men superior to us; and therefore I had the stronger desire to resemble them; to imbibe their spirit, and imitate their manners; I therefore embraced every occasion of improvement; and every new thing that I observed I treasured up in my memory.[54]

But Equiano is only too aware that, whatever his linguistic and cultural acquisitions in relation to English, the claim to be an English-man is a politically volatile one, particularly in a context where the white man continues to have an economic and political investment in denying him freedom (any time up until 1833). The second volume of Equiano's autobiography opens with the high drama of his bid to purchase his freedom; he is poised on the brink of failure and disap-pointment, but eventually delights in recording the official testimony that from 11 July 1766, his then master, Robert King, does agree to 'manumit, emancipate, enfranchise, and set free, the aforesaid negro man-slave, named Gustavus Vassa', [55] However, despite his long delayed moment of delight, captured in his triumph with his new name ('to me the most desirable in the world . . . Freeman'), Equiano is under no illusions about the realities of freedom for him. Indeed, the nearest he comes to receiving a flogging is when he is a freeman, not a slave. He invites the reader to find it cautionary that the law continues to over-ride considerations of freedom and slavery with those of skin colour and

[54] Equiano, *The Interesting Narrative* (1789), i. 132–3.
[55] Ibid. ii. 18. The name Gustavus Vassa, that of a Swedish military man, had been conferred on Equiano by the English sea captain, under whom he served. When Equiano is granted his freedom, he hints that the name Freeman is preferable to his previous one (which signifies, presumably, bondage and the act of appropriation) See Costanzo, *Surprizing Narrative*, ch. 4, for more on the issue of names imposed by slave owners: 'In the eighteenth century, all black autobiographers are given Anglicized slave names. Gronniosaw is called James Albert, Cugoano is baptized as John Steuart (sometimes spelled Stuart or Stewart), and Equiano is ironically named Gustavus Vassa, the name of the Swedish king who freed his country from the Danes in the sixteenth century . . . Gronniosaw, Cugoano, and Equiano prefer their African names because they wish to emphasize their new identities as freemen. (para.) Equiano's identity quest is revealed by his attitude toward the succession of names he bears during his lifetime. (para.) On board the slave ship, Equiano loses his African name when the sailors call him Michael. Later, on the Virginia plantation, he is known as Jacob, and he barely gets used to this name when Captain Pascal purchases him and renames him Gustavus Vassa. Equiano's attitude toward the importance of his name reveals itself when he refuses to be called by the new name and tells Captain Pascal "that I would be called Jacob; but he said I should not, and still called me Gustavus; and when I refused to answer to my new name, which at first I did, it gained me many a cuff; so at length I submitted, and was obliged to bear the present name, by which I have been known ever since" ' (69).

racial origin. The legislation of the Assembly of Barbados, for instance, continued to enshrine the edict that any testimony of a black person against a white was banned, and that the punishment of a white person for murdering a negro, whether slave or free, was the pitifully meagre fine of £15.[56]

It is significant that when in *Obi*, the sugar planter, Ormond, announces his decision to free his slaves, he does so in order to drive a wedge between Quashee and his comrades on the one side, and Jack on the other.

My gallant hearts, your courage shall not go unrewarded; and as the first proof of my bounty, no more my slaves—be free! (*Negroes shout.*) Fear not his wily stratagems—his magic art—all will fail before the arm that's nerved by freedom and by gratitude. This night continue your feast; let not my sorrows taint the few moments you have of mirth. Nay, 'tis my command. To-night celebrate your new-found liberty, to-morrow for vengeance!

The benign master does not visit his personal grievances on those in his charge, but he does still 'command' them to take pleasure, and then vengeance, on his behalf, and against their own kind. Liberty, as the master well knows, is in his gift and only to be dispensed where recognition of his condescension is achieved and celebrated.

### George Colman's *Inkle and Yarico*

When Thomas Clarkson's travels on behalf of the abolition movement took him to Manchester, he found the people of the city particularly 'moved' by 'the peculiar terrors of the slave trade: loss of kin, hearth and community'.[57] This could be accounted for, in part, by the mobility of the population of Manchester and consequent identification with the feelings accompanying loss of roots and social displacement. George Colman the Younger's *Inkle and Yarico*, based on the supposedly true story of a merchant, Inkle, and his shipwreck off the North American coast, draws on such a sense of identification and empathy, as did a large number of poets and playwrights across Europe in response to the story.[58]

---

[56] Ibid. i. 217–19, in which Equiano records that this law is enshrined in the 329th Act of the Assembly of Barbados.

[57] Drescher, *Capitalism and Antislavery*, ch. 4.

[58] *Inkle and Yarico, a comick opera, the words by George Colman Esq., the musick composed by Dr Arnold, organist and composer to his majesty, first performed at the Theatre-Royal in the Haymarket, on Saturday, August 11th, 1787* (Robinson, London, 1787). The

Although the date of the initial performance of the play predates the period under scrutiny here, I make reference to it because of its enormous popularity and influence throughout the period. Initially, Colman's plot keeps to one version of the original, in which Thomas Inkle is rescued and hidden from tribal warriors by a North American Indian woman, Yarico, until the moment when he can board a passing British ship which will take him to safety. In the meantime, charmed by the fair Inkle and his knowledge of the fine civilization of Europe, Yarico has been persuaded to depart with him, thus abandoning her own people. However, the passing ship is bound for the West Indies rather than Europe, and instead of holding to his promises of dressing Yarico in silk and ermine and introducing her to the rich material and cultural life of Europe, Inkle succumbs to the profit motive and sells her into one of the most brutal of all slave regimes.

Colman transforms the material into comic opera, opening the play in an American forest with a satirical exchange between Trudge and Medium of Threadneedle Street, respectively Inkle's manservant and uncle, both also shipwrecked in this version. Colman adopts similar strategies to those later deployed by Fawcett in *Obi*. For instance, Sir Christopher Curry, the governor of the West Indies, far from being an authoritarian overseer of an oppressive regime, is a man of deep, empathetic sensibilities, driven at one moment to tears by the callousness of Inkle's behaviour. Like Ormond, the plantation owner in *Obi*, Sir Christopher is represented as having the interests of slaves at heart and is instrumental in a version of the story which thwarts Inkle and accommodates Yarico to a supposedly happy ending. Whilst the play falls short of questioning white supremacy in Barbados, settling for the familiar trope of benign paternalism (with a chivalric heart, particularly towards the female sex), it does succeed in scrutinizing the mechanisms and ethics of trade, to the extent that it can be put in the context of the movement against the British slave trade. There is increasing evidence to suggest that the play, first performed at the Theatre Royal in the Haymarket in 1787, situated itself directly in the context of the abolition movement. Certainly, its performance ten years later in

play was Colman's first great success. Steele records in *The Spectator* (Henry Morley edition, Routledge, London, 1888) Tuesday 13 March 1711, 21 n., a version of the Inkle and Yarico story as from "'A True and Exact History of the Island of Barbadoes. By Richard Ligon, Gent.," fol. 1673. The first edition had appeared in 1657.' See Lawrence Marsden Price, *Inkle and Yarico Album* (University of California Press, Berkeley, 1937), for versions of the story in different genres and different countries.

Wisbech, and soon after in other East Anglian towns, must have been connected directly to the Clarkson wing of the abolition campaign.[59]

It is not that the spotlight of the play itself is on slavery, although it does feature rather gruelling, if crude, satire on slavers watching for slave ships from Barbados, and audiences might well have known of the story itself and have had their own felt and moral responses to the gross act of betrayal by Inkle of Yarico.[60] What is more significant is the extent to which the play engages with the subject of how British citizens should conduct themselves, in ethical terms, as perpetrators of a trade in people; and with the whole question of the standards by which 'British subjects ought to conduct business around the world'.[61]

Support for the anti-slavery movement in Manchester had not just been about sympathies for displaced persons, but about this very question, of how a city thriving on the economic benefits resulting from the international market could reconcile its supposedly civilized values with some of the practices resulting from the exchanges of that market, and validated in its name. Manchester's very confidence as a mercantile centre, renowned for productive trading and relative prosperity, appears to have been accompanied by a civic conscience about those implicated, and particularly those who were victims of commercial exchange and the accumulation of profit.[62]

Adam Smith had focused the debate over the possibility that the economics of slavery might not necessarily profit the colonial power, and the question of how the rationale to slavery in relation to productive uses of labour-power breaks down over trade is raised in the Equiano autobiography.[63] A demoralized, dispirited, and suffering

---

[59] Wisbech was Clarkson's birthplace and the museum there contains memorabilia not only of Clarkson and his family, but of this production of *Inkle and Yarico*. Wisbech's theatre company, Eastern Angles, recently revived the play in a rehearsed reading. I leave to historians of theatre performance what might be a very interesting set of distinctions between audience reception of the 1787 production in London and that of the 1797 production in Wisbech (at one of the lowest points of the war against France, the year of naval mutinies and of insurrectionary activity by groups such as the United Englishmen). My more general argument about changes in audience reception over the 1790s might, however, cut across some of the local detail.

[60] See Price, *Inkle and Yarico Album*, for the ubiquity and popularity of the story.

[61] Drescher, *Capitalism and Antislavery*, 87–8.

[62] See Thomas Haskell in Bender (ed.), *The Antislavery Debate*, particularly ch. 2, 'Capitalism and the Origins of the Humanitarian Sensibility', for more on the debate over capitalism.

[63] Equiano, *The Interesting Narrative* (1969), particularly the introduction by Paul Edwards.

people may be compatible with the act of colonization itself, which brings them under the yoke of the imperial power for the purposes of working the land. But such a broken and, at best, passive people are of little profit to the market system and its dependence on the energetic initiatives required to circulate goods. (So argues Equiano; and it is not necessarily a cynical argument in relation to the British government, but a knowing one.)

From the moment Colman's play opens, Inkle's motives in having travelled to America are under scrutiny. The audience is introduced to Trudge and Medium as the advance guard, separated from Inkle in the forest after the shipwreck, but also in the sense of being commentators on the whole expedition. Medium bemoans his own rash departure from London, commenting on Inkle's motives and character: 'This it is to have to do with a schemer! a fellow who risques his life, for a chance of advancing his interest.—Always advantage in View! Trying here to make discoveries that may promote his profit in England. Another Botany Bay scheme, mayhap.'

Both *Obi* and *Inkle and Yarico* open with characters other than the central white male protagonist, but the preparation of the audience for the entrance of Ormond is very different from that of Inkle, who, as he appears, is immediately held in critical perspective, the terms of his expedition in question. (Ormond, in contrast, is greeted with a shout of acclamation from his slaves.) In the process, the motives of British merchants travelling abroad are themselves held up to view. It is significant, too, that the exchange acquires an authority from crossing classes. Medium, of the same class as Inkle, reproaches Trudge for his lack of insight into his master. Trudge, partly nostalgic for his time as Inkle's factotum in London, yearns to be reunited with the master from whom he has been separated. Medium satirizes this attachment of Trudge to the office of factotum, retorting that it was certainly no fine position, but more a matter of shining the master's shoes 'with an ink bottle' and 'writing an invoice in lampblack' than being, as Trudge would have it, 'king of the counting-house'. (Darkness, in this play, functions as a metaphor for oppression, not evil, as in the more conventional *Obi*.) After this exchange, Inkle enters, and Medium reveals himself as no less of a critic in his nephew's presence than in his absence.

MED. Zounds, one wou'd think, by your confounded composure, that you were walking in St James's Park instead of an American forest, and that all the beasts were nothing but good company. The hollow trees here, sentry boxes, and the lions in 'em soldiers; the jackalls, courtiers, the crocodiles, fine women and the baboons, beaux. What the plague made you loiter so long?

INKLE. Reflection.

MED. So I shou'd think; reflection generally comes lagging behind. What, scheming, I suppose? never quiet. At it again, eh? What a happy trader is your father, to have so prudent a son for a partner! Why, you are the carefullest Co. in the whole city; never losing sight of the main chance, and that's the reason perhaps you lost sight of us here on the main of America.

In framing the play in this way, in contrast to the triumphalist noises which surround Ormond at the beginning of *Obi*, Colman sets up audience expectations of Inkle in a critical manner, before the audience perceives the particular dilemma of shipwreck. The background is there, through the filter of London and its alienation from jackals and crocodiles, and as in *Obi*, the black participants are invoked in crude stereotypes of and references to 'the natives'. However, the establishing of dramatic distance from Inkle is such that the play's issues are inflected in a crucially different way; this foregrounds a critique of the worst aspects of British mercantilism, its propensity for inflating commodities and people, and the grossness with which it trades in both. Colman's puns in the mouth of Medium—'main chance' off the 'main', 'advantage' always in view—establish the problematic vocabulary of what Carlyle was calling 'the cash nexus'. They may be the cheap jokes of pantomime, but they are also central to the play's dramatic and political vocabulary.

For all that the play sets the frame around a critique of mercantile values, though, the perspective remains that of the white man. Yarico is conceptualized in terms of the white man's fantasy of the exotic other;[64] and the representation of the American forest, as we have seen, sets the wildness of North American 'natives' against the urbane values, however satirically presented, of metropolitan London. The perspective which

---

[64] The debate about 'the exotic other' is too extensive to reference minutely here, but commentators central to originating discussion have been Rana Kabbani, *Europe's Myths of Orient*, Susheila Nasta (ed.), *Motherlands*, and Edward Said, *Orientalism*. Ferguson, *Subject to Others*, focuses on British women writers' responses to the story. Ferguson records that the Countess of Hertford was the first woman 'to adapt the legend of Inkle and Yarico (in two poems)', focusing on Yarico, rather than the couple. The poems were published in 1725, and nine years later an anonymous female poet approached the subject again, with an even more stringent attack on Inkle. Obviously, the precedents were there for Colman!

remains closed to Colman is that of the black man (let alone woman) who is able to question and invert the vocabulary of savagery.

It was not, though, that that model of inversion did not exist, and Equiano, for one, provides it in his autobiography. After having been kidnapped from his African village as a boy, Equiano first encounters white men in the form of the slavers who force him onboard ship. When he later records this, with the benefits of his fluency in English, he depicts the white men not only in terms of the shock of perceiving their skin colour, but also in an inversion of the vocabulary of racial expectation. Their behaviour towards the slaves locates them as 'savages', and the 'refinements' of cruelty which they introduce during the voyage are not the refinements of that European civilization which is supposed to define its representatives as advanced in manners and cultivation, but rather the mark of barbarism. That perspective, though, is not open to Colman, who can only go so far as setting criticism in the context of dialogue between white men.

Much more could be said, and indeed is in the process of being written, about the detail and performance history of *Inkle and Yarico*,[65] but the significance of the play for this account is primarily in relation to its critique of mercantilism and as witness to the range of theatrical and literary languages and genres articulated to abolition and emancipation politics. If Colman could produce spectacularly successful dramatic material out of issues related to the abolition movement, it was, as I argued earlier, because drama can exploit the immediacy of visual impact and the implications of appearance and disguise for questions of racial origin and identity. That the representation of racial stereotypes

---

[65] A production of the play, directed by Simon Godwin and produced by Emma Stenning, was staged at Cambridge Festival Theatre, England, for two nights in April 1997. Under the auspices of Straydogs theatre group, Simon and Emma then reworked the play in a new production at Battersea Arts Centre, London, in August 1998. Whilst rehearsals for the Cambridge production were taking place, we heard that we had been just pre-empted, in terms of reviving the play for staging, by a production in Barbados earlier in 1997. The play is clearly generating increasing academic interest in relation to performance. Frank Felsenstein, who participated in the Cambridge conference, 'Theatre and Politics in the Age of Reform', connected to the Cambridge production of the play, told of his plans to work on an *Inkle and Yarico* companion for Johns Hopkins University Press. Other conference contributors included Peter Raby, J. S. Bratton, Jean Chothia, Ann Featherstone, Jane Moody, Brian Ridgers, Richard Schoch, Rachel Wyndham, Simon Featherstone, Ato Quayson, Tim Cribb, Simon Godwin, and Emma Stenning. Conference organizers were also extremely pleased to welcome Roxanna Panufnik, the composer of the music of the recent production in Barbados, who attended one of the Cambridge performances.

could make for comedy should provoke concern, not least about the extent to which 'the cause of the negro', as it became known in the later Victorian period, could be accommodated and trivialized through laughter.[66] By the same set of devices, though, comedy could be effective in challenging such stereotypes. Comedy could explore, through visual and oral disturbance, that territory of racial difference about which audiences were ignorant and actively or potentially prejudicial.

As we have seen, the autobiographer, Equiano, could conceal the colour of his skin, thereby modifying the impact of his African identity, mediating it through Englishness.[67] The playwright cannot conceal the appearance of his performers, nor the immediate impact of their entrance on stage. However, it is that very inability to hide appearance which renders visual representation and revelation particularly forceful and immediate in its power to confirm or to explode audience expectations. Colman plays with the languages and faces of race, knowing that these are related powerfully to performance meanings. At worst, he abuses his skill in this territory, opening up the play to accusations of racism and misogyny. At best, he invites his audience to explore their assumptions about racial difference, enlighten their ignorance, and question their prejudiced attitudes, particularly over those habits of calculation and advantage which have been so far to the profit of the white man, and so damaging to the interests of the indigenous peoples of the colonies.

The versions of abolition rhetoric used by Equiano, Clarkson, and others could be powerful in the theatre as well as from the soapbox and memoir. Situating *Inkle and Yarico* in the context of widespread support for the abolition movement was no doubt a piece of opportunism on the part of the playwright, famous for his ability to seize the popular moment.[68] However, it was also a testimony to the ability of contemporary drama, and particularly the forms of comedy and melodrama, to shape some aspect of the rhetoric of anti-slavery to dramatic ends.

---

[66] Christine Bolt, *Victorian Attitudes to Race* (Routledge, London, and University of Toronto Press, Toronto, 1971).

[67] The usual literary convention for concealing identity is the sobriquet, one of the most notorious cases being that of the Bronte sisters. By contrast, Equiano's autobiographical strategy depends, in part, upon revealing his racial origin. My argument, though, is that the impact of race on a readership of autobiography is mediated by language rather than skin colour, and here that language is the English of the English.

[68] There is more said in Ch. 6 about audience, and the extent to which theatre audiences, like the abolition movement, crossed class.

Having been massively successful, *Inkle and Yarico* appears hardly to have been performed again after the Emancipation Act, until recent productions in Barbados and Cambridge.[69] This seems to lend force to the idea that the play had served its turn in the abolition movement. In retrospect, it is all too easy, but also too facile, to see as naïve (or worse) that which contemporary audiences acclaimed as reflecting a necessary humanitarianism, and as crossing class and racial differences in countering slavery.

### Thomas Morton's *The Slave*

Thomas Morton's *The Slave*, performed at Covent Garden in 1816, is significantly placed historically between the abolition of the British slave trade and the Emancipation Act.[70] The choice of Surinam as a setting for the play was almost certainly informed by the use of that location in Aphra Behn's *Oroonoko*, which had pioneered a version of the anti-slavery narrative over a hundred years earlier. Thomas Southerne's dramatized version of Behn's novella was extremely popular in stage productions until the early years of the nineteenth century.[71] In being 'a musical', it is also possible that *The Slave* was influenced by the success of the operatic *Inkle and Yarico*.

*The Slave* draws on the complex changes in international trading arrangements which had taken place in the late eighteenth and early nineteenth centuries, particularly with the abolition of British trading

[69] See n. 65.

[70] Thomas Morton, Esq., *The Slave; a Musical Drama, in Three Acts* (Miller, London, 1816).

[71] Aphra Behn, *Oroonoko, or The History of the Royal Slave*, ed. K. A. Sey (Ghana Publishing Corporation, Tema, Ghana, 1977). Thomas Southerne, *Oroonoko*, a tragedy, acted at Drury Lane and Covent Garden (Wenham, London, 1778), adapted from Aphra Behn's novel. See Sandiford, *Measuring the Moment*, ch. 2, on the subject of Thomas Southerne's *Oroonoko*, 'the subsequent stage history of that production was nothing short of phenomenal; the play was performed at least once every season until 1801. The relation of the Oroonoko legend to antislavery . . . rests more in the metamorphosis wrought through changing audience interpretation over the years than in what its original authors proposed. It established the tradition of the "Noble Negro," an image that, although highly sentimentalized and unrealistic, stirred most English citizens' consciousnesses to consider more seriously the plight of the African and the ineluctable proofs of Britain's complicity in crimes against humanity' (61–2). The other source for Morton's dramatic adaptation was John Gabriel Stedman, *Narrative of a Five Years' Expedition Against the Revolted Negroes of Surinam*, ed. Richard Price and Sally Price (Johns Hopkins University Press, Baltimore, 1988).

in 1807. Since the Treaty of Asiento, England had gained progressively greater control over slave trading throughout the eighteenth century, replacing the Netherlands as 'the greatest slave-trading nation in the world'.[72] Thomas Morton's play, described as a musical drama in three acts, derives much of its significance from the interplay of nationalities and national interests between the English and Dutch colonizers, and the Surinam slaves, particularly the heroic African, Gambia. Additional characters, including a Londoner, a Scot, and a Yorkshireman, interact to form a largely comic commentary, running parallel questions of regional alongside those of national identity.

The plot hinges on a love triangle, in which Gambia loves the slave woman, Zelinda, described as a quadroon. However, Zelinda does not return Gambia's affections, and has had a child by Clifton, who is an English captain. One might expect Clifton to develop into the familiar villain of the later Victorian melodrama, and he does have some of the incipient characteristics, but this plot requires him to be functional to the nobility of Gambia's cause, to which I shall return. In short, Clifton acknowledges his child by Zelinda, and pledges to marry her. Initially, Gambia deplores Clifton's bond with Zelinda and swears vengeance on the Englishman. It is significant, though, that even at this early stage, and with Gambia threatening to shed the blood of the English, the playwright endorses Gambia's position. Gambia's speech is the poetic vocabulary of the libertarian poet:

Mark my words—Europe's cold sons may sink into nerveless apathy; but Afric's fiery children know no sleep of passion—Liberty lost, love unrequited, hope extinguished!—what remains to fill this bosom, but revenge, precious, sweet revenge! Let your proud son of freedom tremble at the vengeance of a slave.

In dialogue with Clifton and despite her fears for his safety, Zelinda supports Gambia's claims, with the explanation that 'to his nation, revenge is virtue' (and his nation has every cause for revenge!). However, Gambia is no three-fingered Jack, but rather, as a protagonist of English romanticism, a Byronesque figure in his nobility. When Clifton is threatened by slave uprisings in Surinam, Gambia does not take the part of the other slaves, but, out of his love for Zelinda, protects Clifton against violence. Furthermore, when Clifton is imprisoned for debt,

---

[72] Christopher Hill, *Reformation to Industrial Revolution* (Collins, London, 1985), 227–9, cited in Ferguson, *Subject to Others*, 71.

Gambia plays the martyr, selling himself back into slavery in order to buy Clifton's release—all for Zelinda. In response to Gambia's actions on his behalf, Clifton is given the language of the British abolitionist: 'And is that the being with whom the proud European denies fellowship? if we are not brothers, let the white man blush that he is alien to the blood that mantles in that noble breast.'[73] But, in the very process of romanticizing Gambia, Thomas Morton fuels the European perspective against the African. The implied criticism is not of the individual slave, who is romanticized, but of slave resistance as a collective act. As in *Obi*, the slave protagonist is separated from his male counterparts and is seen to be distancing himself from their activities and interests. The audience is told that the uprising by slaves comes not from that justified vengeance articulated by Gambia at the individual level, but from fury 'against the slaves of this plantation, for their fidelity to their mistress'.[74]

It is also significant that the English governor of Surinam, like governors in both *Obi* and *Inkle and Yarico*, is a benign influence, and even more forcefully, a spokesman for Enlightenment and Christian values:

Yes, slavery must fall before the Christian warrior;—the arena he combats in, is the human mind; Revelation unfolds his banner;—Truth forges his shield;— his armour is rivetted by Reason, and his lance is tempered by Mercy.

And later:

True liberty is the offspring of peace, the nurse of humanity, the parent of benevolence; its home, the world; its family, mankind; its allegiance, Heaven.

Thus the English escape censure, leaving slavery and slave owners to be indicted through the Dutch villain of the piece, Lindenburg, apparently desirous of seeing everyone, perhaps even his own mother, in chains. The historic struggle between the Dutch and the British for control of international trading is foregrounded here by Thomas Morton, perhaps with a suggestion that a British audience might rather enjoy the enactment of the upholding of English interests as against Dutch ones, even after the abolition of the British slave trade (and perhaps because of this?). The supposed winner of the piece is Gambia,

---

73 'Am I not a man and a brother?' was the logo of the abolitionist movement as recorded by Thomas Clarkson in his *History of the Abolition of the Slave Trade*, 1808.

74 Thomas Morton is leaning on Aphra Behn again, in that she represents slave insurrections in Surinam.

in that he gains his freedom from slavery, together with the chance to leave Surinam, but it is also English nationalism and the supposedly irreproachable virtues of the English. In the play's denouement, Gambia is required to eulogize England and its supposed promises:

England! shall I behold thee? Talk of fabled land, or magic power! But what land, that poet ever sung, or enchanter swayed, can equal that, which, when the slave's foot touches, he becomes free—his prisoned soul starts forth, his swelling nerves burst the chain that enthrall'd him, and, in his own strength he stands, as the rock he treads on, majestic and secure.

And that speech does not even need to conclude with a question mark, because its rhetoric is so secure.[75] The slave thus ventriloquizes the voice of the colonizer, in this case the Englishman, while England stands steadfast, supposedly the rock of liberty. However, the play is not this simplistic in its complete message. Within the English camp, there is internal criticism. As in *Inkle and Yarico*, there is the class challenge to mercantilism and particularly to the English aristocracy. It is Sam Sharpset, the Yorkshireman, from whom the comic commentary derives most force: 'there's a New Market made on purpose for them: they all deal in summut—as coals, pictures, lead, parliament, men, brimstone'. Some of them, he claims, have been, 'known to sell their voices'. In terms of the play's own voices, there are significant dramatic questions. Dialect is reserved not for the slaves as in *Obi*, but for the British regions, represented in the Yorkshireman (Sharpset), the Scotsman, and the Londoner. The slave protagonists, Gambia and Zelinda, have access to varieties of standard English, equating their concerns at one level with those of the governor and Clifton. At the same time, the satirical commentary of Sam Sharpset not only focuses class difference, but sets up some manner of critical perspective on the supposed language of

---

[75] In the 1816 production of *The Slave*, William Macready, the famous actor–manager, performed the part of Gambia, for which, of course, he would have had to blacken his skin. It is significant that, in the 1820s, the black actor, Ira Aldridge, about whom Rachel Wyndham spoke at the Cambridge conference in 1997, 'Theatre and Politics in the Age of Reform', appeared in London and was asked to play the lead in Southerne's *Oroonoko* (Royal Coburg Theatre, October 1825). Aldridge is described on this first playbill as 'Tragedian of Colour, from the African Theatre, New York'. See Herbert Marshall and Mildred Stock, *Ira Aldridge—The Negro Tragedian* (Rockliff, London, 1958) for biographical detail. Later in 1825, Aldridge was invited to play Othello. The extent to which the powerful and widely performed Shakespeare play had influenced playwrights and performers of the late Georgian period in relation to questions of theatricality and race is important, but beyond the scope of this account.

liberty as articulated in various discourses of standard English. It could be argued that this prevents Gambia, for instance, from being entirely accommodated to an unproblematic proclamation of English nationalism. Sam Sharpset knows it differently: that the 'fabled land' is largely about goods, creditors, and commodities; and that unless Gambia is lucky, he will be treated more like the last than as an independent subject, standing 'in his own strength'.

The play also focuses the issue of liberty, critically, around questions of gender. Thomas Morton revisits *Inkle and Yarico* in the sense that Zelinda, like Yarico, is enamoured of an Englishman (who is mostly at sea). Like George Colman, Morton sees not only the romantic potential, but also the power relations of these alliances, in terms of race as well as gender. Like Yarico, Zelinda is not a black African. The description of her as a quadroon suggests that she is primarily of white descent, which gives her a status above Gambia, and we must suppose that it in part explains her attraction to Clifton. Like Colman, Morton subsumes the oppressed woman in the love interest while in the very process of seeming to assert her rights.

However, there is one moment in *The Slave* where the question of liberty is put into very stark relationship with ideas of love and marriage. The audience has already been treated to Sam Sharpset's setting of his 'precious liberty' against being lured into marriage, but a less stereotypical version occurs in the particular form that Clifton's dilemma takes when the governor offers him the right to grant freedom to one slave. He chooses Gambia over Zelinda, implying that within marriage, particularly to him, Zelinda will not *require* liberty. In Yarico's case, this had been the trap that had threatened to ensnare her.[76] Neither is Zelinda given much chance to speak back to the case, so enthralled is she with Clifton.

It has been argued that the abolitionists had strong investments in the family unit, as potentially embodying the new social order after the abolition of slavery,[77] and both George Colman and Thomas Morton do seem to support this conception. However, the destinies of Yarico and Zelinda, even when accommodated to utopian perspectives on the future, leave audiences at best uncertain of the character of their liberty.

---

[76] As we shall see in subsequent chapters, it is not the view of contemporary feminists that marriage procures liberty for women.

[77] John Ashworth in Bender (ed.), *The Antislavery Debate*, 274.

Within marriage, Zelinda is, of course, Clifton's property, and there is one moment in the play when Morton, allowing her to voice the dilemma, inflects her anxiety in the direction of Clifton as well as the tyrannical slave-owner, Lindenburg: 'To what fate am I reserved?[78] The slave of him, who is himself the slave of passion—Oh that my humble voice could reach those hearts who pity the children of affliction.' It is apt, too, that further suggestion of and movement towards Zelinda's freedom comes from another woman rather than English men. Lindenburg's mother, even though she is one of the unspeakable Dutch, speaks of Zelinda with affection and concern, as if the women of the colonial power might well have had slave women's interests at heart on occasions, and might have been the only people interested in suing for their emancipation.

## A Concluding Word on Audience

As I demonstrate later, the terms of class as applied to late Georgian history are complex, but what is clear is that the involvement of black people, women, and working men in the abolition movement, expressed not only in petitioning but also in their support as audiences for speakers, translated into theatrical activity. George Colman, Thomas Morton, and other playwrights of the period would, of course, have known of the potential for a mass audience. To argue that their plays are superficial and lack political charge would be to misunderstand both the commercial character of theatre at this time and the growing evidence of an audience which was both politically informed and integrated in its approach to issues of abolition and ethical questions around emancipation. What has been overlooked, then, is not only the importance of working people in their contribution to the pursuit of liberty, across class and racial interests, but also their existence as a substantial yet serious component of audiences, outside and inside the theatre. Leeds labourers, women and men, in whose collective mind the pursuit of liberty was taking a prominent place, were signing petitions against the slave trade and assembling to hear Thomas Clarkson, American abolitionists, and others speak. Popular playwrights were ready to capitalize on their knowledge of this potential theatre audience.

This analysis would appear to lend weight to two crucial arguments:

---

[78] Ferguson, *Subject to Others*, esp. ch. 4, explores comments on slavery within marriage.

first, that the drama of the period could rely, in relation to plays which raised or touched on the abolition issue, on audiences from across what E. P. Thompson describes as the plebeian–patrician continuum;[79] second, that those plays would not have been popular if they had not taken the radical propensity of the audience, informed by its knowledge and involvement in abolition and emancipation movements, seriously. Theatre historians should not be duped by the popularity of these plays and their comic and musical characteristics, into believing that the drama lacked political force, and a capacity to work alongside the political movements, in mutual reinforcement. In the context of its own home-grown movements towards political change, British theatre used comedy and the legacy from French melodrama, with its origins in and continuing capacity for declaring the people's demands for liberty, to examine some aspect of those racial differences dramatically highlighted by the anti-slavery movement, and to explore related ignorance and prejudicial assumptions about race.[80] Though limited to the perspective of white playwrights and audiences made up, for the most part, from those who had not even personally witnessed the distant slave scene, let alone participated in it, the drama helped to forge a rhetoric that could distinguish racial difference from denigration. In doing so, theatre gave its help to the glorious causes of abolition and emancipation.

[79] The reference is developed in Ch. 6.
[80] References to the legacy of French melodrama are developed in Ch. 6.

CHAPTER THREE

# Dark Satanic Mills, Transforming the Face of England

There are at least two other areas, both related to the reform movement, where the discourses of anti-slavery assume a powerful significance. One is the specific use of the lexicon of slavery in application to the role of women, particularly within marriage and the household. In 1825, William Thompson and Anna Wheeler named the problem directly by equating the absence of women's enfranchisement, and of any significant position for them in civil society, with their domestic slavery.[1] British women throughout the late eighteenth and early nineteenth centuries, as well as producing a wealth of anti-slavery poetry and prose, had used the analogy between women and slaves repeatedly.[2] Mary Wollstonecraft, among them, tells a version of the Inkle and Yarico story in a lesson to a readership of women and girls.[3]

The other area where the vocabulary of anti-slavery gained a particular and explicit purchase was in the equation of the master and slave with the employer and employee in the factory. Henry Whiteley's *Three Months in Jamaica* makes reference to the British factory system as 'a domestic counterpart' to colonial exploitation.[4] E. P. Thompson reminds us that factory workers constituted only a fraction of the number of working people, and that what became known as 'the standard of living' debate amongst historians has contested notions of the

---

[1] William Thompson and Anna Wheeler (1825) *Appeal of One Half the Human Race, Women, Against the Pretensions of the Other Half, Men, To Retain Them in Political, and Thence in Civil and Domestic, Slavery,* ed. and with a new introduction by Michael Foot and Marie Mulvey Roberts (Thoemmes Press, London, 1994).

[2] Ferguson, *Subject to Others,* for a thorough exploration of the subject.

[3] Mary Wollstonecraft, *The Female Reader* (Johnson, London, 1789).

[4] Blackburn, *The Overthrow of Colonial Slavery,* ch. 11, cites, Whiteley (Hatchard, London, 1833).

particular economic oppression of factory hands.[5] Nevertheless, as Thompson suggests, it was not necessarily primarily for economic reasons that the mill was one of the dominant images of oppression of the period to be captured later, particularly in early Victorian literary and political writing.[6] Reasons for the association of the factory, and particularly the cotton mill, with slavery were connected with the particular character of industrial relationship operating within them, and with the symbolic force of the dark, Satanic mills.[7]

The mill was particularly characterized by its *visibility* as a domain of labour and by what Thompson describes as 'the transparency of the process of exploitation'.[8] Factory workers and the factory itself were marked out distinctly, creating their own community in which the poverty of the workers was also manifest, as was the wealth of the manufacturer, often accumulated rapidly over one generation.[9] In the factory, the reduction of man to the status of an 'instrument', described by Thompson, was all too visible to critics of the system.[10] It was this instrumentality, together with its observability, which lent such powerful evidence to the accounts of Engels and to Marx's theory of alienation. In 1818, a worker in the cotton industry in the north of England, describing himself as a journeyman cotton spinner, went so far as to describe working in a factory as less preferable to slavery:

The negro slave in the West Indies, if he works under a scorching sun, has probably a little breeze of air sometimes to fan him: he has a space of ground, and time allowed to cultivate it. The English spinner slave has no enjoyment of the open atmosphere and breezes of heaven. Locked up in factories eight stories high, he has no relaxation till the ponderous engine stops, and then he goes home to get refreshed for the next day; no time for sweet association with his family; they are all alike fatigued and exhausted. This is no over-drawn picture: it is literally true.[11]

---

[5] Thompson, *The Making of the English Working Class*, ch. 6, 'Exploitation', for an account of the cotton mills.

[6] Charles Dickens in *Hard Times*, Elizabeth Gaskell in *Mary Barton* and *North and South*, Frederick Engels in *The Condition of the Working Class in England*, Karl Marx in *Capital*, to name a few.

[7] William Blake, 'Jerusalem', for the much-publicized Satanic mill. The North American cotton fields also yield a very powerful image of the relationship between cotton and slavery.

[8] Thompson, *The Making of the English Working Class*, ch. 6.

[9] Ibid.        [10] Ibid.        [11] Ibid. 218–21.

In 1830, Richard Oastler published an attack, to which I shall return, on what he described as Yorkshire slavery, which primarily addressed the exploitation of children and women by Yorkshire mill-owners.[12] In doing so, he brought together both sets of analogies with slavery, that of workers in the British factory, and of women and girls; the exploitation of the female sex was not confined to household slavery, but was a particular feature of factory work. The journeyman cotton spinner had recorded something of the dilemma, in invoking the old days before the steam engine in relation to the new:

The brokers sold it (cotton) to the merchants, by which means the master spinner was enabled to stay at home and work and attend to his workmen. The cotton was then always given out in its raw state from the bale to the wives of the spinners at home, when they heat and cleansed it ready for the spinners in the factory. By this they could earn eight, ten, or twelve shillings a week, and cook and attend to their families. But are thus employed now; for all the cotton is broke up by a machine, turned by the steam engine, called a devil: so that the spinners' wives have no employment, except they go to work in the factory all day at what can be done by children for a few shillings, four or five per week.[13]

By implication, the account also draws attention to homeworkers and outworkers, probably those most exploited economically outside chattel slavery. From 1800 onwards, the concept and practices of the small master gave way to manufacturers and their middlemen, who tended to operate on a larger scale. Weavers and stocking- and nailmakers were pressed into precarious employment as outworkers, much of whose labour was invisible in that it was performed outside the factory.[14] The disenchantment of outworkers was less palpable than that of factory workers, more difficult to perceive from the outside, and less fully documented.[15]

---

[12] Blackburn, *The Overthrow of Colonial Slavery*, ch. 11, makes the connection between factory-owner and mill-owner.

[13] Thompson, *The Making of the English Working Class*, 218–21.

[14] The invisibility of work in the home is an issue which has figured in much feminist writing. For this particular period, the arguments are there in Thompson and Wheeler, *Appeal of One Half*. Barbara Taylor, *Eve and the New Jerusalem* (Virago, London, 1983), ch. 4, ' "The Men are as Bad as their Masters . . ." Working Women and the Owenite Economic Offensive, 1828–34' looks back searchingly on that history.

[15] In the early Victorian period, novelists and social commentators attempt to represent the outworker; notably, Elizabeth Gaskell in her novel *Ruth*, and Henry Mayhew, *The Morning Chronicle Survey of Labour and the Poor: The Metropolitan Districts*, (1850; Caliban Books, Sussex, 1981).

The relationship between wage labour, outworking, and chattel slavery was quite a debate in the period, as it has been subsequently, but it is invidious to create a hierarchy of oppression.[16] In terms of the *experience* of alienation, what characterizes all three most powerfully, and connects with women's objections to the eighteenth-century marriage market too, is the psychology and sociology of being commodified by those in control of one's labour, whether through factory work, or through being literally the property of someone else, as in the case of women as well as slaves. This is what William Thompson and Anna Wheeler had most vehemently taken issue with in their appeal against the particular configurations of eighteenth-century and early nineteenth-century marriage.[17] Writing his anti-slavery pamphlet in Cambridge in 1785, Thomas Clarkson was no doubt enraged in part by what became known as the Zong case in 1783. A slave ship had got into difficulties and had adopted as a solution the horrendous course of throwing slaves overboard in order to save the ship, in conditions where the slaves could only drown.[18] In Britain, the circumstances were debated almost exclusively in terms of mercantilism and the extent to which the death of a huge number of slaves represented a loss of property.[19] What appears to have fuelled all reform movements of the period was a sense that such acts were gross and that it was no longer acceptable for a humanitarian society, and indeed ran counter to any spirit of liberty and equality, to treat people as commodities.

## Staging the Factory

How far did the plays of the period capture these analogies with slavery in the project of transforming the cultural face of England? There *was* clearly a relationship between the new factory, the dark Satanic mill, a very public institution, and a theatre seeking, even at its least idealistic, to seize opportunities for representing novelty and trauma. The particular case of the visibility of the factory and factory workers influenced theatrical imagery and representation. Additionally, the theatre in other

---

[16] See Bender (ed.), *The Antislavery Debate,* for versions of the subsequent debate.

[17] Thompson and Wheeler, *Appeal of One Half.*

[18] Sandiford, *Measuring the Moment,* ch. 1, comments that it was Equiano who had brought the case to Granville Sharp's notice.

[19] Drescher, *Capitalism and Antislavery,* ch. 3, for a version of the tragedy.

domains, such as in relationship to the abolition movement, was showing every evidence of wanting to engage with experiences of oppression.
1832, the year of the Reform Act and a time when women emancipationists were at their most active and articulate, also saw a number of
plays on the subject of the factory as a problematic institution. Two of
these were Douglas Jerrold's *The Factory Girl* and John Walker's *The
Factory Lad*.[20]

*The Factory Lad* has been described as one of the most interesting of
the factory plays, in which 'the themes of class hatred, social injustice,
and industrial unrest' are unprecedented in the power of their representation.[21] As in many of the anti-slavery plays, the employing classes
appear to be constructed out of two models; here the contrast is
between the benign paternalist who, however condescendingly, appears
to have the interests of his employees at heart, and the new industrial-
ist, who characterizes the new age of steam, prioritizing machines over
men and profits over labour relations. In the Westwood family firm, the
ruthless son has taken over ownership from the departed father (and the
only hint of justification of the new master's actions is that there is less
demand than in his father's time for the goods manufactured in the
factory). His characteristic habits, including sneering at his employees,
carry the playwright's critique of a capitalism unmodified by the soft-

---

[20] Douglas Jerrold, *The Factory Girl, An original domestic drama in two acts* (Lord
Chamberlain's Office, 42,918, 1832), fos. 410 to 791, pp. 476–506. Stephens, *The Censorship of English Drama*, ch. 3, cites a *Times* reviewer objecting to the Lord Chamberlain's
Examiner for having allowed *The Factory Girl* to be performed, on the grounds that 'a
more ticklish subject (colonial slavery alone excepted) could not have been selected for
scenic representation'. There is more on the subject of Douglas Jerrold on
http://www.spartacus.schoolnet.co.uk/Jerrold.htm. John Walker, *The Factory Lad*, first
performed at the Surrey Theatre, 1832, in *Victorian Melodramas*, ed. and introduced by
James L. Smith (Dent, London, 1976).

[21] Michael R. Booth (*English Melodrama*, Jenkins, London, 1965), 137–9. See Hart-
mut Ilsemann, 'Radicalism in the Melodrama of the Early Nineteenth Century' in
Michael Hays and Anastasia Nikolopoulou (eds.), *Melodrama: The Cultural Emergence of
a Genre* (Macmillan, London, 1996) for a more detailed account of the play's merits, the
first performance of which took place within months of the Reform Act. Ilsemann
comments on reminders in the play of the Bristol riots in 1831 and the Luddite movement in 1811–12, and on the play's capacity for generating 'an emancipatory potential' in
the process of pre-empting 'received modes of reception'. (191–2) Ilsemann situates his
interpretation of the play in an analysis of melodrama: 'the developmental tendency is
for the English melodrama to move away from the narcissistic structures of illusionistic
performance towards . . . reality-oriented psychological modes of understanding' (205).
For more on the reclamation of melodrama as radical, see Ch. 6, particularly references
to the work of Elaine Hadley.

ening and shaping influences of humanitarianism.[22] The men who are about to be displaced by the introduction of a new steam-loom, articulate the consciousness of their own instrumentality: 'what are working men like us but the tools that make others rich?' And, as with the anti-slavery plays, the playwright endorses the discussion of vengeance as a course of action legitimated by the injustices perpetrated against victims, even drawing, if somewhat invidiously, on specific analogies with slavery. The character William Rushton, a poacher and an outcast, hides and listens into the disgruntled conversation of the factory workers as they make their way home after dismissal.[23] His comment speaks for agricultural workers as well as those in the factory: 'the slave abroad, the poor black whom they affect to pity, is not so trampled on, hunted, and ill-used as the peasant or hard working fellows like yourselves.' The analogy takes an even more lugubrious turn when Jane Allen, wife of one of the threatened factory workers, George, suggests they seek employment in a different place. The spectre of emigration is immediately evoked. George Allen is horrified, asserting that Will Rushton has been crazed by his one-time experience of life in the colonies, where his eldest child was 'slaughtered by the natives, who hate white men, and live on human flesh'.

John Walker's representation of the colonies through characters expressing just grievances is a much more pathological one than that entertained in any of the anti-slavery plays. It is as if the claims on the playwright of a highly melodramatic language of industrial relations puts other discourses of oppression under pressure. Richard Oastler's impassioned contribution to the discussion of the factory can be illuminating here. In that same, significant year of 1832, Oastler had been persuaded to write to the Duke of Wellington, raising objections to the factory system.[24] Oastler's primary argument is that both the landed

---

[22] See Haskell in Bender (ed.), *The Antislavery Debate,* for the discussion of humanitarian sensibility.

[23] See Thompson, *Whigs and Hunters: The Origin of the Black Act* (Allen Lane, London, 1975), for plenty on the subject of rural defiance.

[24] Richard Oastler, *Eight letters to the Duke of Wellington, a petition to the House of Commons, and a letter to the editor of the agricultural and industrial magazine* (Cochrane, London, 1835), from *Richard Oastler, King of Factory Children,* in *British Labour Struggles, Contemporary Pamphlets 1727–1850* (Arno Press, New York, 1972) In his introduction to the letters, Oastler challenges the assumption that the Duke of Wellington is only to be consulted about military matters. He approaches him as a member of the government who has concern for peacetime Britain.

aristocracy and the factory worker are being abused by the manufacturing classes in the interests of money and machinery. The argument is a conservative one to the extent that, in the name of their English national heritage, it exempts the gentry from any blame for labour relations. However, what is most characteristic of Oastler's position is the intensity and drama of the language which he uses to represent the plight of industrial workers; such dramatic techniques, although connected to a particular emphasis, have been learnt from the abolition movement.

### Richard Oastler and Yorkshire Slavery

In the postscript to his introduction to published letters to the Duke of Wellington, Oastler comments on Althorp's 'wicked' Factory Bill, which had 'made slaves of masters, as well as of poor factory children'.[25] In 1832, Oastler had joined with thousands of other Yorkshiremen to petition for the Sadler Bill, which had proposed a range of factory reforms, but was never presented. The 'all important question', argues Oastler in the postscript, is the reform of relations between labour and capital. In his introduction, Oastler draws on fiction and on drama to represent this 'great question'. He tells the 'blood-chilling' story of a poor man, compelled to be 'idle' at home, whilst his children fall victim to exploitation, disease, and death in the factory. The story concludes with an appeal to the Christian Reader to contemplate the fate of a poor man forced into destitution, theft, and violence. As the first-person narrator finishes his 'heart-rending tale', Oastler conjures a panorama of characters who, each in turn, attempt to give him advice. They include Macauley, Russell, Hume, the Mayor of Leeds, the Mayor of Huddersfield, Cobbett, and others. All advocate some kind of reform, but none of it meets the requirements of the poor, starved man, until Ashley and Sadler arrive, charming the children out of their sadness, and leaving the reader with the moral and economic message of Oastler's piece, that the only really appropriate reform consists of introducing 'a fair day's wages for a fair day's work'.[26]

At a key moment in the drama of the poor man, his children are threatened with emigration, where they will be 'flogged at the will o' th'

---

[25] Oastler, *Eight letters to the Duke of Wellington.*
[26] Ibid. 9.

master'. Oastler's argument is that the problems posed by factory labour should be solved at home. He opposes the idea of surplus labour and its concomitant solution of emigration, arguing that the aristocracy should 'cherish its people', not banish them. Although his argument is at times a nationalistic one, invoking Englishness and Yorkshire in particular in highly lyrical terms, it is essentially humanitarian, refusing the reduction of working people to functions of their own labour, without subjectivity and without rights. His stance *vis-à-vis* abolitionist and emancipation rhetoric carries this ambiguity, seeking to highlight the double standards of the government ('That infamous Parliament wept over the Black Slaves, and laughed at the sufferings of the poor Infant White Slaves'[27]) and to expose the evils of emigration, whilst sometimes appearing, in its eagerness to plead for poor Infant White Slaves, to verge on hostility to all those outside home:

And why should our labourers work more than EIGHT hours per day? Surely, with the assistance of our 'unrivalled machinery,' *their* labour is at least as valuable as that of the slaves in the West Indies;—and Earl Grey's son-in-law, the 'Whipper-in' of the House of Commons, Mr. Charles Wood, told us at Halifax, a week or two ago, that the black slaves,—I ask their pardon,—the black *servants*, were only now to work eight hours a day in the West Indies! . . . What a happy change, say all our poor *white* slaves, it would be, if our skins were suddenly turned black!—But, my Lord, what sin have the white servants in England committed, that they should be refused the *same* protection from the *same* Government? And are the white slave holders here, more guilty than the West Indians, that they are obliged to suffer the LOSS of longer labour from their servants?[28]

Objections to Sir Robert Peel's proposals to ameliorate the condition of children employed in cotton factories by regulating the working hours of children under the age of 16 and prohibiting employers from hiring children under the age of 9, were raised noisily, and equally vociferously contested. In a submission made in favour of Peel, thought to be drafted by Samuel Taylor Coleridge, the comparison between slavery and factory work is invoked in a language which both aknowledges Oastler's equivocal tone, and seeks to establish the equation on a firmly principled basis.[29] We would be 'treacherous', the statement argues, if

[27] Ibid. 121.      [28] Ibid. 79–80, in Oastler's typography.
[29] [Samuel Taylor Coleridge[, 'Remarks on the objections which have been urged against the principle of Sir Robert Peel's bill' (W. Clowes, London, 1818), from *The Factory Act of 1819, Six Pamphlets 1818–1819*, in *British Labour Struggles*.

we were to ignore the similarity between arguments made against changes in factory legislation and those made against the abolition of the slave trade. The argument had been that slaves were 'happy and contented', a claim now made for the English peasantry. So strong was such prejudice that 'little less than the united power of all the governments of the Christian World was and is requisite to remove it'. Signing themselves 'the Sincere Friends of Industry, to the Mutual advantage of Master and Labourer', the subscribers conclude their statement with an impassioned recognition of the common cause of the slave and the labourer:

The argument founded on the danger of establishing a precedent for other claims is so far realized, that we, in the present instance, are appealing to a precedent instead of making one; and that every argument of any force, which the opponents of the Bill have urged against it, has been declared invalid, as applied to the continuance of any system *admitted* to be cruel and unjust, and solemnly negatived by the British Parliament, in the glorious precedent of the Abolition of the Slave Trade.[30]

Other defenders of Peel's proposals make reference to 'African emancipation' as a glorious precedent, and as an instance of that 'humane feeling, and enlightened self-interest' which should inspire the factory movement. The reference is invoked particularly in the context of objection to those who seek to oppose factory reform on the grounds that any decrease in working hours will damage productivity and therefore jeopardize foreign markets. It is rather the case, argue Peel's defenders, that profits from the sale of British cotton yarn are absolutely guaranteed ('uniform and certain'), so that, even on economic grounds, the objectors have no firm argument. And when it comes to the responsibilities of a Christian government, for 'the rights of humanity and of our common nature', there is no case to argue.

John Walker's *The Factory Lad* shares the intensity of Oastler's concern. The workers speak the language of rights and vengeance, invoking, just as Jack does in the slave play, *Obi*, defence of the absent and abused family as grounds for a justified attack on the oppressor. At the same time, Walker shares some of Oastler's conservatism: accusations made against the younger Westwood are framed in terms of his having deviated from the path of the true Englishman.

---

[30] *British Labour Struggles*, 3–4.

HATFIELD. Squire Westwood? Squire Hardheart! No man, no feeling! Call a man like that a squire! An English gentleman—a true English gentleman—is he who feels for another, who relieves the distressed, and not turns out the honest, hard-working man to beg or starve, because he, forsooth, may keep his hunters and drink his foreign wines.[31]

Earlier in the play, Hatfield had defined a true English gentleman as 'he who had feeling for his fellow creatures'. Walker confers grievance language on factory workers, agricultural workers, and indirectly, trade unionists, as the suffering men draw up their plots in a spirit of machine-breaking and Combination; but in order to cover that panorama of labour and oppression, Walker, like Oastler, cannot quite seem to avoid making invidious comparisons, so intent is he, again like Oastler, on resisting the idea that emigration can be a solution to problems for British working people (and implying that the British government operates double standards in relation to abroad and home). Like Oastler, Walker dramatizes the lot of the poor working man, whose home is an English home, and whose family represents that which he most values and seeks to preserve. The threat of starvation to George Allen's wife and children is, for instance, contrasted with the factory owner's employment of a new French cook complete with valet. The third scene of Act 1 is a moving cameo, in which the young girls of George Allen's family strive to welcome him home by showing him the lace that they have made during the day. Their choice of moment is wrong and the irony is dramatic as George, having just heard from Westwood of his dismissal, tramples the lace under foot. As a loving father, he soon sets out to console his daughters, but the point has been made, that children and outworkers are caught up in the fortunes of the factory, and that the home is very far from being sacrosanct or protected, in the emotional or the material senses.

The drama of the factory as a domain of exploitation reaches its highest pitch in the play when the workers decide to take their revenge by firing the factory, which the audience sees burning in the distance throughout the first scene of Act 2 (Oastler's poor man had also been driven to use incendiary devices). As the factory is highly visible, so is the drama of its demise. The domestic topography of the play, though, is in tension with the rich language of rights used to justify the wielding of

---

[31] The definition of the English gentleman as one 'who feels for another', connects with the discussion of sensibility and the moral actor in Ch. 6.

firepower. Will Rushton prophesies that 'the sky shall be like blood' and that the land will be blasted by lightning, but Jane Allen looks upon the factory in flames as a horror and a dreadful portent of her husband's destiny. In the final scene in a courtroom, the two sets of dramatic discourses play off each other powerfully. Will Rushton, held as the ringleader, refuses to be silenced, scorning the treatment that leads to 'speaking out' being regarded as a criminal offence. He upbraids Justice Bias for his previous occupation as an overseer in a workhouse, arguing that in such a role, the judge should have protected the poor, not abused his office by receiving goods intended for them. His taking of the stand in the courtroom, as in much subsequent drama, operates to seize the political moment as well as the dramatic one:

'Twas I broke into and destroyed the engines of power. 'Twas I set fire to the mass, and reduced to ashes what has reduced others to beggary. Think you I regret—think you I fear? No; I glory in the act. There! I have confessed; and as in me you see the avenger of the poor man's wrongs, on me and me alone heap your vengeance.

However, Westwood, whilst accepting the confession, will not exempt the other factory workers. Jane Allen intervenes to plead for her husband: 'Mercy—mercy! To you I kneel: pity my poor husband, and I will pray for thee, work for thee; my children, all, all, shall be your slaves for ever—ever, but spare him!' But, as Rushton soon recognizes, the resort to invocation of the domestic, together with the explicit analogy with slavery, is not sufficient in securing the poor man's justice, just as his own heroism has failed in that cause. The curtain falls on a set of tableaux, with Rushton firing a gun at Westwood and Jane in the arms of George; the other accused men stand in surprise, as soldiers level their muskets at Rushton. The implication is that industrial relations are intractable, and that there is no redress except violence to persecution by the new style of employer, who is fixated with machinery, cheap commodities, and cheap labour. At times, Walker uses madness and drunkenness as alibis for violence and insurrection; there is a set of references to crazed states of mind at moments of crisis, not only in relation to Will Rushton, but also to George, and Jane Allen. The play's concluding sound is of Rushton laughing hysterically, as the muskets are levelled at him. But the political message remains clear, that the factory creates legitimate grievances, however aggressively expressed, of the men against their masters. The spirit of appeal to the humanity of an audience appreciating the glorious precedent of abolition is there, alongside the warning that fire and insurrection will follow if labour relations at home, in the sense of both hearth and nation, are not given proper consideration.

The twentieth century saw a persisting acclaim for *The Factory Lad*, which was taken as a precedent for the factory play as it developed in the nineteenth century. It is even thought to have anticipated the problem plays of Galsworthy and Shaw.[32] At the same time, there has been a tendency, as with other politically informed plays of the period, to patronize it as a particular kind of melodrama, which relies on 'black and white morality'. However, John Walker's moral scenario in the play is not so black and white. He even allows the sneering factory-owner, Westwood, to draw on a rational discourse as he invites his men to consider that machinery is bound to replace workers one day; it is inevitable. And certainly, Will Rushton, the crazed poacher, is very far from being an uncomplicated, heroic protagonist with whose actions the audience is entirely comfortable. Even Jane Allen, whilst being irreproachable in her virtue as a wife, goes beyond the stereotype. She is given access to a knowing language of oppression, and attempts to intervene in the courtroom to demand mercy and family rights.[33]

This is indeed 'an uncompromising drama of industrial unrest', but it cannot and does not rely on the stock formations of melodrama in order to be so. The play raises questions, which it does not resolve simply, about the use of violence in industrial relations, about the insecurity of England as home, in both its senses, about the judicial system, and above all, about the embattled relations between men and their masters. The tableau which freezes the final scene, *before* George and Jane Allen, man and wife, are separated, *before* the audience is allowed to witness whether or not Rushton has been successful in assassinating Westwood, *before* the rifles take aim, is a powerful dramatic rendition of the failure of English law and government to address the questions posed by Richard Oastler and others.

Both Walker and Oastler dramatize the plight of the poor man, in order to confront their audiences and readers with the atrocities of the factory system. The use of the factory, its torching, its illumination,

---

[32] James L. Smith, introduction to Walker's *The Factory Lad*.

[33] I wonder if this sets the precedent for heroines like Elizabeth Gaskell's Mary Barton to intervene at moments of high drama in the courtroom, on behalf of the men they love?

draws dramatic attention to the politics of the scenario: the symbolic and real power of the master, the desperate measures of resistance of the men. Much of *The Factory Lad* is set in moonlight or in darkness where men discuss dark deeds, but its moment of brightness is the burning factory, viewed from the threatened Allen home. The factory in flames illuminates the stage as it illuminates the English landscape, the changing face of England, in such a way as to pose dramatic questions about the responsibilities of British manufacturers and of the British goverment, both for those changes, and *to* those whom their actions threaten to drive out of their homes and reduce to the worst conditions of slavery.

## Douglas Jerrold's *The Factory Girl*

In his introductory memoir to his father's works, W. Blanchard Jerrold writes of the strong political feelings which informed Douglas Jerrold's writing.[34] The direction which the latter's professional career took is highly indicative for this account. Jerrold's small claim, 'but mine own', is that in the early years of his professional life, writing on a broad range of subjects, he founded a genre of 'domestic drama', especially with his *Black-eye'd Susan*, one of the most popular plays of the period, if to some extent later disowned by him.[35] By 1841, Jerrold had more or less stopped writing for the stage, and was devoting his energies to fiction and to popular, satirical journalism, particularly through *Punch*, which was founded in that year. According to his son, only about half of his dramatic works were republished, and even so, his output was considerable. The son pays tribute to his father's political radicalism, both in journalism and in life. He was 'the friend of the tenant and not of the landlord', and his writings 'abound in bits of most eloquent pleading for the helpless and the oppressed'.[36] The particular character of Jerrold's

---

[34] *The work of Douglas Jerrold, with an introductory memoir by his son W. Blanchard Jerrold* (Bradbury and Evans, London, 1863). It is apt to note a comment by M. H. Spielmann, who wrote about Douglas Jerrold as a colleague on *Punch* magazine, 'With his soft heart melting for the poor, and his fiery hatred of oppression warping his better judgment, he was led into that unreasonable attack upon property and authority to which Thackeray depreciatingly alludes. Because the poor are unhappy, according to his philosophy, therefore are the rich, most of them, their direct oppressors, and ruling bodies, tyrants. It was he, more than anyone else, who forced on Punch that mixture of Radicalism and Whiggery.' http://www.spartacus, schoolnet.co.uk/Jerrold.htm.

[35] Blanchard Jerrold, *The Work of Douglas Jerrold.*           [36] Ibid.

political satire endorses this impression, as does testimony to his popularity with working-class people. His son records occasions on which
Jerrold was cheered by crowds; he was presented with an onyx ring by
Birmingham working men, and praised in the language of the abolition
movement as a man and a brother.[37] Given these political affiliations, it
is significant that Jerrold found it difficult to sustain his activity as a
dramatist. His career as a playwright runs parallel with the period under
scrutiny here and terminates more or less with it. In his satirical letter
in *Punch*, dedicated to the Lord Chamberlain, he gives some idea as to
why he might have made the move from drama to journalism:

> I have flourished under the benignity of your neglect. I pitch my stage where-
> soever I will, in Westminster or not, without your warrant: I act my plays with-
> out your license. I discourse upon the world as it is, on the life that is moving
> about us, and on the invisible emotions of the heart of man, and pay no penny
> to your deputy. I increase in social importance, for I am not withered by your
> patronage.
>
> Had fate made me, for these last two hundred years, the master of a play-
> house, how different might have been my condition![38]

Douglas Jerrold's consciousness of the inhibiting presence of the Lord
Chamberlain, together with the abandoning of his career as a playwright and the republication of only half of his plays, are factors which
have to be taken into consideration in any explanation of the contemporary drama, and the pressures under which it laboured.

Jerrold's *The Factory Girl* , dated 1832 like Walker's play and many of
Oastler's letters, is currently held in manuscipt form in the British
Library.[39] The setting and some of the scenarios of the play are significant, particularly in relation to the influence of Richard Oastler. The
play opens with wild, romantic scenery in Yorkshire, specified by scene
3 as the West Riding. Throughout the first act, the cotton factory is
evoked, through the sound of factory bells and the description of the
destitution of the spinners and weavers. The factory itself is not represented until Act 2, and even here, much of the action takes place up on
the moor. As in the case of John Walker, the primary focus of the visual

---

[37] Ibid.

[38] Ibid., 'Punch's letters to his son, dedicated to the Lord Chamberlain', 403–4.

[39] Ibid. It is difficult to establish how seriously Jerrold took the play as a finished
form. Certainly, there are unamended spelling mistakes in the manuscript and it lacks a
sense of completion, giving too little space and time for dramatic resolution.

message of the play lies in the contrast between 'rustic, picturesque' scenery, and the dark blot of the factory. The play carries strong reminiscences of Oastler's story of the poor man, which could well have been current beyond the actual narrative of Oastler himself. The male protagonist is Skelton, father of the factory girl, Catherine. As the play progresses, but not until nearly the end of Act 1, the audience learn the reasons why there is no longer any work for Skelton at the factory. He has assaulted Master Husk, who has a rather indeterminate role in the play, but is probably the overseer.[40] It is not until the final scene of the play, though, that the occasion for this act of violence is explained, in terms of Skelton's righteous indignation at Husk's aggression towards an orphan girl in the factory. Even before the audience knew Skelton's motive, Jerrold had appeared to sanction Skelton's action, through other characters who discuss the possibility of assassinating Husk. The timing of Skelton's revelation of his motive reinforces the audience's sense of his having had legitimate cause.

In the interim, between Skelton's exclusion from the factory and his revelation of the reasons behind it, his daughter Catherine has herself been subjected to unjust as well as sexually suggestive treatment by Master Husk. Again, this carries reminders of what happens in Oastler's story of the poor man, where the beloved daughter dies, victim of factory labour and ill treatment. On this occasion, though, Catherine survives to be united, in a classic trope of melodrama, with a wealthy cousin of whom she had had no previous knowledge. This is Jans Hartman, significantly experienced in travel in Holland and America, and visiting Yorkshire to inspect the new innovation of the cotton factory. The stereotypical denouement of the potential marriage into wealth, though, does not entirely distract from the distinctiveness with which Jerrold represents Catherine. The unusual aspect of the character is that she is literate, and a lover of books. Whilst this leads the factory masters to mistrust her, the emphasis on education and literacy for working people is entirely endorsed by Jerrold. The very last item that Skelton pawns in his poverty is the remaining book of the household. Interestingly, Jerrold does not specify that the text is scriptural, rather having Skelton say that the book is 'the only thing within the poor man's house

---

[40] The play carries some impressive imagery in relation to 'overseeing'. The moon is described as 'the illustrious overseer of this world's rogues and vagabonds—like many overseers too—caring as much for oysters as for men'.

upon which hunger did not dare to lay its fingers'. In other words, the book's value does not only reside in its content. Ideas about the civilizing values of reading are further developed around a character of rather odd name, Wynkyn de Worde, a book trader, who describes himself as 'a humble illuminator of the people'. There are suggestions of the comic clown about him, but he is clearly a touchstone for better values. Not only does he keep to his promise of retaining Skelton's last book in pawn, but he also gives, in an act of kindness, a present of *Beauty and the Beast* and *Jack the Giantkiller* to Skelton's two small sons, who can also read.

In some ways, this central concern of the play with the rights of the workers to literacy and ownership of reading matter, and by extension, to education, carries more force than the representations of factory conditions themselves. Although Jerrold firmly condones retaliatory violence in the play, running parallel with John Walker in *The Factory Lad*, he appears somewhat uncomfortable with the dramatic representation of it. It is not accidental that acts of violence are reported action, happening offstage. As in *The Factory Lad*, there are suggestions of firing the factory, and Skelton is accused of this in the final scene, only to be vindicated against any such charge, but dramatic force comes rather from Jerrold's aesthetic concerns on behalf of Catherine and her father, their appreciation of the beauties of the Yorkshire scenery, and their love of gardening (yes! particularly planting tulips) and books.[41] Skelton is something of a precursor of the autodidact, the working man with a passion for nature, later developed in the context of fiction by Victorian novelists, particularly Charles Kingsley and Thomas Hardy.[42] The other way, besides the Yorkshire context, in which Jerrold's play is reminiscent of Oastler is in relation to a defence of children; here he is perhaps open to charges of sentimentality, but can be defended on the grounds that, like Oastler, he makes the case against child labour. As well as the reported incident in which Husk has beaten an orphan child for falling asleep at her task, the play opens with an image of a child suffering sickness, the pretext for Skelton's soliloquy on the preciousness of family. In the final scene, Skelton's little sons are found sleeping in the factory, babes in the wood transferred to the industrial setting. It is

---

[41] The offsetting of the factory with English Romanticism and its aesthetic concerns is an idea to which I shall return in Ch. 4.

[42] Charles Kingsley, *Alton Locke* (1850) and Thomas Hardy, *Jude the Obscure* (1895).

their presence in the factory which vindicates Skelton against the charge, from even the most cynical adversary, of having been involved in setting fire to it.

*The Factory Girl* is a play in which neither character, nor plot, are fully formed. There is too much suggestion of contrivance, and too little dramatic coherence. Nevertheless, Jerrold's concerns in the play match significantly with those of John Walker and Richard Oastler, in their attempt to dramatize both the ugliness and injustice of the Yorkshire cotton factory, and, symbolically, the factory system in general. Henry Whiteley, a member of the Leeds Committee on the Factory System, left England to see if he could find work in Jamaica.[43] His work with the Leeds Committee and his experience of Yorkshire factories had convinced him that the working and living conditions of the negro slave in the West Indies must be preferable to those of English factory children. He records that, after a very short time, 'the enchanting scenery and beautiful humming birds no longer amused me'.[44] The account which follows documents the most barbaric and harrowing conditions imaginable. Whiteley is subsequently persecuted in the West Indies for his Methodism and his hostility to slavery, and returns to England with a changed mind. He concludes that whilst the position of the factory child is 'very bad', that of the plantation slave is 'INFINITELY WORSE' (his emphasis). However, the shock to his previous judgement occasioned by direct observation and personal suffering does not lead him to abandon the cause of the factory child, but serves to reinforce his conviction that the factory and emancipation movements should work together on behalf of each other: 'I shall most cordially rejoice to see the friends of Negro Emancipation co-operating with the friends of Factory Regulation, in carrying the Ten Hours' Bill speedily through Parliament.'[45]

Both Oastler and Whiteley had seen the analogies between factory workers and slaves, and had, in different degrees, been forced to see necessary distinctions. There were grievous problems to be solved abroad, but also at home. Playwrights, despite the constraints under which they were working in relation to the Lord Chamberlain and from elsewhere, seem nevertheless to have been determined that they would add their energies to that endeavour, by dramatizing, however inadequately, the scene of the oppressive factory as well as that of the slave trade.

---

[43] Whiteley, *Three months in Jamaica in 1832.*
[44] Ibid. 3.                    [45] Ibid. 22.

CHAPTER FOUR

# Distressed Tenants and Rural Landscapes

It has already become apparent, from studying some aspects of the factory movement and its drama, that there is more at work in the representation of the plight of industrial workers than an exclusive concern with the factory itself. Part of what Richard Oastler and others who campaigned against the factory system and against enforced emigration were defending, as well as the rights of labourers and their children, was the English rural landscape and its charms.[1] In John Walker's *The Factory Lad*, and in particular, in Douglas Jerrold's *The Factory Girl*, rural landscape figures strongly, as we have seen. There are two central considerations which emerge here in relation to agricultural life and work; one relates to agricultural labour itself, the other to aesthetic concerns with the rural landscape.

Between 1790 and 1830, the largest group of workers in any sector were those participating in agricultural labour.[2] Twenty-eight per cent of all families in Britain constituted these workers.[3] By the 1790s, rural labourers had begun to feel the force of their loss of common land, after enclosure. William Cobbett comments, significantly for this account, that labourers had become *slaves* under the emergence of the gentleman farmer.[4] Successive governments were not oblivious to, nor entirely unconcerned about, the dilemma. In 1796, William Pitt had registered his opposition to a minimum wage for agricultural workers, but the introduction of the controversial Speenhamland system appears to have

---

[1] Oastler, *Eight letters to the Duke of Wellington*. On p. 16 of his introduction, Oastler renders an account of the beauties of Yorkshire.
[2] Thompson, *The Making of the English Working Class*, ch. 7, 'The Field Labourers', 233 ff.
[3] Ibid. 233 n..
[4] Thompson, ibid., cites Cobbett on p. 256.

marked some attempt, at least, to protect farmworkers as wage-earners, and prevent them from being dependent on gentlemen farmers and effectively the property of the latter.[5] Another move which reinforced analogies with slavery was the introduction of gang labour into the fields, initiated in Castle Acre in Norfolk in 1826; for a modern reader this is reminiscent of descriptions of chain gangs in North America and elsewhere.[6] Workers were particularly destitute in the south-west of England, where employers did not have to compete with industry to the extent that they did in the north, and an outstanding feature, not alleviated by the introduction of the Speenhamland system, and reinforced by gang labour, was the exploitation of women and children. Evidence gathered at a later date can give some indication of developments which had taken place over the period.[7] Alfred Austin, one of the commissioners of a report published in the 1840s, was delegated to report on the southern counties of Wiltshire, Dorset, Devon, and Somerset, which were taken to be some of the most beleaguered in the country. One of the impressive aspects of Austin's account is that he invites and publishes the testimonies of women workers themselves, including servants and field labourers. The testimony of Mary Puddicombe is one example:

I worked more in the fields than in the house. When my master died, I went as servant at Blackston for two years. I was treated very bad there: the people beat their servants. I used to be beat black and blue. The servants beat me; my master used to bang me. I never was much hurt. I never complained to a magistrate. I told my father and mother, and they told me to be a better maiden next

---

⁵ Although there remains a discussion about how far the introduction of a family wage, through the Speenhamland system, was discriminatory against women and children. There is controversy, too, amongst historians, as to whether or not the new system led to increased poverty. G. E. Fussell, *Landscape Painting and the Agricultural Revolution* (The Pinder Press, London, 1984), whilst acknowledging the extensive documentation of the economic conditions of the period, beyond the scope of that account or indeed this one, assumes that it did—'the workers had already been pauperised by the Speenhamland system' (46).

⁶ Jennifer M. Frances and Karen Sayer, 'The Forgotten Labourers, Women in the Fields in the Nineteenth and Twentieth Centuries: The UK Experience', paper presented to the fifth annual conference on rural and farm women in historical perspective. The paper documents the introduction of gang labour, its consequences and implications, very thoroughly and persuasively. Also, see W. Hasbach, *History of the English Agricultural Labourer* (1908), for the East Anglian labour-gangs, cited by Thompson, *The Making of the English Working Class.*

⁷ *Parliamentary Reports of Special Assistant Poor Law Commissioners on the Employment of Women and Children in Agriculture* (Hansard, London, 1843).

time. Apprentices were treated worse; two, without fathers to look after them, were beat with a stick for anything that happened. One maiden had her arm cut to the bone with a stick the young master cut out of the hedge at the time, for not harrowing right, for not leaving enough for harrow to go back again. That went to a justice: master was fined 5 pounds, and had to pay the doctor's bill.[8]

Alongside the scene of injustice and abuse, there emerges a powerful aesthetic movement, English Romanticism, associated in particular with William Wordsworth, but influential well beyond his work. Some of the commissioners appear to find irresistible the conceptualizing of their study, of the conditions in which women and children are working, in terms of the Wordsworthian encounter with nature. They support the perceptions, elicited from farmers, village vicars, and the local gentry, that agricultural workers' experience of the 'congenial scene', is primarily one of 'free and bracing influences of air, light, beauty, and occupation, which must re-act favourably on the mind'.[9] Not all the testimonials given by women agricultural workers are at odds with this version of agricultural work, although their language does not betray any sense of the fields as a 'scene', nor its influences on the mind. Many of them comment, as they have clearly been asked to do, on their children and on the difficulties of reconciling fieldwork with childcare, but more than one testifies to the relative acceptability of agricultural labour. Mrs Britton comments: 'I never felt that my health was hurt by the work. Hay-making is hard work, very fatiguing, but it never hurt me. Working in the fields is not such hard work as working in the factory. I am always better when I can get out to work in the fields.'[10] Jane Long also comments, 'I was always better when working out in the fields than when I was staying at home.'[11] The poet John Clare refers to fieldwork as a relatively liberal sphere of activity, in his case compared with gardening, where constraints from employers are more direct, and personal freedom of activity more confined.[12] It is worth noting, though, that the image of the noble rustic emerged in the north rather than the south of England. Perhaps this was not accidental, given the evidence of particularly grim conditions in the south-west. In

[8] Ibid. 109.        [9] Ibid. 146.        [10] Ibid. 66–7.
[11] Ibid. 70.
[12] *John Clare's Autobiographical writings,* ed. Eric Robinson with wood engravings by John Lawrence (Oxford University Press, Oxford and New York, 1983); 'Sketches in the life of John Clare', 1–28.

his *Lyrical Ballads*, and the manifesto statement in the preface, Wordsworth popularized the notion of the moral superiority of the untutored mind communing with nature.[13] His choice of subject-matter for the ballads is that of 'low and rustic life', because:

In that situation the essential passions of the heart find a better soil in which they can attain their maturity, are less under restraint, and speak a plainer and more emphatic language; because in that situation our elementary feelings exist in a state of greater simplicity and consequently may be more accurately contemplated and more forcibly communicated; because the manners of rural life germinate from those elementary feelings; and from the necessary character of rural occupations are more easily comprehended; and are more durable; and lastly, because in that situation the passions of men are incorporated with the beautiful and permanent forms of nature.[14]

In *The Prelude*, Wordsworth was to go on to document this set of commitments in terms of his own life experience.[15] In Books 3 and 6, in which Cambridge University features, he offers the reader an opposing figure to the ethical rustic in whom resides the superior sensibility—the tutored mind, educated at Cambridge. The relationship with Cambridge, where the student Wordsworth is confined to his 'unlovely cell', remains an unreal one compared to the poet's relationship to nature. He writes not only of his own preferences, but of the 'delusion of young scholars', who deal in 'languages that want the living voice'.[16] In establishing this radical trope, in which ethical constitution derives from proximity to land and nature, rather than scholarship, Wordsworth continues until the present day to be credited for his 'levelling language', for transcending 'the barriers of class', and for his 'honourable link' with Revolutionary France.[17]

In taking up the rustic as his *cause célèbre*, Wordsworth dignifies the

---

[13] William Wordsworth, *Preface to the Lyrical Ballads* (1800 and 1802, Methuen, London, 1963).                                                                    [14] Ibid. 244–5.

[15] William Wordsworth (text of 1805), *The Prelude, or Growth of a Poet's Mind* (Oxford University Press, London, 1970).

[16] Wordsworth, *The Prelude*, Book 6, lines 105–14.

[17] Michael Foot (Sunday 9 July 1989), 'The Nearly Revolution' in *Observer Review* (Guardian Media Group, London): 'The English people . . . could look to a true revolutionary tradition; they had learnt to start to speak to one another across the barriers of class in the language of Milton and Marvell, of Bunyan and Swift. Everyone, even his critics on the Left, acknowledged the "levelling" tendency of Wordsworth's language. And here was a genuine and most honourable link between the best in his English inheritance and the exhilaration he drew from events in France.'

lot of the agricultural worker at the very moment when the latter was, arguably, experiencing the worst vicissitudes in English history, not least the events leading to the Captain Swing riots of the 1830s.[18] It is important, then, to explore what some of the drama of the period does with this interesting but uneasy juxtaposition, in which agricultural workers participate in popular agitation, but also symbolize the more durable passions and morals. On the one hand, labourers' revolts were met with 'the same sense of outrage as a rising of the "blacks" '.[19] On the other, and perhaps under the influence of the Wordsworthian aesthetic, the middle class supported rural workers after their revolt of 1830, and the claim is that such support contributed to agitation for reform in 1831 and 1832. William Cobbett comments: 'The middle class, who always, heretofore, were arrayed, generally speaking, against the working class, are now with them in heart and mind . . . Among the tradesmen, even of the metropolis, ninety-nine out of a hundred are on the side of the labourers.'[20]

## J. B. Buckstone's *Luke the Labourer*

J. B. Buckstone's *Luke the Labourer*, first performed at the Adelphi in 1826, figures the eponymous Luke as its protagonist.[21] Like Jerrold's *The Factory Girl*, the play is set in Yorkshire, in this case in a village, from which there is a distant view of the city of York. Luke is described as a big, hefty man, and he speaks a blunt, Yorkshire dialect. As with Will Rushton in Walker's *The Factory Lad*, the audience learns of a past which has reduced Luke to destitution. In the language of melodrama, he describes his wife's deathbed scene, as she invokes the absent farmer who employs Luke, appealing to him, via her husband, to alleviate their suffering. However, the resemblance between Will Rushton and Luke ends with the shared experience of a cruel past. Luke has few of Rushton's redeeming characteristics, and is remorseless in his pursuit of revenge on his old employer, Farmer Wakefield. Even as the play

---

[18] See Frances and Sayer, 'The Forgotten Labourers', for more on the subject of Captain Swing. Thompson, *The Making of the English Working Class*, also documents riots, the torching of corn-ricks, and attacks on threshing machines.

[19] Thompson, ibid., citing *Wellington Despatches*.

[20] William Cobbett (4 Dec. 1830), *Political Register*, cited in Thompson, ibid., 253.

[21] J. B. Buckstone, *Luke the Labourer, A domestic melodrama* (Cumberland, London, 1826).

opens, the audience learns that Luke's pursuit of vengeance has turned the tables by reducing Wakefield to poverty and imprisonment for debt. In its adoption of the revenge motive, *Luke the Labourer* has more in common with *Obi; Or, Three-Fingered Jack* than with *The Factory Lad*.[22] Luke shares with the negro protagonist, Jack, a clear motive for vengeance, deriving from a personal history which has been characterized in terms of victimization and abuse heaped on a member of an oppressed class; but in each case, the dramatic action progressively leads the audience to lose sight of justifying causes. Luke turns to ever more villainous courses of action, not least plotting with the Squire to abduct the heroine of the piece, Farmer Wakefield's virtuous daughter, Clara.

Another idea which the play shares with the factory drama, in addition to and as a function of the rural setting, is that of the possibility of escape from country to town, from agricultural hardship to perceived urban pleasure. This is also conceived in terms of moving south from the north of England, and as in Jerrold's *The Factory Girl*, specifically from Yorkshire to London. Bobby Trot, something of a clown or bumpkin, makes several attempts, on each occasion thwarted, to escape to London, or as Buckstone has him call it, Lunnon. There are a number of wry comments about how Bobby would not survive the vices or temptations of the great wen, if he were ever to get there. His knowing lover, Jenny, is a reliable witness here, and tempts him to stay in Yorkshire, with the promise of the culinary delight of cold pudding. Unlike Jerrold, Buckstone treats comically the idea of mobility as a possible solution to the problems of Yorkshire labourers. This distinguishes his attitude clearly from that of Jerrold. Indeed, neither of the central representatives of agricultural labour, Luke and Bobby, invite much congenial treatment from Buckstone *vis-à-vis* the plight of the labouring man. Even allowing for the ironizing propensities of comedy, and the melodramatic qualities of the revenge motive, audience sympathies are unlikely to flow their way. From the beginning, the playwright's emotional investments are in Clara Wakefield and her father, and thereby in the more middle-class members of the farming community. Buckstone retains his commitment here, but even this is to some extent displaced or overtaken as the play progresses, and the audience begins to see that the play's

    [22] W. H. Murrey, *Obi; Or, Three-Fingered Jack*.

theatrical energy is at its most sharply realized in another direction, that of Philip, the sailor, who does not make his appearance until the last scene of the first act.

Whilst the character of Philip is that of the stereotypical Jolly Jack Tar of the period, his language, or lingo as he prefers to call it, is a theatrical *tour de force* on Buckstone's part.[23] The playwright clearly has an ear for naval metaphor and Philip's speeches are replete with it; and it is quite beguiling, if somewhat irritating in its ubiquity. Beyond this, though, Philip, the son of Farmer Wakefield, sold to the gipsies by Luke when he was a boy to the devastation of his parents (his adult existence unknown to them and his sister Clara), is a character who functions with an obvious set of plot devices in mind. His return to the Yorkshire village ultimately brings wealth as well as happiness to his beleaguered family, after the requisite set of concealments of identity and tearful asides to the audience. His first appearance on the scene is appropriately heroic, as he rescues Clara (brother and sister are unknown to each other at this moment, of course) from imminent abduction by the lustful and predatory Squire, who, inviting Luke into the conspiracy, wishes to force himself on Clara and abscond with her to London. In the dark wood, with a storm raging, the navy enters to rescue the aforesaid damsel in distress, by exercising the art of combat and dealing a number of blows to the heads of Luke and the Squire. From this point onwards, Philip takes over the stage.

At one level, the play is much more successful as a piece of theatre than, say, Jerrold's *The Factory Girl*. Buckstone creates musical effects quite beyond the requirements of the Lord Chamberlain, to enhance melodramatic entry and exit.[24] Scene 2 of Act 1 opens with musical accompaniments to the entry of each character, reinforcing their mood

[23] J. S. Bratton, *Acts of Supremacy, The British Empire and the Stage, 1790–1930* (Manchester University Press, Manchester, 1991), particularly ch. 1 for the subject of Jack Tar and the nautical melodrama. It is interesting to note, too, that theatre audiences of this period were constituted in no small measure from those who had lived through and served in the Napoleonic Wars, which ended in 1815. No doubt, Philip as the hero of the piece would have appealed to them, and to others who might wish to remember or to celebrate British nationalism.

[24] Theatre managers had to include at least five songs into the three-act structure. Many theatres attempted to escape the patent system by submitting a manuscript to the Lord Chamberlain with five songs present for the sake of official sanction and then either dropping some of the material or changing the words to incude material previously censored. See Joseph Donohue, 'The Burletta and the Early Nineteenth-Century Theatre', in his *Theatre in the Age of Kean* (Basil Blackwell, Oxford, 1975).

and persona. Dame Wakefield has a soliloquy on the subject of her husband's imprisonment. The music changes. Clara enters in a mood of anxiety mixed with troubled pleasure, having been delicately smuggled some money by her benefactor and aspiring lover, Charles. The music changes. Farmer Wakefield enters in a state of elation, released from prison with the help of Charles's money. The music changes. Luke is heard knocking at the Wakefield cottage door, and again the music changes. Philip endorses the use of music on Buckstone's behalf, by eulogizing the art of song, and there are solos, duets, choruses, even some rather interesting lyrics, and of course, loud claps of thunder. Formally, the play is interesting, drawing on this wide range of devices to enhance characterization and mood. However, in the process of pursuing these effects, the play loses sight of what even the most inadequately realized of Jerrold's dramatic conceptions retain, a sense of the plight of the agricultural worker and its configurations. Buckstone invests energy in the Wakefield farming family, and very briefly in anathematizing the landed gentry through the villainous Squire, but his dramatist's heart is in the navy, and for what Philip can yield in terms of theatricality *per se*. The village scene and agricultural hardship recede, as the heroic and irrepressible sailor, the lost son regained, defender of duped daughters, vanquisher of villains, gathers in momentum, steals the role of protagonist from Luke, and takes command of the play.

However, some of its contemporary critical commentary reclaims the play for the socio-political context.[25] Buckstone has shown his audience, indeed 'posterity', that we should not trifle with 'the poor man's only hope and dependance—his character'. Luke's depiction of his state of destitution and the death of his wife is described as 'truly heart-rending'. The commentator seizes the occasion, in a reading which is certainly in keeping with textual detail, to inveigh against the evils of alcohol, and the reduction of Luke, under its influence, to a social burden and 'pest', but the crucial message is that he has been *driven* to these circumstances. This particular commentary offers two further observations of significance to this account. One is that Buckstone has captured the spirit of the age in depicting 'scenes of every-day life', which approximate to the circumstances of the audience. Entering into the debate about reforming the drama, and drawing on some of the sentiments which, as we shall see later, characterize Edward Bulwer-

---

[25] Buckstone, *Luke the Labourer*, 'Remarks', on pp. 5 and 6.

Lytton's approach in *England and the English*,[26] the commentator writes: 'The truest sympathy is excited by characters and events that come under the general observation of mankind. The public have no relish for magnificent woe—they are little moved by crowned and sceptered personages vaunting their triumphs, or bewailing their sorrows, in blank verse.'

The other strategy adopted by the commentator is to invoke the Romantic poets, both for their ability to represent the plight of the common man, and for the lyricism with which they depict the rustic scene. The eponymous hero of P. B. Shelley's *Peter Bell* is held to be an exemplar of the honest, ordinary man, as against the conquerors and tyrants whom the drama might have celebrated in earlier years. Crabbe's poetry is given as an example of plain narrative combined powerfully with 'poetic fervour'. Significantly, the commentary compliments Buckstone for having met the challenge of bringing social and dramatic tension to the pastoral scene. Some poets, the argument goes, have been too inclined to represent the countryside exclusively in terms of 'the last precious remnants of the golden age'. Reference to the poets, and to the debate amongst poets about the role of the pastoral, pays testimony to the extent of their influence, and gives some indication of the extent to which dramatists are also engaging with the aesthetics of Romanticism, an issue which is of more obvious significance in another play set conspicuously in the rural context, Douglas Jerrold's *The Rent Day*, a much more fully developed script than his *The Factory Girl*.[27]

## Cottage Sensibilities in Thomas Morton and Douglas Jerrold

Before turning our attention to Jerrold's *The Rent Day*, which neatly inverts some of the tropes of Buckstone's *Luke the Labourer*, it is worth spending some time on one of the very popular plays of a slightly earlier date, Thomas Morton's *Speed the Plough*.[28] The play is a gentle satire on the fashions and the pretensions of the aristocracy *vis-à-vis* the rural community. Sir Abel has allowed himself to be lured into matrimony

[26] Edward Bulwer-Lytton, *England and the English*, ed. by Standish Meacham (1833; University of Chicago Press, Chicago and London, 1970). For more on Bulwer's observations, see Ch. 6.

[27] Jerrold, *The Rent Day*.

[28] Thomas Morton, *Speed the Plough: a comedy, in five acts*, first performed at the Theatre Royal, Covent Garden (Longman, London, 1800).

with Nelly, taking her to be 'a simple rustic, unsophisticated by fashionable follies, a full blown blossom of nature'. Instead, he finds her, once married, overbearing, talkative, and likely to succumb to any financial or sartorial temptation.[29] Sir Abel also has scientific aspirations for the rural scene. He has invented the curricle plough, which he is trying to patent. It meets its demise in the ploughing competition, where, despite its relatively competent driver, it veers off in the direction of the northern counties, from Hampshire where the play's action is set. However, Morton's comment on the landed interests of the gentry, whilst set in the supposedly beleaguered context of the south-west of England, is for the purposes of theatrical delectation and benign comedy rather than being a serious exposé of any kind. Where aristocratic figures are not buffoons, they are prey to gothic horrors and histories, as in the case of Sir Philip, who believes, until all is revealed, that he has murdered his own brother, and cannot bear to enter the room in his not insubstantial castle where the weapon of violence still resides. The play's values are inclined to favour the landed gentry, and the romantic hero, Henry, is of their stock.

Morton's heart, though, is with Farmer and Dame Ashfield, and the latter's imaginary rival, the infamous Mrs Grundy. In terms of status, the Ashfields bear some relation to the Wakefield family in *Luke the Labourer*. Both farmers carry the playwrights' sympathies, and both families are central to the values espoused by the two plays, ennobling rural cottage life, and upholding cottagers as virtuous, if slightly corruptible in the case of the women (Nelly, who had been a servant with the Ashfields, and Dame Ashfield, who competes gently with Mrs Grundy for social and sartorial status). The difference, perhaps deriving from Morton's comedy as distinct from Buckstone's melodrama, is that the Ashfields speak in dialect, in a not too obliquely parodic version of the Hampshire rural accent. Whilst the use of dialect does not always lend the farmers dignity when compared with smooth-tongued aristocrats,

---

[29] Thomas Morton is all too inclined to represent women as unable to control or guard their tongues. Indeed, this is something of an obsession of his. Another vivid example is Templeton's wife in *Education, A comedy in five acts*, as performed at the Theatre Royal, Covent Garden (Longman, London, 1813). Like Nelly, Dame Templeton is held to be 'a loyal subject' to 'the monarchy of fashion'. Interestingly enough, though, she has had what Templeton, and perhaps Morton, takes to be 'a perverted modern education', in which 'the unassuming domestic virtues' have been 'jostled into a corner'. Hmm!

neither does it make for a simple caricature of rural life or farming itself. It is more a form of sentimentalism, justified in the play's comic scheme. Rather like Trudge in George Colman the Younger's *Inkle and Yarico*, Farmer Ashfield is the play's most virtuous conception, born of a slight condescension, perhaps inescapable, on the playwright's part.

*Speed the Plough* is a stylistic lucky bag, unashamedly combining chambers of horror with comedy, romance, and exorbitant spectacle (like that of the ploughing competition, which appears to take place on stage). It delighted audiences, no doubt with its energy, its variety, and its obvious theatricality. It is a sort of staged game. It makes no serious pretension to socio-political comment, nor even to a realistic representation of rural life, but it does register mildly that the aristocracy are being displaced from the drama's centre of value, and that, in one kind of play, the farming community, answerable for their rent and their living to the Squire, are taking their place. With a different kind of rural drama in mind, A. E. Green argues that the mummers' play is a nineteenth-century invention and that it is 'the expression of an agrarian proletariat, not a peasantry'.[30] Green's case is that the mummers' play emerged out of the need, in a period of dramatic change in agrarian and industrial relations ('social upheaval and demographic change'), to re-create a sense of belonging and community. *Speed the Plough* is no mummers' play, but the analysis is pertinent to Morton's vibrant and humanitarian attempt, in the first year of the new century, to invite an audience into the farming household, where friendship, community, and family loyalty are clearly prioritized over any efforts by privileged gentry to intimidate or demoralize their tenants.[31]

Out of the three plays by Buckstone, Morton, and Douglas Jerrold, it is the last which carries the force of the argument on behalf of rural workers, although both *Luke the Labourer* and *Speed the Plough* are probably each, in their different ways, plays where performance possibilities are more easily imagined. The first and most obvious contrast to be made between Jerrold's *The Rent Day* and Buckstone's *Luke the Labourer* is over the way in which each of them represents the nautical element. In *The Rent Day*, the navy, represented in Jack, wears a much more dubious

---

[30] A. E. Green, 'Popular Drama and the Mummers' Play' in David Bradby, Louis James, and Bernard Sharratt (eds.), *Performance and Politics in Popular Drama* (Cambridge University Press, Cambridge, 1980).

[31] At least, I think this favourable analysis, under pressure from Morton's misogynistic tendencies, just about holds.

aspect than in *Luke the Labourer*. Jack's first appearance on the scene leads the audience to believe that he is cast in the heroic mould, but as time passes, it becomes clear that Jerrold is not being quite so generous with the navy.[32] The audience is invited to condemn the character when he succumbs to the temptation to pursue Rachel Heywood sexually, against her will. (Rachel, though, is distinctly pre-Victorian in her feisty response. She defends herself against Jack with a woodcutter's bill.)

More important than Douglas Jerrold's dramatic investment in the navy (although Jack does project some of the vitality of Philip in *Luke the Labourer*) is the clear investment in the cottage farmers, Rachel and her husband, Martin. The family is recognizable in Wordsworthian terms, its members being morally and aesthetically educated and civilized by their proximity to the rural landscape. Their status in socioeconomic terms is quite interestingly ambivalent, somewhere between that of Buckstone's agricultural labourer, Luke, and his farming family, the Wakefields. Jerrold appears to take some pains to avoid class stereotypes, and to highlight a common dilemma for labourers and cottagers.[33] As William Cobbett had argued, the gentleman farmer, in the worst circumstances, had made slaves of his tenants, not only of his casual workforce. Tenancy could form one of the worst versions of dependency. However, it would be a mistake to interpret the Heywoods too closely in terms of a naturalistic representation of the experiences of cottagers. Rather, the characters are conceived poetically, out of images taken from contemporary Romanticism.

---

[32] Douglas Jerrold joined the navy at the age of 10, 'but he was deeply upset by the way the officers treated the men on board ship. Jerrold was particularly horrified by the way officers flogged the men for minor offences and this gave him a life-long hatred of authority . . . After a couple of years in the navy, Douglas Jerrold left to become a printer's apprentice' http://www.spartacus.schoolnet.co.uk/Jerrold.htm (p. 1).

[33] John Barrell, *The Dark Side of the Landscape: The Rural Poor in English Painting 1730–1840* (Cambridge University Press, Cambridge, 1980), argues, 'If we can be sure of anything about the eighteenth century, it is that English society at the time was minutely stratified and subdivided, and there is no level at which a line can be drawn around the social pyramid, marking off, the "rich" from the "poor" or the consumers of Britain's wealth from its producers' (2). It is possible, I think, to see the drama both recognizing and operating quite confidently across these minute stratifications, in a capacity to give a broad sweep to the argument against injustice and for reform. I suppose it is only fair to say, though, that on the whole labourers are handled less favourably than cottagers and farmers, implying the superior social status of the latter groups. It is not as simple, though, as conferring dialect, say, on one group rather than another. For example, Morton gives Farmer Ashfield dialect, but Jerrold's cottagers speak in something resembling standard English.

The play also invokes the spectre of emigration, drawing both on knowledge of and fears about the horrors of distant slave regimes which informed, as we have seen, the abolition movement, and on the comparative attachment to the relative pleasures of England, as in the writing of Richard Oastler and in the factory play. John Walker, in *The Factory Lad*, had also inveighed against emigration. Jerrold is not so interested as Oastler is in extolling the virtues of England or Yorkshire, but has the same investment in defending the rights of the free-born Englishman and woman to stay in their cottage, their home. The implicit message is that home is about more honourable and deeper feelings than those occasioned by property ownership.[34] It is about history, roots, and community, together with what Wordsworth had identified as the more enduring and permanent feelings. For these reasons, the audience knows that when Martin Heywood, victim of failing harvests, poverty, and a neglectful landlord, raises the issue of emigration with his wife, he does so in bad faith, and only out of the worst vicissitude.

MARTIN. What, say you, shall we cross the sea?
RACHEL. What! leave the farm?
MARTIN. I am offered a place on an estate, far away in the Indies. What say you?
RACHEL. Leave this place? . . . Would you quit our home?
MARTIN. Our home! where is it?—the work-house!

The Wakefield family had also articulated their fear of the workhouse. Two scenes later, Martin reveals, in a soliloquy, that even posing the question to his wife had been to act against all his deeper feelings. The cottage home, occupied by his father and his grandfather before him, is as 'a living thing' to him. (Indeed, in a very transparent device at the end of the play, Martin makes the accidental discovery in the cottage of Grandfather Heywood's gold, bequeathed to his grandsons.)

As well as ennobling the cottage farmer and his lot, the play mounts a systematic criticism of the absentee landlord. Toby, a character of slightly indeterminate rank, is a touchstone for reliable values, and is the mouthpiece for these criticisms. The Squire, on this occasion, is away from home, 'feeding the gaming-table'. If he must do so, declares Toby, it should not be 'with money wrung, like blood, from the wretched'.

[34] Green's argument (n. 30) is pertinent here.

Whilst 'he shuffles his cards', he should 'remember the aching hearts of his distressed tenants'. The idea of solving rural problems by a move to London is there again, but on this occasion, the project does not involve escapism or fantasy. Toby decides to go to the metropolis in order to look up the Squire and tell him that, 'if landlords are too proud or too idle to look after the comforts of their tenants, and to live upon their own lands, why 'tis a great pity that Providence should have entrusted them with any'. As with the Heywoods, Jerrold does not claim to represent Toby naturalistically. His is the character of the Romantic polemicist, a Peter Bell, an orator, a spokesman for the playwright's judgements, speaking with the voice of political radicalism and even reform, challenging landlords, and by implication, other property owners, to take their responsibilities seriously.

Other characters derive from a more comic and satirical mould, particularly in relation to Jerrold's attacks on mercantile and other financial exploitation, which is reminiscent in some ways of George Colman the Younger's *Inkle and Yarico*. The force of the satire is carried by a character with the not too subtle name of Bullfrog. He describes himself as a prudent capitalist, but the trustworthy Toby has a different opinion of Bullfrog, whose occupation consists of taking possession of cottages where occupants are failing to pay the rent. Like Colman, the playwright brings the critique of trading directly to bear on slavery, in this case via the equation with the impoverished tenant, neglected by the Squire. Toby proposes, sardonically, to Bullfrog that instead of smashing up tea-cups and wooden bowls in the homes of English cottagers, he should:

TOBY.  . . . go to the colonies and sell the blacks.
BULLFROG.  Are blacks mortals?
TOBY.  Virtue is especially marketable in the West Indies. There, it's worth while being a constant husband and a doating parent; for one sells for a few dollars extra. Go to Jamaica by all means.

## Painting Rural Scenery

The play's commitment to the pastoral scene operates in the visual dimension, as well as through the poetic and polemical tropes of Romanticism. It is dedicated to the painter, David Wilkie, and specific references to the two paintings, *The Rent Day* and *Distraining for Rent* foreground and support the action (see Plates 11 and 12). Act 1 of the play is framed by the two paintings, opening with reference to *The Rent Day*, as well as taking its title from that painting, and closing with a direction to the players to arrange themselves as a tableau, in imitation of *Distraining for Rent*.[35] A contemporary commentator provides a detailed note on both paintings, offering insight into past attitudes to Wilkie's work.[36] On the subject of the earlier one, *The Rent Day*, the commentary sets the scene in:

> The comfortable steward's room, in the mansion of his noble master, where preparations have been made to receive the rents of his humble tenantry . . . the tenants all appear of the humble class . . . a pathetic, almost painful, feeling pervades this group. [37]

The passage goes on to describe a 'sweet widow' with her children, 'a group pleasingly painful as we anticipate in idea the distresses that too probably await those who have hitherto been living in the lap of affectionate security'. It appears that it might have been in relation to his conception of the Heywood family that the painting caught Jerrold's attention. The later painting, *Distraining for Rent*, takes the action inside the home of the cottager, and is described in the following terms:

> Perhaps we may be justified in thinking that distress, rather than want of thrift or economy, has produced the catastrophe; that the poor man before us, sunk in listless moody misery, upon whom falls the desolation of wife and bairns, is the victim of unavailing struggle with misfortune . . . The half-rifled bed—the open cupboards—the air of disorder and discomfort cast over the whole, inspire a feeling of desolation, speak of the loss of home, and of the darkening prospects of the ruined family.[38]

The moment when the painting is invoked in Jerrold's play is the highly melodramatic one at which Martin Heywood is most fearful about the imminent loss of his cottage, and announces his passionate love for the family home. The freezing and friezing of the action in the form of a tableau operates in interestingly tense relationship to the impassioned vitality of the dialogue, inspired with what Wordsworth describes as 'the

---

[35] Alan Cunningham, *The Life of Sir David Wilkie* (John Murray, London, 1843) records that *The Rent Day* was painted in 1807 and *Distraining for Rent* in 1815. Wilkie exhibited his paintings at the Royal Academy, from the late 1820s onwards.

[36] In *The Wilkie Gallery: A Selection of the Best Pictures of the Late Sir David Wilkie* (George Virtue, London and New York, undated).

[37] Ibid. 20.
[38] Ibid. 77, 78.

living voice', eloquent, in this instance, with the cottager's defence of his home. The moment, together with Douglas Jerrold's signalling of his interest in Wilkie in relation to the framing of the play as a whole, gives rise to speculation about how coherently the drama has managed to draw in aesthetics, painting as well as poetry, to the more active forms of stage dialogue and movement, and to what purpose.

Douglas Jerrold's direct reference to painting can be examined both in relation to the growth of popular painting, and in the context of a developing interest in the representation of the rural poor.[39] It was no accident that a particular kind of English tradition of painting, as distinct from European classical art, emerged from the Drury Lane area in the early part of the eighteenth century. By the second half of the century, there was a growing public for this art, particularly for genre scenes of everyday life.[40] Hogarth, an 'unapologetic advocate of English art', had friends amongst the scenery painters at Drury Lane and other theatres, and it is possible to suppose that artists like Zoffany and Loutherbourg, who worked primarily in theatre, were able to perform a bridging operation between the academic painter and the commercial artisan.[41]

The drive to represent the rural poor had emerged, energetically, out of the 1790s, which had displayed a 'remarkable' interest in rural-subject painting.[42] The development of a new kind of rural subject in art can

[39] Barrell, *The Dark Side of the Landscape*. David Wilkie is a Scottish painter and therefore does not conform to Barrell's titular description of English painting.

[40] Brewer, *The Pleasures of the Imagination*, ch. 5, 'The Market and the Academy'.

[41] Ibid. It is possible that Brewer somewhat underestimates the importance of the movement as a whole, in giving almost exclusive attention to the one advocate, Hogarth, whose influence, Brewer argues, was ultimately rather constrained by rash temperament. Despite the attractions of Brewer's account of Hogarth, this dismissal seems a little disappointing.

[42] Barrell, *The Dark Side of the Landscape*, introduction. For further reading about British landscape art at this time, see Charlotte Klonk, *Science and the Perception of Nature: British Landscape Art in the Late Eighteenth and Early Nineteenth Centuries* (Yale University Press, New Haven and London, 1996); Klonk comments in her first chapter, 'Aesthetics, Philosophy and Physiology: The Road to Phenomenalism' that 'The development of sympathy is the necessary means by which humanity moves from a coercive to a cooperative political order' (18–20, in relation to the culture of sensibility in Scottish painting). This connects with the commentary on sensibility in Ch. 6 (and in relation to Burke, Paine, and Wollstonecraft in Ch. 1). In her conclusion, Klonk comments that 'the heyday' of panoramic art was over by the 1830s (150). Also, Ann Bermingham, *Landscape and Ideology: The English Rustic Tradition, 1740–1860* (Thames and Hudson, London, 1987); Andrew Hemingway and William Vaughan, (eds.), *Art in Bourgeois Society, 1790–1850* (Cambridge University Press, Cambridge, 1998).

be explained in part in terms of the type of argument that Richard Oastler makes in his letters to the Duke of Wellington, that the landed interest and the labouring interest are both 'in distress', with the advent of the factory system, and that gentry and labourers need to work together in a recognition of the mutuality and interdependence of their interests.[43] Whether the Duke of Wellington, or other members of the aristocracy, were convinced by this particular argument or not, they would be likely to share Oastler's commitment to representing a relationship between their estates and the labourers in their hire that had a capacity to produce an image, at least, of harmony and contentment. The primary market and audience for this painting would be members of the aristocracy, perhaps enthusiastic to reassure each other that such a spirit was possible, and that their golden estates could withstand the imminent blot of the factory. This might explain the apparently paradoxical element of the paintings, which do not always overtly register the distress of which Oastler writes.[44] The agricultural labourers are often derived not from the painter's observation of agricultural work itself, but from Romantic conceptions of the noble rustic and the pastoral scene. The apparel of figures in the paintings is frequently drawn not from life, but from art. The workers do not labour, they pose, even whilst holding a scythe or loading a hay-cart.[45]

Through more popular forms, such as engraving and indeed, theatrical scenery, such paintings had begun to reach a public beyond the connoisseur and the aristocratic viewer. The subjects of the paintings, like the developing public for their viewing, were beginning to operate, like the drama, across the classes. Also like the drama, this style of painting gives a particular emphasis to peopling the landscape, and to using costume in which to do so, and apparently unconstrained by the later, Victorian debates about realism. Painting thereby aestheticizes the agricultural worker, sharing the project of theatre, in an attempt to give status and dignity to the rural subject. However, the drama can avoid

---

[43] Richard Oastler, first letter to the Duke of Wellington in 1832.

[44] See Barrell, *The Dark Side of the Landscape*, for a reading of the complex messages carried by the paintings: 'For the most part the art of rural life offers us the image of a stable, unified, almost egalitarian society; so that my concern in this book is to suggest that it is possible to look beneath the surface of the painting, and to discover there evidence of the very conflict it seems to deny' (5).

[45] There is also a gender discussion to be had here. The women, as in the drama, are often clothed in particularly elegant and elaborate costume.

the passivity and incongruity of the static image of painting by giving voice to the subject—in other words, by introducing dialogue and transforming the subject into the actor. The labourer and the farmer, however aestheticized in the static, visual image, are brought to speak on the stage. However far the playwright constrains them and dictates the terms, characters have agency where the subjects of painting do not. Even where they are clothed in costumes taken from pastoral painting, stage cottagers can speak, can articulate the condition of the oppressed. Even where dramatists fail to show the exploitative conditions in which they work, labourers as characters can *act* with a sense of wrong and just grievance. *The Rent Day* utilizes these forms, and there is evidence to suggest that other plays of the period used this reciprocity of genres, the visual image exploiting painting's capacity to aestheticize the subject, alongside the notion of agency, the actor able to articulate the agrarian cause.[46] To at least one recent commentator, though, Jerrold's choice of Wilkie's paintings is something of a puzzle. John Barrell comments on David Wilkie's *Village Politicians*:

The customers at Wilkie's alehouse are grotesquely and condescendingly portrayed, but in what we are clearly invited to recognize as the 'realistic' manner of Teniers or Ostade, so that the painting was much admired for the truth of its representation. We have learned to be wary of approval on those terms—what was it, we must ask, that its admirers wished to believe was true about the rural poor, and that is apparently confirmed by this image? In this case, the answer is clear; for Wilkie's picture seems immensely eager to reassure us that whatever interest the poor may take in politics, it can be a naive and ignorant interest only, and that these 'politicians' are too stupid to initiate any action which their opinions however radical might prompt them to...[47]

However persuasive the interpretation is of this particular painting, it must not be conflated with an account of David Wilkie's work as a whole. Nor can it explain his attraction to a playwright of such radical persuasion as Douglas Jerrold. Another commentator sees beyond this particular picture to Wilkie's other work, highlighting his capacity for arousing audience sympathies for cottagers and their distress (precisely that word which Barrell had said was not in evidence), ubiquitous in his

---

[46] There are connections here with my concluding argument about the status of the moral actor in the period.

[47] Barrell, *The Dark Side of the Landscape*, 114–15.

portrayals and particularly reinforced in the working relationship with Jerrold.[48] Martin Meisel describes Wilkie as an innovating domestic realist, the idea of the *tableau vivant* being mutually influential between the drama and the painter.[49] As the commentator on the two paintings chosen by Jerrold testifies, this is particularly the case in relation to *Distraining for Rent*, which was chosen for exhibition in the British Institution with telling consequences: 'The great excellence of this picture had, at first, induced the Directors of the Institution to buy it as soon as it was seen at Somerset House. But they were afterwards frightened at what they had done, on its being suggested that the subject was a satire on landlords.'[50] C. R. Leslie's autobiographical writing, from which this passage is taken, also records the effect of viewing the painting on Washington Irving: 'I was present at the time, and I remember that he stood for some minutes before it without saying a word; and when he turned round tears were streaming down his cheeks.'[51]

At a later stage, Queen Victoria was to find *The Rent Day* affecting.[52] Perhaps Jerrold had become acquainted with the paintings themselves through exhibitions, particularly those held at the Royal Academy in 1829 and 1831, just before he wrote the play. Or perhaps he, like many other people, was familiar with the etchings of Raimbach, who had popularized *Distraining for Rent* with his engraving of the painting.[53] However he came to them, Douglas Jerrold's *The Rent Day* uses David Wilkie's paintings to draw together the age's most significant aesthetic conceptions of rural life into the political, polemical context of the aggrieved cottager and labourer. Wilkie shared Jerrold's commitment to a popular aesthetic, believing that audiences for his art should transcend class, not be confined to the private, aristocratic viewer as owner. Theatre could lend its aid to creating this broader audience for painting, a move which is beginning to occur, as 'an effect of liberty'.[54]

---

[48] Martin Meisel, *Realizations: Narrative, Pictorial, and Theatrical Arts in Nineteenth-Century England* (Princeton University Press, Princeton, 1983).

[49] Ibid.

[50] William Boyne, *Sir David Wilkie* (Walter Scott Publishing, London and New York, 1903), 71, cites C. R. Leslie, in *Autobiographical Recollections*.

[51] William Boyne, ibid.

[52] William Boyne, ibid., records how the Queen became engrossed by the painting when she saw it exhibited in Dublin in 1853.

[53] Mrs Charles Heaton, *The great works of Sir David Wilkie* (Bell, London and Cambridge, 1868). Her preface records that Wilkie's pictures were 'as familiar to us as household words', because of prints produced by engravers.

[54] John Barrell, *The Political Theory of Painting from Reynolds to Hazlitt* (Yale

Wilkie's paintings are an important dimension, but they are only one dimension of Jerrold's dramatic techniques in *The Rent Day*. A discussion of the play can be situated in the broader context of the politics of domestic drama, 'with its serious treatment of suffering and joy in humble circumstances, and its habitual location of the sources of undeserved suffering in the local agents and unworthy possessors of property and power'.[55] Whether or not the play works in performance, given its wide range of styles and devices, is another question. Would, for instance, the arrangement of tableaux endorse and enhance the action, or merely slacken the pace? Would the relationship of melodrama to pastoral tableau intensify feeling, or result in a theatrical contradiction in terms? How could the Wordsworthian sentiments of endurance and permanence be reconciled to the drama's emphasis on exploitation and discontent? What the answers are, audiences of 1832 might have known; but it is possible that all these apparent contradictions would have been reconciled with ease, and that spectators would have revelled in the range of effects, finding them nicely ambitious, in Jerrold's style, and actually quite appropriate to the complex cause of agricultural workers, whose lot and whose struggle could not simply be summarized in terms of the difficulty of their labour. The opportunity which Jerrold had seized from Wilkie was that of popularizing art and aesthetically dignifying the action of the domestic drama, presenting a combination forged out of humanitarianism, on behalf of the rural worker and the agrarian cause.

University Press, New Haven and London, 1986). In his introduction, Barrell conducts a lengthy discussion about the rise of painting, which was, 'invariably understood as, pre-eminently, the effect of liberty: not just the political liberty of a state which is not subject to the dominion of another, and not just that kind of personal freedom which is enjoyed by all who are not slaves; but the freedom, political and personal, which is enjoyed by free citizens who are able to participate in the government of themselves' (33).

55 Meisel, *Realizations*, ch. 8.

# CHAPTER FIVE

# *Women Players and the Protection Racket*

Earlier chapters have made reference to women's central involvement in the political agitation of the period. As has already been mentioned, women, together with black activists, were in many ways the prime movers in the abolition movement, carrying over arguments about slave ownership and slave labour into other domains, and in particular creating a set of analogies between slavery and the condition of women in marriage and the household.[1] In the aftermath of the French Revolution, there was an intense foregrounding of feminist activism across all the central freedom movements of the period as they found expression in Britain. Documentation has begun to be quite extensive in relation to Mary Wollstonecraft as an important *individual*, and is accumulating more gradually in terms of the *movement* itself.[2]

---

[1] See Midgley, *Women Against Slavery*, for evidence supplementary to my earlier chapters and much fascinating material generally about women's involvement in the anti-slavery campaigns; 'Women participated in the anti-slavery campaign in Britain from its earliest stages. Enslaved women brought to Britain from the sixteenth century onwards joined in black resistance to slavery through running away from their owners; white women became involved in campaigning against the slave trade from the 1780s onwards through supporting local and national abolition societies, abstaining from slave-grown produce, and writing anti-slavery verse' (9). Louis Billington and Rosamund Billington, ' "A Burning Zeal for Righteousness" : Women in the British Anti-Slavery Movement, 1820–1860', in Rendall (ed.), *Equal or Different*, comment on how mid-19th-c. feminism claimed abolition in terms of its 'precedents'.

[2] *The Works of Mary Wollstonecraft*, ed. Janet Todd and Marilyn Butler (William Pickering, London, 1989) provides a very useful service here. Also, Clarissa Campbell Orr (ed.), *Wollstonecraft's Daughters* (Manchester University Press, Manchester, 1996) with particular reference to Pam Hirsch, 'Mary Wollstonecraft: A Problematic Legacy'. See Barbara Taylor, *Eve and the New Jerusalem: Socialism and Feminism in the Nineteenth Century* (Virago, London, 1983) for the early 19th-c. and the legacy from the late 18th. Similarly, see Ruth and Edmund Frow (eds.), *Political Women 1800–1850* (Pluto, London, 1989).

At the same time, women's activity both in and outside the home remained heavily circumscribed by particular notions of male patronage and protection. The French Revolution had given rise to significant debates in Britain not only about how far royalist ideologies of patriarchy were sustainable, but also about male responsibilities for women in general.[3] Burke had argued that 'the protective patriarchal order' was essential to the well-being of women and that the Revolution had unleashed forces which would enable men to abnegate responsibility for women.[4] The supposed post-Revolutionary liberation of women was, in his view, no more than 'a ruse that reduces the female to an object of male sexual will-to-power'.[5] Burke's argument is not readily dismissed as sexist, as he identifies a significant dilemma for women in any male-dominated and male-orientated revolutionary or reforming movement. However, his position does rather rely on the acceptance that the old patriarchal order was a reality rather than mythological in its supposed protection of women. Mary Wollstonecraft, along with women playwrights of this period, challenged the mythology of patriarchal protection significantly, demystifying Burkean ideas about the sublime and the beautiful for their problematic gender assumptions.[6] Although it is more difficult to trace a women's movement as such than the other political movements in late Georgian Britain, women's individual and collective critique of the established patriarchal order was both crucial to the reform movement and an intriguingly explicit form of theatre.

The unfinished autobiography of Mary Darby Robinson, performer and writer, provides a graphic account of one instance of both royalist ideology and the supposedly protective patriarchal order.[7] Commentary

[3] See Blakemore, *Burke and the Fall of Language*, ch. 3 for more on the subject of Burke and Patriarchy.

[4] Ibid. For more on the subject of Burke and gender, see Linda Zerilli, *Signifying Woman: Culture and Chaos in Rousseau, Burke, and Mill* (Cornell University Press, Ithaca, NY and London, 1994) and Tom Furniss, *Edmund Burke's Aesthetic Ideology: Language, Gender, and Political Economy in Revolution* (Cambridge University Press, Cambridge, 1993).

[5] Blakemore, *Burke and the Fall of Language*.

[6] See Blakemore, ibid., for an interesting account which is not simplistically critical of Burke.

[7] *Memoirs of the late Mrs Robinson* written by herself, from the edition edited by her daughter (Hunt and Clarke, London, 1826). Introductory comment includes, 'Autobiography of this class is sometimes dangerous; not so that of Mrs Robinson, who conceals not the thorns inherent in the paths along which vice externally scatters roses.' For a recent edition, *Perdita: The Memoirs of Mary Robinson*, ed. M. J. Levy (Peter Owen,

1. Frontispiece from Moncrieff's *Reform*. J. Bull: 'The sycophants!—the blood-suckers!—but I'll have a thorough reform. (British Library)

2. *The Riot*, p.31 of Louis James (ed.), *Print and the People, 1819–1851* (Penguin, Harmondsworth, 1976). (Cambridge University Library)

3. *The Reformers' Attack on the Old Rotten Tree*, from *Print and the People*. (Cambridge University Library)

4. *Political Showman*, p. 245 of *Print and the People*, which uses the format of a playbill to publicize (and satirize!) political debates. (Cambridge University Library)

5. Frontispiece from George Colman the Younger's *John Bull*. (Cambridge University Library)

6. Géricault, *La traite des nègres*. (Ecole Nationale Superieure des Beaux-Arts)

7. *Am I not a man and a brother?*
The logo of the abolition movement.
(Wisbech and Fenland Museum)

8. Frontispiece from Murrey's *Obi; Or, Three-Fingered Jack*. (British Library)

9. *A Factory Victim*, p. 115 of *Print and the People*. (Cambridge University Library)

10. P. J. de Loutherboug's *Coalbrookdale by Night*, 1801. (Science Museum)

11. David Wilkie, *The Rent Day*. (Cambridge University Library)

12. David Wilkie, *Distraining for Rent*. (Cambridge University Library)

13. *Florizel* and *Perdita*, from the 1894 edition of Mary Robinson's *Memoirs*. (Cambridge University Library)

14. *Am I not a woman and a sister?*, from Robin Blackburn, *The Overthrow of Colonial Slavery* (Verso, London, 1988). (Cambridge University Library)

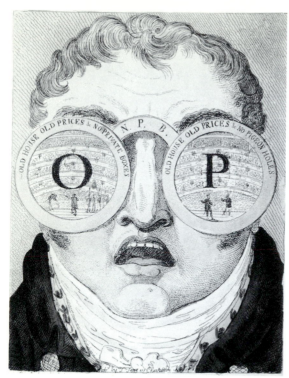

15. *The OP Spectacles.*
(Theatre Museum, Victoria
and Albert Museum)

16. *The NP Spectacles.*
(Theatre Museum, Victoria
and Albert Museum)

on the subject of Mary Robinson has tended to focus on her fame as a stage performer, but she was also involved in writing for the theatre. It is on her significance as a writer for the stage that I intend to focus.[8] She recounts that, at the age of 15, whilst completing her education at a school in Marylebone where the dancing master was also a ballet instructor at Covent Garden, she entertained ambitions to write dramatic verses and a tragedy. Robinson was recommended, first to Mr Hull at Covent Garden, and later to David Garrick, as 'possessing an extraordinary genius for dramatic exhibitions'.[9] In her memoir, Mary Robinson is careful to prepare the ground for considering the stage as a profession. The context is one of family vicissitude, where a beloved mother has been all but abandoned by her husband, who is a merchant, seemingly rather reckless in his pursuit of colonial adventures and of illicit love.[10] If it were not for financial debt and lack of an independent income, the mother would not have even considered a stage career for her daughter (one of the strategies of the father was to object to his wife's attempts to earn money by teaching). As it is, she does so under her husband's threat, before another of his volatile departures for America, that she should 'take care that no dishonour falls upon my daughter'. He promises his wife that, 'If she is not safe at my return I will annihilate you!'[11]

When Mary Robinson does take to the stage, it is very much as a beautiful performer, with little further mention of her aspirations to write.[12] Initially, she is the child protégée of David Garrick, billed to

London and Chester Springs, 1994); Levy describes Robinson as one of London's leading literary radicals in the late 1790s; also, 'she was a feminist, a hater of the government of William Pitt, a firm believer in the idea of progress and an opponent of what would eventually turn out to be a long and arduous war with France. Among her friends were the anarchist William Godwin and Mary Wollstonecraft, the author of the notorious *Vindication of the Rights of Woman*' (p. vii).

[8] I therefore use the term 'player' in the sense of contributor as well as performer.

[9] *Memoirs*, 25.

[10] Ibid. 14–17, Mary Robinson describes how her mother discovers that her husband has taken a mistress on his expedition to establish a whale fishery off the coast of Labrador. The Indian population rebels against the colonizer's attempt to exploit their labour, and commercial losses follow.

[11] *Memoirs*, 26.

[12] See Carlson, *In the Theatre of Romanticism*, ch. 4, 'Romantic Antitheatricalism: Surveilling the Beauties of the Stage' for more on the implications for women in theatre of 'the new prominence of beauty as a social and political category' (136). Carlson also very interestingly cites William Hazlitt's *Liber Amoris* for what it demonstrates about 'the violence that underlies romantic aesthetics' (147). Whilst critical attention to the ideo-

play Cordelia to his Lear, and later she is under the supervision of Richard Sheridan, of whom she is deeply in awe. From the moment she appears in public, she is treated as a sexual and aesthetic object presented for pursuit, besieged by admirers, including her husband to be, who turns out to be feckless and adulterous from the beginning of their marriage. Initially, her husband insists that she retire from the stage, and so she never performs her Cordelia to Garrick's Lear. It is only when Mr Robinson finds himself in debt that he agrees that his wife should return to her stage career. Ironically, it is during one of these periods of debt, in sharing imprisonment with her husband, that she finds time to turn her attention to writing verse.

Later in her professional career, she is drawn into just as disastrous a relationship with the lovelorn Prince of Wales, who has admired her from the boxes, and has cajoled a third party into bearing messages of love between the two of them. It is in her role as Perdita in *The Winter's Tale*, in a performance commanded by their majesties, that she first attracts the Prince's 'fixed attention', followed by a note from him signed in the name of Florizel. Mary Robinson comments drily that her reader will know enough Shakespeare to be aware of what Perdita means to Florizel (see Plate 13). Her autobiography founders at the moment when the Prince terminates the liaison, giving her no information as to why he has chosen to do so. It is as if the autobiographer is literally unable to recall more of these painful memories. In the meantime, Mary Robinson has retired from the stage at the Prince's request, as well as having chosen to separate from her husband, on the Prince's behalf. The Robinson memoir is taken up by 'a friend', who documents subsequent events in Mary Robinson's life story, commenting that Britain is a place where 'an unprotected woman rarely fails to become the victim of calumny and persecution'.[13]

---

logical construction of the woman performer has been urgently necessary, the more recent move of exploring the contribution of women playwrights to late Georgian theatre has perhaps been still more pressing; refer particularly to Donkin, *Getting into the Act*; Catherine B. Burroughs, *Closet Stages: Joanna Baillie and the Theater Theory of British Romantic Women Writers* (University of Pennsylvania, Philadelphia, 1997). Caroline Franklin gives welcome attention to Mary Robinson as writer in a new edition of *The Poetical Works* (Routledge, London, 1996). My point is that the pressures were on women to be performers rather than producers, but that the former gave some access to the latter.

[13] *Memoirs*, 123. Levy, *Perdita*, records that 'although the Memoirs are traditionally ascribed solely to Mary Robinson, only the first part is fully autobiographical; the second

Mary Robinson is very much preoccupied with the concept of *protection* in her account, constantly invoking the term, nearly always in relation to the gender politics of the period, which dictate that a woman should not act without visible male protection.[14] Mary Wollstonecraft is another who constantly voices complaint and complexity on this issue. In the absence of women's rights, he who offers genuine protection, as is the case of Darnford, the virtuous hero of her novel, *The Wrongs of Woman*, is undertaking the best possible course of action for a woman, especially where this means friendship as well as taking financial responsibility.[15] However, in circumstances where a woman eschews unwelcome support from a man or has protection withdrawn, she can quickly be condemned.

The situation of a woman separated from her husband, is undoubtedly very different from that of a man who has left his wife. He, with lordly dignity, has shaken off a clog; and the allowing her food and raiment, is thought sufficient to secure his reputation from taint. And, should she have been inconsiderate, he will be celebrated for his generosity and forbearance. Such is the respect paid to the master-key of property! A woman, on the contrary, resigning what is termed her natural *protector* (though he never was so, but in name) is despised and shunned, for asserting the independence of mind distinctive of a rational being, and spurning at slavery.[16]

In other words, protection is set against that independence which is difficult to attain while property laws and social practices connive in women's dependence. Similarly, for Mary Robinson, the male protector often proves illusory, whilst in the very process of being perceived as a necessity. She is only permitted to further her career in writing and performing at moments when the men in her life acknowledge that *they* benefit from her doing so.[17] *They* need, if not her protection, her financial support. The male protector is a polite fiction, designed to promote the illusion of male respectability and chivalry, and to justify existing property relations by appearing to ameliorate, in a vocabulary of care

part, comprising roughly a third of the text, was mostly contributed by a "friend", who may or may not have been Maria Elizabeth Robinson, the original editor and Mrs Robinson's only surviving daughter' (p. ix).

[14] Or, perhaps, as we shall see, *act* is all they can do.

[15] Mary Wollstonecraft, *The Wrongs of Woman: Or, Maria* (1798), ed. Gary Kelly (Oxford University Press, Oxford, 1976), 188, 'As her husband she now received him, and he solemnly pledged himself as her protector—and eternal friend.'

[16] Wollstonecraft, *The Wrongs of Woman*, 157–8. My emphasis.

[17] See Pascoe, *Romantic Theatricality*, for commentary on some of the writings of Mary Robinson. Also, Franklin, *Mary Robinson*.

and friendship, the stark fact of the husband's ownership of the wife. The reality, of course, is the continuation of female subordination and dependence, together with absence of independent rights for women. As Ellen Donkin demonstrates in her book about women playwrights, the theatrical relationships of the period are characterized by these arrangements, which carry over from the household to the professional sphere.[18] Two of the most influential theatre managers of the previous generation, David Garrick at Drury Lane (who had officially retired by the time Mary Robinson came into contact with him) and George Colman the Elder, mentored by Garrick and later manager of the Haymarket Theatre, were instrumental, at one level, in encouraging some women playwrights, and giving them protection.[19] However, as Ellen Donkin shows, their support was double-edged, relying as it did on the promotion of their own personae, together with their investments in the commercial interests of theatre.

The focus of this account is on the era after Garrick's death,[20] when the notion of the female coterie surrounding the charismatic male manager had to some extent dissolved, and women playwrights were confronted with the realities of what the absence of male protection could mean (as well as the ambivalence of what it *had* meant). As Ellen Donkin stylishly puts it, 'The power to confer legitimacy is predicated on the power to take it away.'[21] It is the case that the late eighteenth century, which saw an increase in print production generally, and more women than previously entering the sphere of literary activity, also saw a limited number of women emerging as theatre managers and playwrights.[22] However, although there is also plenty of pictorial and written

---

[18]  Donkin, *Getting into the Act.*

[19]  Donkin, ibid., documents how Garrick's relationship to women playwrights was often constructed in either paternalistic or seductive terms. Ch. 2, about Frances Brooke, reveals tellingly that he experienced very real problems with any woman who regarded herself as his peer or his critic. Donkin also makes reference to a matter to which I shall turn—that both George Colman the Elder and his playwright son wrote plays satirizing women playwrights.

[20]  David Garrick, 1717–79, stopped managing Drury Lane in 1776.

[21]  Donkin, *Getting into the Act*, 'Afterpiece', 184–91.

[22]  Donkin, ibid., makes crucial reading in her retrieval of women dramatists. Also pioneering is J. S. Bratton's work on the theatre manager, Jane Scott; refer to her paper read to the conference, 'Women, Writing and the Public Sphere 1680–1830', held at Cambridge University, July 1996; also, her paper 'The Adelphi, 1807–1832, a Study in Institutionalised Opposition', given at the conference, 'Theatre and Politics in the Age of Reform', held at Homerton College, Cambridge, April 1997.

evidence to suggest that women made up a sizeable proportion of theatre audiences in the period, as well as being a spectacle in themselves both as performers and within the audience,[23] there is still a strong sense in which the writing and production of the play itself is gendered male, and any intervention from prospective women playwrights takes the form of muffled opposition.[24]

There are analogies to be made between painting and theatre, and between viewer and audience. John Barrell argues that, although the popularizing of painting in this period was in keeping with the enlarging spirit of democracy in Britain, women's supposed attachment to 'personal ideas' put the sphere of 'the higher, the public genre of art' out of their reach and relegated them to the more lowly domain of portrait painting, not only as artists, where they were able to be such, but also as critical viewers.[25] Mary Wollstonecraft, inveighing against a set of assumptions whereby the entirety of women's relationship to the public sphere is held to be characterized in terms of their having a lower status than men, lends credibility to Barrell's analysis. He cites Wollstonecraft for her despairing thought that women are held to be incapable of drawing 'comprehensive conclusions from individual observations'.[26] Art can be compared with theatre, in that both attach significance to women as subjects to be viewed, exhibited as spectacle. The woman performer attracts reverence and financial rewards in the period, but, as the response to Mary Robinson on stage shows, this appreciation is of a dubious character.[27] The idolizing of the performer, Sarah Siddons, to the point of Siddonsmania is even more graphic.[28] A cynic might see

[23] Davis, *Actresses as Working Women,* documents women as spectacle in audience as well as on stage in the later period.

[24] Donkin, *Getting into the Act,* cites Fredric Jameson, *The Political Unconscious* for 'muffled oppositional voices', and applies it to women playwrights, 'But there was opposition being staged, not so much in the plays, as I read them, but submerged in the day-to-day details of their production and pre-production experiences . . . the formulations of feminism which were to follow in the late nineteenth century were not yet sufficiently established to lend any conscious structure to their experiences' (28).

[25] Barrell, *The Political Theory of Painting,* 66.

[26] Ibid.

[27] Thanks to Helen Nicholson, Homerton College, Cambridge, though, for the information that it was open to women performers to subvert their parts—not so easy in the case of a subject of a portrait painting (though not impossible?)!

[28] As well as the influence of Siddons on the representation of Marie Antoinette, referred to earlier, and the wide range of literature about her stage appearances, there is now some quite explicit information about her role in the political as well as theatrical sphere. Pascoe, *Romantic Theatricality,* devotes her first chapter to 'Sarah Siddons and the

the relationship as an inverse one, in that the more highly the woman is *viewed* as spectacle, the less she is credited with the ability to be a critical *viewer*.

This is stating it too baldly, though, because the distinguishing feature of theatre is that the viewer is more than an individual—the audience is a collective entity and to some extent an unpredictable and ungovernable one. However far high art can determine a lesser status for the woman viewer, individualizing her in her gender category, theatre cannot necessarily determine the role of the women members of its audiences. In theatre, 'individual observation' cannot easily be separated from 'the comprehensive conclusion'. The audience can and do bring down the play with their condemnation, and the theatre can, in this way, give a kind of licence to its women members. Response cannot easily be silenced, and eighteenth-century theatre was a noisy and riotous place. Reaction from men, whilst they on the whole have louder voices, cannot be clearly distinguished from the reaction of women in an audience.

Some theatre men were clearly rattled, not only by women playwrights, but also by the behaviour of women in the audience, and perhaps by their very presence. Contemporary commentators, together with those writing subsequently, have tended to imply hostile judgements about women in the audience, not reserving their censure, with its famous double standards, for prostitutes, who were known to use the theatre to attract and consort with clients. The theatre historian, Allardyce Nicoll, as well as citing George Colman the Younger for his objections to 'disturbances' in the audience among 'blackguards and women of the town', reproduces uncritically William Hazlitt's complaints about 'elderly gentlewomen' in the audience talking too loudly.[29] The implication is a fear that neither women's behaviour as part of an audience, nor their influence on the reception of a play, can come entirely under male influence.

Performative Female'. Amanda Foreman, *Georgiana, Duchess of Devonshire* (HarperCollins, London, 1998) writes of Mary Robinson and Sarah Siddons being invited by Georgiana to perform on behalf of the Whig cause. Georgiana's own participation in the 1784 Westminster election had been noted for its theatricality and for challenging sex/class assumptions by ignoring the conventional proprieties about women's behaviour.

[29] Allardyce Nicoll, *A History of English Drama, 1660–1900* (Cambridge University Press, Cambridge, 1952), iv. 8–9.

In this period of political vitality, with feminism emerging as a shaping force, theatre audiences were receptive to the work of women playwrights. Prologues and epilogues appealed to members of the audience to support plays, a process of address inescapably gendered, it seems, in the case of women playwrights. Elizabeth Inchbald's *To marry, or not to marry*, an interpretation of which I shall turn to later in this chapter, serves as one instance where a significant transition occurs, in the course of one play, from a prologue addressed primarily to the men in an audience, to an epilogue spoken by a woman, addressed primarily to women.[30] The subject-matter of the play, for reasons which this account will explore later, has allowed this shift in perspective and change of address to occur. The prologue prioritizes the critic, by definition male at that time, and asks for kindness to the female author. The epilogue, whilst proceeding to admit that the speaker has temporarily forgotten the play, prioritizes the woman observer and the feminist issues raised in the play, commenting on the fickle characteristics of man. It is significant, in this context, that neither George Colman the Elder's *The Separate Maintenance*, nor George Colman the Younger's *The Female Dramatist*, both of which lampooned women playwrights, were popular with audiences. With the latter, hissing was the order of the night. Indeed, it could well have been audiences' refusal to sanction too much hostile stereotyping of women playwrights which had prompted theatre managers, with *their* view to the market, to realize that there were possible audiences for works by women writers. Certainly, a tension existed between audiences with their taste for women playwrights, and those men—playwrights, managers, critics—who were uneasy about that interest, particularly in circumstances where audience judgement went counter to their own, or where women playwrights threatened to elude their control.

Thomas Morton, referred to in previous chapters, introduces in more than one of his plays the trope of the woman who needs to be silenced. In his comedy, *Education*, the idea is there again, in the form of Templeton's complaints about his wife, who has had 'a perverted modern education', which has jostled 'the unassuming domestic virtues . . . into a corner'.[31] The anxiety experienced by the man playwright,

[30] Mrs Inchbald, *To marry, or not to marry*, a comedy in five acts, as performed in the Theatre Royal, Covent Garden (Longman, London, 1805).

[31] Thomas Morton, *Education*, a comedy in five acts, as performed at the Theatre Royal, Covent Garden (Longman, London, 1813).

anticipating that women's access to new educational opportunities will lend her 'the weapons of satire', as has happened in the case of Mrs Templeton, is all too evident, and is perhaps akin to that felt by managers, such as Garrick and Colman the Elder, at moments when women playwrights threatened to assert too much autonomy for them and too little dependence on them.[32] This is primarily an intellectual and political question, rather than an economic one. As we have seen, there is evidence, although even that can be overestimated, of women performers earning not insubstantial amounts of money from the stage. The more important issue is that the woman playwright who could be seen to operate independently, without visible male protection, was challenging the orthodoxy of the period's gender politics, demonstrating not only how such independent initiative was possible, but also that it might be preferable to male patronage, and indeed incompatible with the latter. Ellen Donkin focuses the matter very sharply when she writes of Frances Burney's attempts to make her mark on the drama as a playwright.

As I sift through the materials of this book, I come back again and again to Frances Burney's letter to her father, to the way it names certain patterns of obedience and defeat. I no longer find it surprising that Burney was forty-seven years old when she finally called him to account for his deadly masquerade of protection: it takes a long time to make the transition from attendant daughter to self-authorized woman. For me, Burney's letter marks that quiet, incandescent moment in which the woman writer becomes steel, and she finally understands that she can write to or even about this father without writing *for* him. (her emphasis) [33]

## Becoming Steel—the Plays

In 1787, six years after her separation from the Prince of Wales, and after a long visit to France, where she had retreated after his rejection of her,

[32] I have written elsewhere, in Pauline Polkey (ed.), *Women's Lives into Print* (Macmillan, London, 1999) about how Mary Somerville, who comments favourably on the work of the playwrights, Miss Mitford and Miss Baillie, had criticized attitudes to the education of women in the late 18th and early 19th c., when her own schooling took place. Her daughter Martha comments on how those attitudes had changed, even between her mother's generation and her own. Somerville, *Personal Recollections.*

[33] Donkin, *Getting into the Act*, 'Afterpiece'. (Frances Burney is more well known as Fanny Burney, author of the novel *Evelina*.) Perhaps it was such an incandescent moment which gave rise to Burney's play, *The Woman-Hater*, written in 1800. *The Complete Plays of Frances Burney*, ed. Peter Sabor (William Pickering, London, 1995).

Mary Darby Robinson returned to Britain to pursue what her biographer describes as 'her literary career'. She had never found writing easy, describing it as 'a destroying labour', but she continued to write in the later phase of her life, even against the advice of a physician, who argued, in the typical manner of the period, that her delicate physique and ill health would not withstand the exercise of intellectual faculties. Her autobiography records some of the writing from this period, including a little farce[34] written by her and treated to an interestingly controversial reaction from its audience, but what it does not record is that she did succeed in writing that full-length tragedy which she had aspired to as a child.[35]

*The Sicilian Lover* is formulaic in its gothic setting and melodramatic plot. Alferenzi, the Sicilian of the title, is cast in the Romeo mould, as the ill-fated lover, pursuing the virtuous Honoria, whose father has promised her in marriage to Albert, the son of an old friend of the family. After a series of violent and bloody encounters between most of the male characters, Alferenzi kills Honoria's father, believing that he is responsible for the death of his daughter. In this fatally flawed action lies the demise of all comers. In a passionate speech in Act 4, a clearly alive Honoria explains to Alferenzi why there is no longer the least possibility of returning his affections. She retires to a monastery where, despite encountering her mother, of whose continuing existence she has been unaware, Honoria proceeds to die from grief. Alferenzi, once he learns of her death, follows suit. The plot is not an unconventional one, and death and violence are too casually handled, justifying some of Mary Wollstonecraft's criticisms of post-Shakespearean tragedy.[36]

---

34 *Memoirs*, 140–2, records how the farce, *Nobody*, met with a mixed reaction from an audience amongst which there were some hostile elements, eventually subdued by a more sympathetic reaction to the play. During this time, Mary Robinson was also writing satirical odes for the *Morning Post*, under the name of Tabitha Bramble.

35 Mary Robinson, *The Sicilian Lover*, a tragedy in five acts (Hookham and Carpenter, London, 1796).

36 Mary Wollstonecraft writes on the subject of the theatre in *The Works*, ed. Todd and Butler, iv. 46, 47: 'Death is treated in too slight a manner; and sought, when disappointments occur, with a degree of impatience, which proves that the main end of life has not been considered . . . The hour of death is not the time for the display of passions; nor do I think it natural it should: the mind is then dreadfully disturbed, and the trifling sorrows of this world not thought of. The deaths on the stage, in spite of the boasted sensibility of the age, seem to have much the same effect on a polite audience, as the execution of malefactors has on the mob that follow them to Tyburn.' However, it is also worth noting that in *The Wrongs of Woman* the virtuous Maria loves her visits

However, the various contrivances are quite skilfully and carefully plotted, and Mary Robinson mostly avoids a sense of bathos.[37]

What is powerful about the play, both dramatically and politically, is the character of Honoria and her prominence in the action. From the first moment, she is set in defiance of her father's wishes for her future. She articulates 'a fixed aversion' to the man to whom her father has promised her in marriage, and Robinson maintains Honoria's position with passionate conviction.[38] The argument is conducted very clearly in terms of that feminist radicalism espoused by Mary Wollstonecraft, Anna Wheeler, and others, which was claiming the position of women in marriage as analogous to the condition of slavery, and the marriage-act as a mechanism of patriarchal property relations. In Act 1, Honoria proclaims to her father:

> Does the vain suitor arrogantly hope
> To buy me like a slave? A shackled slave!
> O! impious and presuming! may his days
> Creep slowly on, disastrous and forlorn:
> May the worst demons of despair assail him
> For urging such a deed of dark injustice!

Later in the act, Alferenzi defends his feelings for Honoria in similar rhetoric, and it is very much a question of his language mirroring hers, rather than vice versa, the more familiar version of the trope. His appeal for freedom is on her behalf rather than his own:

> Curst be the sordid wretch whose grov'ling soul
> Wou'd bind, in golden chains, a trembling slave;
> Or, like a dastard, traffic with the base
> To sell that freedom, Heav'n design'd for all!

to the theatre, 'My uncle introduced me to some literary society; and the theatres were a never-failing source of amusement to me. My delighted eye followed Mrs Siddons, when, with dignified delicacy, she played Calista' (144).

[37] Morton, *Speed the Plough*, draws on similar gothic contrivances, with the suggestion of shadowy acts in dark castle corridors. Morton does not conduct resolutions with Mary Robinson's skill, but his play *is* comedy. I suppose it is possible that he is parodying the Robinson plot and similar ones. For further comment on *Speed the Plough*, see Ch. 4.

[38] There is a slight temptation towards a biographical reading here, in relation to Mary Robinson having appeared to express admiration of her own father, whilst representing him as completely unworthy of such. She wrote paeans of praise to him after his death.

Again, the language of the abolition movement is brought together with that of women's rights.[39] Of course, the speech is highly coloured by Romanticism (and its own rhetoric of the rights of true love) but the form remains unusual: a woman playwright defends a woman's rights to freedom as against an imposed marriage contract, through the mouth of a male character in support of the female protagonist.[40] For, despite the title of the play, it is Honoria, the woman character, her perspective, her concerns, who dominates the action throughout all five acts. Mary Robinson had asserted in her autobiography that 'the consciousness of independence is the only true felicity in this world of humiliations', and it is the failing struggle for this that she articulates through Honoria and the play, as well as in her autobiography.

The other interesting feature of the play lies in the extent to which it invokes the word 'reason', again through Honoria. To her father she argues, 'Thy fancy doth beguile thy better reason', and it is a term she repeatedly reverts to in defence of her own argument. On many occasions, female reason is set against male sentiment or lack of reason, inverting the normal Enlightenment order.[41] Similarly, the grand and noble passions are those which characterize women, rather than men, who, even at the height of the noble sentiment of love, are victims of their pursuit of uncontrolled vengeance and violence. Honoria crowns her final speech to Alferenzi with a rhetoric worthy of the reformed King Lear:

---

[39] There is a moment of some poignancy in Mary Robinson's autobiography (1826) where she uses the language of abolition and negro emancipation very directly. She writes of the time when her husband had entered into deepest debt, and this was reflecting very badly on her own circumstances: 'Of our domestic establishment there was only one who did not desert us, and he was Negro!—one of that despised, degraded race, who wear the colour on their features which too often characterises the hearts of their fair and unfeeling oppressors. I have found, during my journey through life, that the two male domestics who were most attached to my interests, and most faithful to my fortunes, were both Negros!' (59).

[40] Of course, there was no shortage at this time of strong women characters or strong speeches for women. I speak, though, of the particular alignment of woman playwright with strong woman protagonist and performance.

[41] Mary Wollstonecraft is another who repeatedly defends women on the grounds of reason. See particularly her *The Wrongs of Woman: Or, Maria* (1798) where she uses madness and incarceration as literal settings and metaphors for those states of mind where individuals, by being deprived of their rights, are under pressure to lose their reason.

> That I have lov'd thee, Heav'n can bear me witness,
> Beyond what truth can paint, or fancy form!
> With thee I could have liv'd and been content,
> Beneath some mountain hovel's rushy roof;
> Have shar'd the busy task of daily toil,
> And smil'd and sung the weary hours away!
> When gaudy summer deck'd the glowing scene,
> I wou'd have trim'd our citadel of joy,
>  Have call'd our humble meal, a princely feast;
> Our myrtle bow'r a canopy of state!

The language may be that of domesticity, but such speeches, plangent and reproachful, define the terms of the action, rather than taking the more conventional form of being subsidiary to the emotional concerns of a male protagonist. Honoria is more of a Lear than a Cordelia, in terms of both the length and critical perspective of her speeches, in carrying that weight usually designed for the male tragedian. (Mary Robinson may have nearly played Cordelia to Garrick's Lear, but in terms of her writing, it was the latter role which appears to have energized her.) Moreover, in *The Sicilian Lover*, it is the female characters who speak with the philosophy of Jean Jacques Rousseau or William Wordsworth, the expression of which is usually reserved for the male voice.

### Elizabeth Inchbald's Satirical Edge

Despite the impressive achievement, both dramatically and in terms of feminist politics, of Mary Robinson's *The Sicilian Lover*, it is something of a relief to turn away from its unrelieved heroic gloom (and indeed, from that of Mary Wollstonecraft's *The Wrongs of Woman*), to the comic and satirical mode which characterizes the style of some other women playwrights of the period, notably Elizabeth Inchbald and Hannah Cowley.[42] Mary Robinson's aspiration to write tragedy, as well as appearing to be in character with her sensibility, can also be understood in terms of the conventions of the age. Shakespearean tragedy was

---

[42] Angela Escott, Birkbeck College, University of London, read a paper about Hannah Cowley's subversive comedy to the conference, 'Women, Writing and the Public Sphere 1680–1830', Cambridge University, July 1996. I am grateful to her for the introduction to Cowley's work, and for comments on her play, *Who's the Dupe?* Donkin, *Getting into the Act*, also includes a chapter on Cowley's theatrical relationships.

promoted as the noblest of forms, to which contemporary playwrights could barely hope to attain an approximation. At the same time, a woman playwright might perceive this as the only acceptable form available to her, in an age where women's activities were judged and circumscribed according to certain expectations of their moral behaviour as well as their intellectual faculties. Writing tragedy, in other words, is compatible with being virtuous, especially where it is unlikely to be performed.

Elizabeth Inchbald, by contrast, whilst appearing to have been aware of such constraints, does not seem to have been prepared to become the victim of them. Out of the women playwrights of this period, with the particular obstacles to their achievements, Mrs Inchbald greatest autonomy.[43] The choice of comedy, whilst being more risky in terms of a woman's moral character, is arguably less ambitious than writing tragedy, where claims to generalize from the particular might be held to be inappropriate to women's world-view (or perceived lack of it). More important, though, the ambivalence of comedy—is the audience laughing *with* these men or *at* them?—appears to have worked to Inchbald's advantage. A reading of her plays gives some insight into how she used comedy and satire both to expose and to ridicule certain prejudices against women. *Wives as they were, and maids as they are* yields one example of how Inchbald managed to frame her plays in terms of the conventional denouement of the happy marriage, thereby circumventing resistance from theatre managers to performing such material, whilst raising, rather trenchantly, some of those issues which so exercised Mary Robinson and Mary Wollstonecraft.[44]

This particular play, a comedy in five acts, is primarily a satire on male protection, masquerading cleverly as an encomium to wifely obedience and duty. The male protagonist, Sir William, has recently returned from India and, for reasons best known to himself, has concealed his identity from his daughter, Miss Maria Dorrillan. The play opens with a discussion between Sir William and his friend, Mr Norberry, in whose care he has left his daughter. Sir William rebukes Mr Norberry for the waywardness of Maria, who, embracing the life of

---

[43] Donkin, ibid., for an account of Elizabeth Inchbald's adroit handling of theatre managers.

[44] Mrs Inchbald, *Wives as they were, and maids as they are*, a comedy in five acts, performed at the Theatre Royal, Covent Garden (Robinson, London, 1797).

the fashionable set, is living beyond her means, gambling at cards and running into debt.[45] This opening dialogue sets the tone of the play before any of the women characters appear. Whilst Sir William is established as a kind of moral touchstone, and even though the male characters have been outlining the women's weaknesses, the bickering over which of the men is and should be responsible for Maria's protection already lends audience sympathy to the women before their appearance. In other words, the issue of male protection is under even greater scrutiny than the fashionable habits of women.

The other characters to take the stage before the audience hears from Miss Dorrillan are Lord and Lady Priory and their entourage, in particular their trustworthy servant, Oliver (who is himself a neat little cameo from that genre in which the servant is well acquainted with the foibles of his masters). Lord Priory takes centre-stage to lecture Mr Norberry and Sir William on the subject of his marital regime. The audience learns that in Lord Priory's perception, his wife is firmly subject to his will. Not least of his controlling measures is to force her to rise from bed at 5 o'clock in the morning, and take to her bed by 10 o'clock at night at the latest. If she refuses to rise, he locks her in her room until the evening. None of this endears an audience to Lord Priory's version of conjugal relations, but this is no simple satire on husband's expectations or misconceptions of wifely obedience. For Elizabeth Inchbald eventually appears to condone wifely duty, as the best of a bad set of options. As Lady Priory puts it to her would-be seducer, Bronzely, 'But, to the best of my observation and understanding, your sex, in respect to us, are *all tyrants*. I was born to be the slave of some of you—I make the choice to obey my husband' (her emphasis). The address at the end of the play, written by one Mr Taylor, seems to miss the ironic nuance and complexity in simply asserting that Inchbald's play is wholly in favour of the ways of the 'ancient dames' over the modern.

In terms of the main action of the play, too, there is by no means a simple censuring of Maria as against her noble father. Miss Dorrillon is surrounded by suitors, but balks at the idea of relieving her financial difficulties by exploiting 'the weakness of a lover'. Instead, she turns to her friend, Lady Mary, proclaiming that the two of them should be

---

[45] See Foreman, *Georgiana*, for an account of Georgiana, Duchess of Devonshire's notorious gambling habits (a possible model for Inchbald).

allies, bound 'by the common ties of poverty'. Thus, Inchbald under-lines a simple message about the wealthy household: that money resides with the men, only lodges with the women as their gift. At the same time, of course, she exposes, as is common amongst eighteenth-century women writers, not least Jane Austen, the extent to which marriage is sustained on the basis of financial and property interests. In the third act of the play, the not very convincing Sir George, pursuing Maria albeit fairly honourably, is given a speech which unwittingly rounds on Sir William, blaming Miss Dorrillon's vices on 'her absent parent'. Thus, Inchbald complicates the moral and dramatic topography, imply-ing that Sir William will not be taking his responsibilities seriously until he reveals his identity to his daughter. The audience grows impatient *with* Sir William, and *for* that moment.

By Act 4, Maria is claiming protection (that word again) from her creditors, appealing to Sir William to shield her. The comedy comes very close to melodrama and tragedy as Inchbald actually imprisons Maria for debt, before her father will take action on her behalf. Even then, he only discloses his identity because Maria inadvertently reveals her passionate feelings for her father, whom she still believes to be in India. Act 5 sees the drama catapulting to a close, with Maria paired off with Sir George, at Sir William's bidding, and Lady Mary with the brazen Bronzely, but the rapidity of the action is unpersuasive, leaving the question open as to how the women are to be best protected, and whether other means than dependence on fathers and men in general might be preferable.

In a later play, *To marry, or not to marry*, Elizabeth Inchbald revisits two of the central ideas of *Wives as they were, and maids as they are*.[46] The question of protection is foregrounded again, as is the related issue of the absent father. The woman protagonist, Hester, has absconded from her cruel guardian's house on the very day of the proposed wedding which has been arranged by him for her. She arrives at the grand house of Mrs Sarah Mortland, whom she has only met once before, at a social event, where the two were charmed with each other. Inchbald makes a passing, cryptic, but telling reference to property laws, as Mrs Mortland, on to whose mercy Hester has thrown herself, does not actually own the house. It belongs, because of patrilineage, to her younger brother, Sir Oswin Mortland (who harbours an antipathy

---

[46] Inchbald, *To marry, or not to marry* (Longman, London, 1805).

to the marriage state, preferring the contents of his spacious and, of course, private library). Thus, in Act 1, the play has already raised the issue of women's dependence, alongside that of the protection of the single woman, at a number of different levels. Hester has appealed directly to Sarah Mortland for protection from a guardian and a suitor, both of whom she believes to be abusing their rights over her. However, as a woman, Sarah Mortland can only mediate and arbitrate. The legal and financial means of offering protection to Hester are open, not to her, but to her brother, Sir Oswin. There is also the question of Hester's absent father, removed from the action and not in a position to support his daughter.

As in the earlier play, the plot revolves around the means by which the father figure is brought back into his daughter's presence, reinstating the 'natural' manner of offering protection to the vulnerable woman.[47] In the process, Inchbald employs comedy to explore how Sir Oswin is going to respond to the test of his principles and scruples. In an interview with Hester, he requires an explanation of why she has abandoned her guardian and her suitor. Her response is that she wishes to *choose* a husband, not to have one imposed upon her. Sir Oswin feigns shock that a woman should acknowledge a wish to initiate love-making, but Hester proceeds to vindicate herself in his eyes, with her frankness and charm. The subtext, of course, is that this young and beautiful girl is weakening Sir Oswin's resolve to abjure love and marriage. When he declares to his old friend, Willowear, who is no other than the aspiring husband of Hester, rejected on the wedding day ('She has flown to this house for protection; and I believe the laws of hospitality oblige me'), he is concealing, even from himself at this moment, his true motive of support for Hester. In other words, Inchbald again implies that the male protector is not motivated by his desire to defend a dependent, or even what he takes to be a weaker species, but by sexual and romantic interest.

It has to be stressed, though, that if Inchbald is at all judgemental, she is so in a very equivocal way. Most of the play persuades the audience to appreciate Sir Oswin's dilemma, to admire his glamour, and to hope for a happy resolution in his prospective marriage to Hester, which

---

[47] The subplot of the play is that Hester's father, Lavensforth, has been banished after a political quarrel with Sir Oswin, of whom he is an inveterate enemy. In the happy denouement, he is reconciled with Sir Oswin as well as with Hester.

is precisely what the denouement promises. Sir Oswin, however far he is under scrutiny for his abjuring of female company, is a charismatic character, waiting to be romantically conquered by the simple and beguiling heroine. However, whilst this is far from being a radical feminist's revolutionary scenario, Inchbald does take the opportunity to expose, if not to condemn, those attitudes to which women can so easily fall victim. The problem with men, if Mrs Sarah Mortland is to be believed, is that they can afford, in more ways than one, to allow their emotions to remain ungoverned. (This is also what makes them unpredictable and unreliable as prospective protectors of women.) By contrast, women, who do not have recourse to the law in protecting any rights to which they might aspire, cannot afford such arbitrariness. On being asked how she knows that he is in love with Hester, Sir Oswin's sister replies:

The reason is—women feel everything. Men's perception lies only in the head; ours comes from the heart. Brother, the sexes are thus contrasted—sensibility gives us wisdom, but takes it away from you men. When man is governed by his heart, he's less than woman—and *we* are the lords of the creation.[48]

Like Mary Robinson, Inchbald inverts the normal Enlightenment trope, insisting that it is women who possess, of necessity, that unifying sensibility which informs the ability to reason, not men, whose treatment of women repeatedly demonstrates that they lack this. However, this is comedy, and the audience can always be excused for laughing at the very idea that women are the lords of creation. Other aspects of the play's comedy must have appealed to contemporary audiences, and indeed theatre managers. 'To marry, or not to marry' puns neatly on 'To be, or not to be', as the central dilemma of a man's life, and carries over elegantly from the male to the female protagonist, being the central issue for Hester as well as for Sir Oswin. Also, the roles allocated to the protagonists, with their witty asides and urbane exchanges, were very attractive to comic players. Indeed, theatre managers like John Kemble could well have been attracted to Elizabeth Inchbald's plays by the charismatic parts for male performers.

Elizabeth Inchbald's plays, as in an example given earlier, were framed by prologues and epilogues, often spoken by male performers, and frequently written by men, nearly always bearing some kind of

---

[48] Inchbald, *To marry, or not to marry*, Act 4.

apology or rationale for the playwright being a woman. One of the more interesting, slightly less patronizing versions of these, by the Reverend Mr Nares and spoken by Mr Farren, forms the prologue to her play, *Every one has his fault.*[49] Nares refers directly to writings such as those of Wollstonecraft, citing Inchbald in the context of women's rights:

> *The Rights of Women*, says a female pen,
> Are, to do everything as well as Men.
> To think, to argue, to decide, to write,
> To talk, undoubtedly—perhaps, to fight.

The text goes on to argue the case for women playwrights, but the significant rationale appears towards the end of the piece, indicating that there is a dire need for new material for the stage in the period:

> Then, drive not, Critics, with tyrannic rage,
> A supplicating Fair-one from the Stage;
> The Comic Muse perhaps is growing old,
> Her lovers, you well know, are few and cold.
> 'Tis time then freely to enlarge the plan,
> And let all those write Comedies—that can.

Elizabeth Inchbald, along with other women playwrights of the period, was extremely adept at other languages besides English, and could be involved in supplying some of this badly needed dramatic material, not least through her skills in translating French. Their entry into the profession could have been accepted, more than for any other reason (including that of the desire of theatre managers for a personal circle of female devotees), in order to supply the insatiable market, which was greedy for imports from the Continent, but particularly for home-grown material.

It is probably the case that the subject-matter of Elizabeth Inchbald's plays does not aspire to the broad canvas of a Colman or Jerrold. Her interest is substantially in the grand mansion and the grand manner, even where its subjects are treated to the satirical mode. When Inchbald introduces a black servant, Amos, into *To marry, or not to marry*, it is with a certain amount of tokenism. He is loyal and devoted to his master, in keeping with Mary Robinson's encomium of black servants,

---

[49] Mrs Inchbald, *Every one has his fault*, a comedy in five acts, as performed at the Theatre Royal, Covent Garden (Wogan, Dublin, 1793).

but dramatically, he is rather sketchy and insipid, stereotyped to a brief role in a revenge motive. To conclude, though, that the emphasis by these playwrights on women of their own circle is a narrow one, would be to run the risk of contributing to those prejudicial attitudes which this account is setting out to challenge. In any case, there is plenty of evidence to suggest that women playwrights related their interest in women to a broad range of concerns, in addition to the feminist commitments of the period, and that they were chastised for doing so. Ellen Donkin writes of the 'termites bellicosus' which Joanna Baillie encountered, once her identity and gender were known, after having published her discourse on plays and playwriting anonymously.[50] Baillie's introductory discourse is a polemic on behalf of the representation of everyday life in the drama. In the course of her argument, she questions those 'well-meaning enthusiastick criticks', who expect a play to imitate the classics. Her view is that they should be concerned, rather, with 'faithfully delineated nature'. It is significant to find this discussion of naturalism and its merits as early as the 1790s, almost a hundred years before naturalistic drama is thought to have arrived on the stage in Britain.[51]

The more widely Baillie's gender was known, the more she met with hostile criticism, both for her audacity at challenging contemporary critics, and for her effrontery in writing a set of plays which she hoped would fulfil the requirements of her aspirations for the drama. She describes herself as being motivated to write tragedy by a desire to free the form of unnecessary and archaic embellishments, and to write comedy in order to counter the 'insipid similarity' of contemporary comedies.[52] Her statements about audience are also radical, upholding the theatre as the most potentially democratic literary or artistic form, in reaching 'a greater number of individuals' than any other writing. She comments on her preference for writing for what her readers will take to be 'the rude and uncultivated', over other forms of audience. In passing,

---

[50] Joanna Baillie, *A series of plays: in which it is attempted to delineate the stronger passions of the mind. Each passion being the subject of a tragedy and a comedy* (Cadell and Davies, London, 1798), 'Introductory discourse', 1–72. Joanna Baillie is the subject of ch. 7 of Donkin, *Getting into the Act*.

[51] And yet her fame has not reached the present day in the way that William Wordsworth's has in relation to his thoughts about everyday life and poetic language (*Preface to the Lyrical Ballads*), or later Emile Zola's has, in relation to his thoughts about naturalism. I return to issues of naturalism in Ch. 6.

[52] Baillie, *A Series of Plays*, 'Introductory discourse'.

Baillie makes apology to the reader for her lack of a scholarly reference system in her discourse. Her explanation in terms of lack of access to a library of any sort is a salutary reminder of the inadequate resources with which women were working, and gives us another take on Elizabeth Inchbald's wry comments on Sir Oswin's attachment to his private library (in *To marry, or not to marry*).

To some extent, Joanna Baillie appears to share Mary Robinson's formula for tragedy, in foregrounding the male protagonist but giving more significance, whether inadvertently or not, to the women of the piece. Her tragedy, *Count Basil*, set in sixteenth-century Mantua, focuses upon the eponymous military hero, whose tragic dilemma is that he is caught between love and war.[53] The contours of his anxiety are rather classic and the arguments about the ethics of this particular choice rather well rehearsed, but as the play progresses, both the female protagonist, Victoria, and to an even greater extent, the Countess Albini, her governess, begin to steal audience interest. Albini is cast in a Wollstonecraft mould. Her view of love, which informs her advice to Victoria, much in the spirit of *The Female Reader*, warns against personal, feminine vanity and in favour of reason and reflection. She upbraids Victoria for her lack of caution towards Count Basil, whose devotion to her endangers his commitment to military leadership, and brings about his downfall. Love interest, as Baillie herself argues in her introductory discourse, is no excuse for dereliction of duty, or for being complicit in such. At the same time, though, Albini is far from being sanctimonious. She does preach the domestic virtues in one sense, but she also shares with those notable women of Renaissance drama, such as Amelia in *Othello*, a capacity to defend her mistress's interests at all personal cost, and does not reproach her for having seduced Basil from his purpose. Baillie has effectively replaced the concept of male protection with the less suspect one of sisterhood and female protection. It is also as if Baillie, once the tragic denouement of Count Basil has taken place, is reluctant to send the women on the same dramatic voyage (unlike Shakespeare in his treatment of the women in *Othello*). Basil's death rather abruptly ends the play, leaving Victoria and Albini distraught, but very much alive and at the centre of the action.

[53] Baillie, *A Series of Plays*, contains three plays, one of which is a comedy and the other two tragedies: *Count Basil*, *The Tryal* and *De Monfort*. The comedy, *The Tryal*, is a neat satire on the aspirations and pretensions of male suitors. The women protagonists, Agnes and Mariane, tease and test the motives of Sir Loftus Prettyman, and others.

In *Count Basil,* Joanna Baillie works hard to create a history play, drawing on documented events, and setting the action in a military context. She is looking beyond the grand mansion and the domestic setting. The play has ambitions beyond those of most women play-wrights. It is perhaps a little ironic then, that Baillie does not altogether avoid those problems raised in her introductory discourse, of tragedy being too derivative and too inclined to ape the classics or the received formula. When she writes outside that formula, that is, in relation to the women characters, the play realizes her theories more profoundly. It would be absurd, though, to imply that women playwrights' successful writing about women should be seen as a weakness, or that they should have to take special account of having written primarily about women. They had more than enough to do to make an intervention into the profession at any level, and even where their plays reached performance, they were under constant pressure from the conviction of many of the theatre men of the time that any talent they had was derived from or subsidiary to that of men. Prologues to the plays make this clear; as Taylor's prologue to Inchbald's *To marry, or not to marry,* states:

> Custom to her [woman] that range of life denies,
> Which ampler views to lordly man supplies;
> He, unrestrain'd, can ev'ry class survey,
> That mark the myriads of the grave and gay;
> Hence can his talents take a boundless sweep,
> And richest crops of character may reap;
> But, woman, fix'd within a narrow scene,
> What Genius slights, must be content to glean.

Women simply could not afford the luxury of drawing on subjects from the factory movement or the abolition cause, at a time when their own legitimacy and the subject of woman as an independent human being was in question and under scrutiny.[54] This, it seems to me, is precisely what Elizabeth Inchbald's work, along with that of Mary Wollstonecraft, addresses. It is also, clearly, the gauntlet which Joanna Baillie and Mary Robinson had to run. Of course, it *is* open to us to form the conclusion that the fight for women's rights was, after all, the hardest political struggle of the time, as well as the most influential on the abolition movement and other areas of political reform, albeit with,

---

[54] Where they did, they came in for heavy criticism, and we do not know how many more scripts were lost to posterity.

until recently and as ever, the least recognition. Certainly, this early version of the women's movement, in theatrical form, was indispensable to any sexually equalizing aspect of reform, required by any society in which attempts to move towards a proper democracy were being made.

CHAPTER SIX

# The Grand Theatre of Political Change, 1789 to 1833

Political movements in Britain following the French Revolution, up until the 1832 Reform Act and the Emancipation Act a year later, were strongly informed and characterized by the vitality of theatrical performance and the ebullience of theatre audience. We have seen how all the glorious causes of 1789 to 1833, including the factory movement, the early women's movement, agrarian reform, the abolition movement, and above all, the movement to reform the parliamentary franchise itself, drew heavily on the rhetoric of the drama and theatrical forms.[1]

However, until recently, theatre historians and social historians had tended to give a decidedly mixed reception to the drama of the period, frequently damning it in the act of ignoring it, or representing it as lacking in artistic merit, vulgar, tasteless, and at best only suited to plebeian audiences.[2] It *is* the case that stage performance of the late eighteenth and early nineteenth centuries in Britain has been difficult to assess, because it was wildly eclectic both in its audiences and in its performers, featuring animals, freaks of nature, the elements (water, fire and earth, as well as air), not to say many varieties of human kind. A plurality of genres, including burlesque, pantomime, comedy, tragedy, mock-heroic comedy, mock-satirical tragedy, musicals, not to mention melodrama, sentimental domestic drama, and others, reflected and encouraged this diversity, sometimes producing, under one playbill, a

---

[1] I have demonstrated the significance of French Revolutionary influences on reform theatre and politics, although in some senses, 1788 could equally well have provided my starting-point, as the anniversary of the Glorious Revolutions of 1688, or 1787 might have served, as the year when Colman's *Inkle and Yarico* was first performed.

[2] Thompson, *The Making of the English Working Class*, 781–915, makes reference to the absence of artistic merit in 'plebeian theatre'. I single out Thompson not because he is particularly guilty, but because of the attractions of the rest of his argument (developed later in my discussion).

multiplicity of performance styles, combining 'in a single evening the appeals of the circus, the concert hall, the gallery, the museum, and the prizefight ring'.[3] Such eclecticism inevitably puts critical criteria under strain.

Another factor that has produced a pressure to maintain critical distance has been the relative infrequency of production of the plays from the period in question, in the late nineteenth and particularly the twentieth century. This is in marked contrast to the intense popularity of many of the plays in their own time. In consequence, where serious attention has been paid in the past, a certain inappropriateness of critical judgement has arisen, bringing to bear aesthetic criteria applied to and deriving from assessments of quite different styles of drama and performance, in particular, the well-made play emerging in the 1880s. The relative unpopularity of the plays in the Victorian period has also given rise to hostile judgements about eighteenth-century audiences, who have been judged lacking in refinement and rigour in comparison with their late nineteenth-century counterparts.

However, the appearance of a startlingly direct relationship between theatre and the political life of the period has caused some discomfort to the most sceptical of critics. The years 1789 to 1833 saw an unprecedented and perhaps unsurpassed interconnectedness of theatrical and political activity, and relations between the two were, arguably, at one of their most vital and significant points in the history of the British nation. This has given rise to the argument, growing in force, that theatricality was crucial to a definition of 'the mental universe of late Georgian society' and that any account of that period of British history would be incomplete without a consideration of the interrelationship between theatre and politics, between stage and State.[4]

---

[3] J. Kinnaird, *William Hazlitt* (Columbia University Press, New York, 1978), ch. 5. Bratton, *Acts of Supremacy*, produces fascinating readings of playbills in her paper, 'The Adelphi Theatre 1807–1832, a Study in Institutionalised Opposition', given to the conference on theatre in the age of reform held in Cambridge, 26 April 1997.

[4] Baer, *Theatre and Disorder*, 39–65. Gillian Russell, *The Theatres of War, Performance, Politics, and Society, 1793–1815* (Clarendon Press, Oxford, 1995) also subscribes to a firm belief in the political character of theatre in the period; 'the socially encoded hierarchy of box, pit, and gallery tended to encourage the use of the auditorium as a forum for political expression', (introduction).

## Reviewing Critical Assumptions

There are methodological and historiographical issues involved in taking plays simply as historical 'sources'. Joseph R. Roach has put it tellingly that 'what historians optimistically call "sources" . . . hold out the false promise of authentic origin'.[5] Theatre historians suffer from 'a wistful sense of incompletion' as the playtext fails to yield adequate evidence of the full event and to capture the elusive properties of performance, because of 'the evanescence of performance itself'.[6] Exclusive analysis of any of the component parts of a play, whether it be the playtext as artefact, or one performance inevitably crafted for a particular kind of audience, then interpreted in a press review for a particular kind of readership (which may or may not do justice either to the script or to the performance, which may not *itself* have done justice to the script), carries its own limitations in terms of adequate forms of historical retrieval.[7]

The playtext, even where it is an accurate or faithful representation of the playwright's script, is of course only a signifier, a witness to a greater idea, which can only be realized through the interpretation of production, with all the accompanying visual, oral, and aural elements of whatever style of performance has been judged appropriate in a given socio-cultural context.[8] Whereas literary criticism tends to privilege the individual writer, any play performance requires a prioritizing of the group over the individual in a co-production. In relation to any play, there are these production as well as performance values to consider.[9]

[5] Joseph R. Roach, 'Introduction to Theater History and Historiography', in Janelle G. Reinelt and Joseph R. Roach (eds.), *Critical Theory and Performance* (the University of Michigan Press, Ann Arbor, 1992).

[6] Ibid.

[7] I emphasize here that an account of performance and rehearsal processes, *per se*, in relation to individual plays or spectacles is not within the scope of my book. I hope that this work may be taken up by others with reference to the lesser known plays retrieved here.

[8] John Rouse, 'Textuality and Authority in Theater and Drama: Some Contemporary Possibilities', in Reinelt and Roach (eds.), *Critical Theory and Performance*, reminds us of the place of semiotics in analysis of theatre, and of the useful distinction, for the purposes of interpretation, between performance texts and dramatic texts. There is also much interesting work emerging, including that of Ann Featherstone at University of London Royal Holloway College, about the relationship between spectacle and audience in this history.

[9] Bruce A. McConachie, 'Historicizing the Relations of Theatrical Production', in Reinelt and Roach (eds.), *Critical Theory and Performance* highlights the significance of

Additionally, claims about artistic merit nearly always reify the art object, often, in establishing formal criteria, driving a wedge between aesthetic and ideological matters, or allowing one to occlude the other.[10]

All of this makes any particular case for theatre in history, especially political theatre (rooted in contemporary concerns themselves not always adequately recorded), extremely problematic, even where the maximum amount of what might qualify as evidence is available. Added to this, the theatre of the 1790s to 1830s carries with it particular reasons for being controversial. It resists critical attachment to playwrights in its promotion of the actor over the author, in its foregrounding of specta-cle over dialogue *per se*, and above all in the fluidity of relations between performance and audience, arguably rendering the dialogic utterances of what Ellen Donkin calls the shouting audience as important as writ-ten script.[11]

Until recently, attention to the playtexts of late Georgian theatre has tended to be either heavily taxonomic, placing plays firmly in thematic categories, or demonstrating how their content pandered to some debased notion of popular taste, at best satisfying the demands of the voracious market. These styles of commentary have been overtaken recently by work which appropriately insists on situating an analysis of the relationship between theatre management and the market economy in a socio-political context.[12] Questions remain, though, about the

the word 'production' itself. Adam Smith's emphasis on the word in relation to political economy in his *Wealth of Nations* (1776) is not mirrored in theatre, where the term is introduced over a hundred years later. ('Before 1894 English writers termed a theatrical event a show, a presentation, or a performance.') The analysis of artistic practices, McConachie argues, often focuses on 'means' rather than 'relations' of production, reflecting a tendency to separate the 'aesthetic from the practical'.

[10] Reinelt and Roach challenge the separation in their general introduction: 'We did not include a section on the pure aesthetics of performance, transcending the realm of ideology, because we could not imagine one.'

[11] Ellen Donkin, 'Mrs. Siddons Looks Back in Anger: Feminist Historiography for Eighteenth-Century British Theater' in Reinelt and Roach (eds.), *Critical Theory and Performance*.

[12] Baer, *Theatre and Disorder*, Ellen Donkin, *Getting into the Act*, and others, write about the intricacies of theatre management and the patent system, which gave more legal and economic stability to the central London theatres, particularly Covent Garden and Drury Lane, than others. The work of Baer, Donkin, and others gives me my reason for not needing to devote much space to the issue of theatre management in relation to the patent system. It is probably the area of scholarship on late 18th- and early 19th-c. theatre to which most attention has been given. Nicholson, *The Struggle for a Free Stage*, is exhaustive on the detail of the patents.

extent to which later critical criteria of the drama have attached too much significance to the written text, failing to recognize spectacle as the more significant element of Georgian theatre, or denying the possibility that visual, oral, and aural elements of the drama, together with audience response, are as potentially integrative of the whole form as its scripted dimension.

Making a case for the plays of this history in terms of aesthetics may well be an inadvisable, indeed, an impossible task. This was a formally eclectic and, at one level, random playmaking, without claims to the finish and finesse that some expect of the artistic artefact. Even pioneers and advocates of this theatre history have made little attempt to claim artistic merit for the plays. One such is Michael Booth, in his impressive task of rescuing melodrama from the enormous condescension of posterity.[13] Those whom Booth describes as the best British writers of the period, including Wordsworth, Coleridge, Shelley, Byron, where they wrote plays, did so in the form of dramatic verse, prioritizing poetry and with no performance expectations. If their dramas were performed, such writers did not expect them to be produced with any integrity, as theatrical performance values were largely inapplicable to dramatic poetry (and the more rarefied critical evaluations appropriate to poetry).[14] In voicing a complaint that theatre audiences contain 'unlettered persons . . . who do not know what an author is', Charles Lamb corroborates Booth's point about disregard in the theatre for any serious concern with writers as such.[15]

However, we have seen that the plays of late Georgian theatre do operate well as 'sources' (even in that simple understanding of the term shared between optimistic historians), often yielding very direct evidence of the political movements of the period. When John Walker writes about the factory, he does so with an informed sense of the debates likely to enlighten and engage those involved in the factory movement.[16] When Elizabeth Inchbald dramatizes the plight of the

---

[13] Booth, *English Melodrama.*

[14] Although, work on the dramatic conceptions of the Romantic poets, and attempts at realization, have been completed since Booth published his book; see particularly Carlson, *In the Theater of Romanticism.*

[15] E. V. Lucas (ed.) 'On the Tragedies of Shakespear', in *The Works of Charles and Mary Lamb* (1912), cited in Loren Kruger, *The National Stage: Theatre and Cultural Legitimation in England, France, and America* (University of Chicago Press, Chicago, 1992), ch. 1, 'Theatrical Nationhood and Popular Legitimation'.

[16] See Ch. 3 for more on John Walker's plays.

woman fleeing from home in the early hours of her prospective wedding day, she does so with an informed intelligence of discussions made public by Mary Wollstonecraft and others of marriage as a state of oppressive property-relationship for women.[17] Similarly, Douglas Jerrold knew much about the critique leading to attempts at agrarian reform, George Colman the Younger made direct connections with the abolition movement, W. T. Moncrieff was well acquainted with debates about the reform of the parliamentary franchise, and so on.[18]

The challenge for playwrights was not only that of engaging with contemporary political movements thematically. Many popular playwrights of the late eighteenth and early nineteenth centuries attempted to address the process of offering a challenge to received notions of rank in society, indirectly as well as directly. The concept of the moral actor, shortly to be explored in more detail, together with a re-creation of the relationship between actor and audience in the period, was to have important implications for how playwrights conceived of dramatic representation in general, particularly on the question of how characterization could provide a new means of articulating relations between actor and audience, between the individual and society. The question, in other words, is about what late eighteenth- and early nineteenth-century playwrights could do to actualize a new system of dramatic representation and performance which would contribute and do justice to the influence of levelling processes, responding to politically-aware and contentious audiences.[19] The task appears to have been no lesser one than that of reconceptualizing and redesigning dramatic representation itself.

So, even if all attempt to apply assessment in terms of artistic merit were abandoned, it would still be possible to show that there was a highly important and mutually influential relationship between the content of the plays and the political movements of the period. Certainly, also, theatre at this time was 'a site of struggle . . . among

---

[17] See Ch. 5 for more on Elizabeth Inchbald's plays.

[18] See Ch. 4 for more on Douglas Jerrold, Prologue and Ch. 2 for George Colman, and Ch. 1 for W. T. Moncrieff.

[19] Edward Bulwer-Lytton's analysis of the people receives more treatment shortly. See Leigh Hunt's *Dramatic Criticism, 1808–1831*, ed. Lawrence Huston Houtchens and Carolyn Washburn Houtchens (Columbia University Press, New York, 1949) on the subject of the educated quality of the people. In his essay, 'Late Hours at the Theatre', 7 July 1831, Leigh Hunt writes, 'that the diffusion of knowledge has been bringing up the uneducated classes to the point where the others left off'.

competing attempts to legitimately define the appropriate relationship between theatre and society'.[20]

However, it would be something of an act of intellectual timidity to abandon the question of aesthetic criteria entirely.[21] Something has to be said and done about the suspicion that posterity's reaction to this theatre history uses aesthetic arguments as a camouflage. Are subsequent critics who bemoan the absence of the well-made play displacing political and social anxieties about the disappearance of early forms of patronage, or of the well-made audience (of later date), sitting hygienically and politely in their seats, adopting the appropriate class demeanour?[22] Certainly, the literary-critical establishment has often appeared to find it extremely difficult to separate its prejudices about class from its judgements about art. As Loren Kruger puts it: 'the leisure habits of dominant classes tend to be universalized as taste, art or theatre, while those of subordinate classes or groups are merely entertainment or potentially unruly behaviour.'[23] Connected and sometimes conflated with the debate about class is one about popularity. Intense interest and support for theatre in the Georgian era apparently provides some critics with that perverse turn, not uncharacteristic of the critical establishment, of consigning that theatre to oblivion *now*, almost as punishment for its popularity *then*. Whether by implication or in direct

[20] Kruger, *The National Stage*, 25.

[21] Hadley, *Melodramatic Tactics*, 1–12, argues tellingly that one cannot simply dispose of questions of aesthetic value in a culture measured in 'units of value'.

[22] I see a distinction here with, say, Renaissance theatre, which, whilst sharing some of these characteristics of audience, was clearly under the patronage of the Crown. In late Georgian theatre, though, the move was towards 'the public as patron' (McConachie, *Melodramatic Formations*) Critical anxiety would no doubt follow about an audience that was not only 'unruly', but also gaining power! There is another argument, beyond the scope of my project here, about the extent to which 18th- and post-18th-century criticism transformed Renaissance theatre, particularly Shakespeare's plays, into 'poetry' for critical purposes. In one sense, late Georgian theatre is critically caught between aesthetic criteria appropriate to poetry and those deriving from the late 19th about the well-made play.

[23] Kruger, *The National Stage*, and see Kruger's introduction, too, on questions of how theatre is an 'exemplary site for investigating . . . cultural hegemony' (12, 13). Later, Kruger argues convincingly that national popular theatre in republican France disrupted 'the theatrical order of the *ancien régime*' (34). However, Kruger does not believe that a parallel challenge existed in Georgian Britain: 'comparable developments in England unleashed a torrent of laments about the decline of the drama, effectively foreclosing any legitimate discussion of the specificity of popular needs and tastes'. Kruger may well be right about the absence of proper discussion, but I would argue that the case for Georgian theatre and the plays themselves in disrupting the old order can be made.

form, the debate about the relations between popular and high art, and their mutual exclusions, continues to have a powerful resonance, since the Victorians named those categories.[24]

Recently, cultural studies analysts have reclaimed fields of popular culture and working-class audience,[25] but the terms of appraisal have often involved recognizing or creating or ratifying a separate category of working-class art or culture, rather than exploring those cultural forms whose audiences cross class.[26] Is the very specificity of eighteenth-century audience—that is, its diversity of class interests, its ability to cross class in a lively exchange, its energy for challenge and change, constituting itself as a new form of public insisting on displacing, or at least, shifting the balance away from old forms of patronage—what critics find most difficult to accommodate, leading to their intolerance of the plays?

### The Politics of Audience

To volunteer a rebellion for the theatrical éclat of the thing

In redressing the balance, in trying to accommodate an understanding of late eighteenth-century and early nineteenth-century theatre which

---

[24] See *Popular Culture: Past and Present*, Bernard Waites, Tony Bennett, and Graham Martin (eds.), (Open University, Croom Helm, London, 1982) for discussion of these relations, including Edward Thompson's article 'Class Consciousness: The Radical Culture'.

[25] The Open University and the Birmingham Centre for Contemporary Cultural Studies are notable initiators in the field, e.g. Waites, Bennett and Martin (eds.), *Popular Culture* and John Clarke, Chas Critcher, and Richard Johnson (eds.), *Working Class Culture* (CCCS, Hutchinson, London, 1979). I must emphasize, though, that much of this work has been very exciting, and critically aware of the political circumscriptions involved in discovering or inventing such categories.

[26] Peter Bailey, *Leisure and Class in Victorian England: Rational Recreation and the Contest for Control, 1830–1885* (Routledge and University of Toronto, 1978). Whilst acknowledging in his introduction that 'the governing classes . . . often patronised' popular village festivities along with 'the common man', Bailey appears reluctant to accept an inference that such festivities attracted a cross-class audience in which all were legitimate participants. Instead, he inadvertently reinforces a solipsistic category of working-class culture by insisting on its separate sphere: 'the authority structure of village society could be temporarily inverted . . . the common man was king for the day and the world was turned upside down, as villagers thumbed their noses (and worse) at their betters.' This type of account, whilst being extremely well intentioned, thus underestimates the potential influence, via cultural hegemony, on both parties (in what E. P. Thompson describes as the patrician–plebeian continuum) deriving from a common audience sharing the experience of a common event.

does justice to the integrated relationship between theatre and political life, an appropriate consideration is a scrutiny of audience in terms of the class politics of late Georgian society. E. P. Thompson's assumption in his early work that theatre audiences of the time were 'plebeian' and lacking in taste, is one which helps to set the argument moving. Had Thompson left the judgement at that, it would have been somewhat curious that a historian of his egalitarian ilk, who has done so much to rescue working people from 'the enormous condescension of posterity' (that metaphor that has seized the imagination so widely), should conflate the term plebeian with bad taste and the want of critical acumen.[27]

However, although it is in his *The Making of the English Working Class* that Thompson makes the most explicit reference to theatre *per se*, the issue of theatricality in the class politics of the Georgian period is one to which he repeatedly returns, constantly refining the reference. Indeed, in his later essay, 'The Patricians and the Plebs', it is as if theatricality increasingly becomes the presiding preoccupation in his attempt to understand and explain class relations in this history.[28] After oscillating over the question of how far plebeian culture was reactive or how far it formed a distinctive culture of its own, Thompson settles for a 'patrician/plebs equilibrium', in which 'cultural hegemony' is produced out of a dialectic between the two class forces. Any explanation of class relations which asserts simple dominance by either the paternalism of Whig aristocrats or the rise of the middle class fails to allow for the complexity of this dialectic, which is enacted through symbolism: 'The reciprocity of these relations (between 'patricians and plebeians') underlies the importance of the symbolic expressions of hegemony and of protest in the eighteenth century. That is why I have directed so much attention to the notion of theatre.'[29] Of course, it is not Thompson's purpose to define theatre itself, as class relations are the focus of the discussion, but his analysis leads in the direction of an understanding of theatre as not only a metaphor, but also a reality in terms of a 'contest for symbolic authority' in this history:

There is a sense in which rulers and crowd needed each other, watched each other, performed theatre and countertheatre to each other's auditorium,

---

[27] Thompson, *The Making of the English Working Class*, preface.
[28] Thompson, 'The Patricians and the Plebs', *Customs in Common*, 19–96.
[29] Ibid.

moderated each other's political behaviour. This is a more active and reciprocal relationship than the one normally brought to mind under the formula 'paternalism and deference'. [30]

Theatre audiences brought plebeians and patricians together in the *actual* space of theatre as well as in the symbolic space of 'the theatre of cultural hegemony', in this mutual influence on political behaviour. There is now much evidence to confirm that theatre audiences, both in London and the provinces, were constituted from members of all classes of society. [31] Theatre architecture, together with the hierarchy of ticket prices charged by theatre managers (at a time when they were highly conscious of economic motives [32]), undoubtedly ensured elements of segregation within the physical space of the theatre itself, but there was also powerful coexistence of the classes, articulated as audience response.

Certainly, there are accounts of factionalism within audience, not just in relation to overt disruption (as in the case of the Old Price riots [33]), but also as a systematic form of response. One such instance is that described by Mary Darby Robinson, some of whose theatrical work was scrutinized earlier. [34] Her autobiographical account of the reception of one of her own plays includes a description of sections of the audience responding noisily to each other as well as to events on the stage.

However, whilst such instances could be interpreted in terms of the different and distinct interests of audience members and groups, they can equally be explained in terms of a certain kind of dialectic, inspired by and protected in the theatre, affording a powerful testimony to the licence afforded by theatre to its audience. Georgian theatre presented its audiences with the possibility of an implied, sometimes overt, political

[30] Thompson, 'The Patricians and the Plebs', *Customs in Common*, 19–96.

[31] I use the word provinces with some unease, believing that critics tend to use it somewhat dismissively, and certainly in too sweeping an aggregation, which I probably also do here. See Sybil Rosenfeld, 'The Georgian Theatre of Richmond Yorkshire and its Circuit' (Society for Theatre Research, London, 1984) for more on Yorkshire audiences of the time (not that Yorkshire people would have regarded themselves as 'provincial', if present-day Yorkshire provides a yardstick—I speak from experience).

[32] Baer, *Theatre and Disorder*, develops arguments about theatre economics usefully, as does Donkin, *Getting into the Act*.

[33] See Baer, *Theatre and Disorder* for a full thesis about the OP riots and their significance to Georgian London. The rioters, at Covent Garden, were responding to attempts by managers to raise ticket prices, following expensive rebuilding of the theatre after a fire in 1808; also, Hadley, *Melodramatic Tactics*.

[34] See Ch. 5.

argument, both within the audience and in relation to performance.[35] Audience response derived much energy and vitality from its ability to generate confident exchange across the classes (and, importantly, sexes) in a relatively protected space.[36]

Although this history predates the advent of the Blue Book and other such governmental records, particularly that of the census returns, making it impossible to know what the precise statistics of the case are, it is clear that working people were extensively involved in political agitation, with its new forms of mass petitioning and mobilization to hear speakers and protest.[37] It is also clear that a proportion of those rallying to hear speakers like Thomas Clarkson (who travelled hundreds of miles to advocate the abolition of slavery[38]), signing up in large numbers to abolition petitions, agitating for reform of the parliamentary franchise, and putting their energies into a range of causes, were also members of theatre audiences. Political activists and agitators were theatre activists.[39] Theatre audiences were political audiences.

William Hazlitt wrote that 'the people are *not* apt . . . to volunteer a rebellion for the theatrical éclat of the thing', and his very assertion of that negative highlights the relationship between rebellion and theatre. Working people gave voice to rebelliousness in theatre, as well as in public protest, and theatre provided a forum for the representation of

---

[35] See my Prologue for questions about the significance of theatre legislation in restricting the expression of political ideas at this time. My contention is that censorship laws never really succeeded in stifling politics in theatres, and there is some question about whether their antiquated character, in this period, and the confused state of their implementation, are characteristics which reveal a lack of firm commitment to any serious control over the expression of political ideas in theatres. Stephens, *The Censorship of English Drama*, ch. 3, records Robert Southey on the issue of censorship seeing the need for it in terms of securing domestic peace and public tranquillity. In the light of Southey's perception, it is interesting to note Shearer West, *The Image of the Actor: Verbal and Visual Representation in the Age of Garrick and Kemble* (Pinder Publishers, London, 1991), ch. 1, airing the possibility that it is suggested by evidence from the earlier part of the 18th c. that if anyone caused disturbance at the theatre, it was members of the aristocracy, as 'fine gentlemen's attendance at the theatre (was) purely gratuitous, whereas the less pretentious sectors of the audience' were more likely to be 'seduced by the play's power'!

[36] See Ch. 5 for a discussion of women's presence in the audience—obviously controversial, at least for critics like William Hazlitt.

[37] Drescher, *Capitalism and Antislavery.* See Ch. 2 for detailed reference to arguments about mass mobilization.

[38] See Ch. 2 for more on this subject.

[39] See Baer, *Theatre and Disorder*, for a slightly different, but related, take on 'activist audiences'.

and participation in political opposition and commitment.[40] 'The dangerous ebullience of the audience' in the theatre, about which Thompson is uneasy in his early work, is also that ebullience of the political agitator and the political crowd which he later celebrates as part of a necessary rebelliousness, even where, and perhaps because, such people are found dangerous by the State.[41]

There are two points of emphasis important for my account which have attracted much critical attention concerning Thompson himself. One is the issue of how far class relations in late Georgian Britain can be solidly categorized and named, as against how far they remained fluid. The other is about the significance of culture and cultural hegemony, as the contexts of theatre, in relation to class formations and political dynamic.

On the former issue, there is now a wide debate, sometimes critical of Thompson's position, about how far class taxonomies can be imposed on a history which predates the industrial factory system.[42] This has particular interest for an understanding of theatre audience. To characterize

[40] Thompson, *The Making of the English Working Class*, cites Hazlitt on the title-page of his introduction to Part Three.

[41] Ibid., ch. 16. In *Customs in Common*, ch. 4, Thompson refines his argument about the crowd and about rebelliousness in terms of 'moral economy'.

[42] Harvey J. Kaye and Keith McClelland (eds.), *E. P. Thompson, Critical Perspectives* (Polity Press, Cambridge, 1990) contains a number of pertinent essays, including Geoff Eley, 'Edward Thompson, Social History and Political Culture: The Making of a Working-Class Public, 1780–1850', 12–49. Eley's premise is that historians should theorize more 'about state formation and political development', and that this has been Thompson's strength. Eley also acknowledges many of Thompson's qualities, including his distinctive contribution to the discussion of the 18th c., but appears to fault Thompson for his failure to find that 'full-blooded socialism' which would give evidence of a 'proper' working class in the 1790s. Eley's search, like that of Thompson, is for class-consciousness in the pre-Victorian period, but he can only find such consciousness in classification itself, i.e. in imposing a class category which belongs to a later period, and therefore is uneasy with Thompson's more fluid categories. Despite this, he registers that 'representation becomes the key question' and hits the mark with his speculation that 'although Thompson shows the existence of a rich and developing radical culture, the unifying power of that radical culture (its impact on the consciousness of the class as a whole) awaits proper demonstration.' See Gregor McLennan, 'E. P. Thompson and the Discipline of Historical Context', in Richard Johnson *et al.* (eds.), *Making Histories: Studies in History-Writing and Politics* (Centre for Contemporary Cultural Studies, Hutchinson, London, 1982) for a particularly rich essay on Thompson. McLennan argues that in Thompson's later work, the term 'struggle' gains ascendancy over 'class', and that this is reflected in his concepts and methodology. The analysis that 'class struggle (occurs) from above as well as from below' would seem particularly applicable to the 18th c.

audience response to theatre as plebeian, or to distinguish a plebeian aesthetic response to theatre from that of a member of the aristocracy or middle class, is to run the risk of being highly reductive about the sophistications and complexities of audience reception and reaction. To explain response to plays in terms of an imposed class position, contrasting a reaction from, say, a member of the aristocracy in the expensive seats, with that of a plebeian, bawling and perhaps brawling in 'the gods', is both to classify spuriously (and perhaps erroneously) and to underestimate the capacity of audience to generate dialogue and dialectic, to override the individual response and to defy classification. If the confident class categories of the later period, by which time it is possible that stratifications in terms of social class did become more literal in relation to dramatic genres and theatrical taste, do not apply in the case of the economic and political conditions of late Georgian Britain, neither do they apply in the case of theatre.[43]

On the question of culture and cultural hegemony, there has been much discussion of Thompson's work.[44] Any objection here, though, would not be the frequent one to culturalism *per se*, but to the extent to which Thompson continues, even if less so in his later work, to operate a double standard over culture and class. Whilst he is appropriately renowned for attributing human agency to the plebeian subject, he is much less likely to attribute to them a capacity for good taste. In other words, there remains something of an élitist reflex to the aesthetic category of culture, as against the egalitarian momentum informing class analysis.[45] Even in his later work, there is a slight sense that the cultural

[43] See Kathleen Wilson, *The Sense of the People: Politics, Culture and Imperialism in England, 1715–1785* (Cambridge University Press, Cambridge, 1995) for details of audiences in the earlier history. I do not wish to imply, in my own analysis, that the 18th-c. British élite did not generate its own exclusive audiences. It is circumstances where it did not do so that are, of course, my concern.

[44] Robert Gray, 'History, Marxism and Theory', in Kaye and McClelland (eds.), *E. P. Thompson, Critical Perspectives* raises important questions about E. P. Thompson and culture. See also, McLennan, 'E. P. Thompson' on Thompson, culture, and culturalism. Thompson, in 'Custom and Culture', ch. 1, *Customs in Common* returns to a scrutiny of the term, describing it as 'clumpish', and reminding us of 'its tendency to nudge us towards over-consensual and holistic notions'. There is perhaps a problem, though, with his turn towards 'custom' in a substitution for culture, in order to discover unifying practices across the working class (the problem referred to already of attempting to discover a unity where, arguably, it does not exist).

[45] Julia Swindells and Lisa Jardine, *What's Left? Women in Culture and the Labour Movement* (Routledge, London, 1990, particularly in ch. 2, 'In a Voice Choking with Anger', trace something of the Thompsonian uncritical acceptance of culture (and

hegemony of which he writes in the eighteenth century involves an inevitable hierarchy, of the Whig polite culture over the plebeian impolite one, which he does not apply in the case of class *per se*. That imposition of class as a fixed category which is avoided by Thompson to the perplexity of some of his critics, is apparently more difficult to escape in relation to culture. Robert Gray makes the case neatly in finding a problem with a particular aspect of *The Making of the English Working Class*: 'I would, however, draw attention to a tendency to treat culture and values as constitutive of polarized worldviews, linked to opposing classes.'[46]

Nevertheless, Thompson's continuing insistence on culture as an important category of class struggle and of historical materialism is very important, particularly to an understanding of theatre.[47] His increasing attachment to theatricality in the analysis of eighteenth- and early nineteenth-century class politics, together with his attempt to register what its symbolic importance was in terms of class equilibrium, is full of potential illumination. What E. P. Thompson had seen was that theatricality was a central symbolic term in the enactments carried out by rulers and ruled in this history. What Thompson had perhaps not seen was that this was operating in more than the symbolic arena; that class relations were being newly forged within the theatres themselves, in ways which were crucial in deciding the character of the British nation, giving a language and form to political as well as dramatic performance and engagement.

## Humanitarian Sensibility

Part of the project, then, in the recent endeavour to restore theatre audiences and performances to a proper, considered place in the critical

---

particularly literature), as against Raymond Williams's lifetime attempt to politicize the term in the interests of class equality; on the subject of Thompson's response to Thomas Hardy's *Jude the Obscure*, 'Thompson shows in his striving to build history around "experience" a passion for Jude and Sue, a passion for literature which shows him deep in that version of culture which Williams is striving to problematize'.

[46] Gray, 'History, Marxism and Theory'.

[47] Gregor McLennan and Ellen Meiksins Wood, 'Falling through the Cracks: E. P. Thompson and the Debate on Base and Superstructure', in Kaye and McClelland (eds.), *E. P. Thompson, Critical Perspectives*, 125–52; Meiksins Wood reclaims Thompson for historical materialism, arguing with persuasive panache that 'an appreciation of ideology and culture' is completely compatible with this and that 'the base/superstructure metaphor has always been more trouble than it is worth'.

panoply, is to find ways of understanding theatre audiences and political agitation which avoid certain rather rigid preconceptions about social and cultural classification, more appropriate, if appropriate at all, to a viewing of a later history. This is not to say, of course, that any rescue operation of the period 1789 to 1833 should carry itself to the opposite pole of claiming the fluidities of class and culture, and the accompanying possibilities of dialectic and reciprocity, as politically liberating *per se*. It is undoubtedly the case that late eighteenth-century Britain was minutely stratified in terms of the holding of property, particularly land, of occupational and social position, and above all, political power.[48] Any amount of cultural hegemony would not have been sufficient to free that epoch of history from class oppressions, tensions, and prejudices (and those of race and gender), however far my thesis about theatre is reliant on an acceptance of the materiality of culture, of the important construction that 'Culture . . . is not epiphenomenal, but constitutive of social relations themselves'.[49]

However, what does appear to be the case with theatre audiences is that hierarchy and differential status were contested, which contributed to the forging of a libertarian rhetoric and ideology. Two rather classic arguments could apply here. First, and continuing to build on the Thompsonian analogy, there is the possibility that this was about the making of the English working class inside the theatre as well as outside it, the dialectics of drama contributing to the process of constituting

[48] See Barrell, *The Political Theory of Painting*, for particular force and clarity over the more general case, now made widely, about 18th-c. hierarchy. Clive Barker, 'A Theatre for the People', in Kenneth Richards and Peter Thomson (eds.), *Nineteenth Century British Theatre* (Methuen, London, 1971) is useful on the subject of how to theorize the historical context of theatre.

[49] Gray, 'History, Marxism and Theory'. There has been much discussion of the relations of culture to materialism and of whether E. P. Thompson's attachment to culture enhances or undermines his credentials as a historical materialist. Raymond Williams, *Culture and Society 1780–1950* (Penguin, Harmondsworth, 1958) represents the most obvious and sustained thesis about 'culture' as a newly explored category in which relations to class and to economics become decisive in the definition of the term. However, the precise relationship of culture to materialism remains interestingly unresolved, despite the many debates about 'base and superstructure' and about language, central in the domain of culture, as a determining category. I suppose my rather flagrant acknowledgement, in the main text here, that the forces of cultural hegemony were not sufficient to counterbalance other determinants of political power is a qualified concession to economic determinism. Nick Stevenson, *Culture, Ideology and Socialism: Raymond Williams and E. P. Thompson* (Avebury, Aldershot, 1995) for analytical engagement with both Thompson and Williams.

class consciousness.[50] Second, there is the argument that conflict within theatres and theatrical spaces *contained* class rebellion and maintained the *status quo* at a time in British history when there was much anxiety about revolutionary attitudes and forces.[51]

Nevertheless, to insist either on an argument about class formation or about the maintenance of the political *status quo* is to be reductive, both about historical hermeneutic and about the character of theatrical constituency and political movement in this era. Rather, there is evidence of theatre generating, through the process of dialectical exchange across theatre audience as well as between audience and performance, that which has been identified as a particular kind of humanitarian sensibility, necessary to the conception of political possibility characterizing and crossing the reforming movements of the time. (Again, it is arguably the later history, from the 1830s, after the concessions of the Reform and Emancipation Acts, and with high capitalism and the hardening of imperialism, which sees Victorian ideology bringing down the curtain on social homogeneity, reinventing segregation and separated compartments, both in social class and dramatic genres.)

Theatre audiences generated a set of responses which could cross classes, could be articulated publicly in sets of exchanges between members from different class positions across the aristocratic–plebeian continuum, and between women and men. Theatre was a rare, if not unique forum, in contrast to, say, Parliament, which was exclusively male and largely aristocratic. Such a set of exchanges was impossible in Parliament, and perhaps anywhere in society except theatre.[52] Most

---

[50] See Thompson, *The Making of the English Working Class*, for the argument about the making of the English working class, obviously.

[51] Baer, *Theatre and Disorder*, puts forward a version of this theory in his introductory chapter.

[52] John Lucas, at a seminar at Nottingham Trent University, 1998, raised the significant question of whether the Church might qualify in these terms. It cannot be my focus here, but questions of the relationship between theology and theatricality are important in the period and are under scrutiny. For the more general case of the relationship of theology, particularly the dissenting sects (Baptists, Quakers, Unitarians) to popular radicalism, see Gerard McCann, *Theory and History: The Political Thought of E. P. Thompson* (Ashgate, Aldershot, 1997), ch. 3. Also, Boyd Hilton, *The Age of Atonement: The Influence of Evangelicalism on Social and Economic Thought, 1795–1865* (Clarendon Press, Oxford, 1988) for the influence of dissenting religions on politics. I broadly hold to Thompson's position (outlined by Gerard McCann), though, that religion, however dissenting, is often compromised by its chiliastic dimension and, in my view, by its relation to existing social and political hierarchies (most obviously in the domain of gender).

important, audience members were not constrained by status-consciousness; rather, debate appears to have been fuelled by differences in social status.[53] An analysis of theatrical language and performance demonstrates that the crucial development was of a *social* consciousness, influenced by, but not explained away in terms of class-consciousness, informed by a diversity of class, gender, and racial interests, and able to be articulated to agitation for constitutional and humanitarian reform. This development was instrumental in producing the homogeneity of humanitarianism, with audiences arriving at a common sensibility out of the arena of contention.

This argument, about the homogenizing propensities of a strategy working across the classes in dialectical relation, can be set alongside, but also in distinction to, the one which claims that it was new forms of capitalist ideology, created out of the fluidity of mercantilism and the market, which produced the conditions for humanitarianism. Such theories tend to confer a monopoly of humanitarian feelings on the middle class, often commenting on the bourgeois origins of social and political reformers in the period. However, this begs a lot of questions about the diversity of audiences for social and political reform outside the theatre as well as inside it. One such commentator, Thomas Haskell, asks us to look away from a class analysis to the conditions of the market economy, where, he argues, the explanation of the source of a new cognitive style resides. He claims that the market fostered 'a certain way of perceiving human relations', because of its encouragement of new 'forms of life'.[54] In the same volume, John Ashworth responds with a critique of Haskell, arguing for the family as the key conceptual tool in understanding late eighteenth-century humanitarianism.[55] However, both explanations are in danger of failing to do justice not only to working

---

[53] There is a tension, to which I have already made indirect reference, in the argument that class-consciousness was in the making between 1789 and 1833, reflected in the tendency to impose a category (working class) and possibly force a separation (in imposing taxonomies) in the very process of arguing for fluidity and interaction between class forces. As well as Geoff Eley and Kate Soper in Kaye and McClelland (eds.), *E. P. Thompson, Critical Perspectives*, see Bryan D. Palmer, *E. P. Thompson: Objections and Oppositions* (Verso, London, 1994) and Gerard McCann, *Theory and History*, on the subject of class-consciousness and human agency in Thompson.

[54] Thomas L. Haskell, 'Capitalism and the Origins of the Humanitarian Sensibility', in Bender (ed.), *The Antislavery Debate*.

[55] John Ashworth, 'The Relationship between Capitalism and Humanitarianism', in Bender, ibid.

people's commitment to political radicalism, aknowledged by another contributor to the debate, David Brion Davis, but also to the production of a social consciousness which crossed classes—a concept of society forged out of cultural materialism, via the expression of difference, not merely out of bourgeois self-interest or the functions of the market.[56] Theatre was formative in producing this group consciousness, which was central to creating the 'moral actors' who could carry forward the cause of humanitarian reform.[57]

Another strategy in relation to crediting the middle class and the aristocracy with a monopoly on humanitarian sensibility is to do so whilst ironizing their motives.[58] 'The hustings, sporting spectacles, theatres, resorts' brought together the aristocrats and 'the mob', and 'the beauty of philanthropy lay in enhancing within the elite the superiority of their own patrician sensibility'.[59] This is nicely cryptic about the toffs, but does not really explain what share working people had in the enterprise, and whether a desire for humanitarian sensibility rubbed off on *them* from the association of plebeians with patricians; neither does it account for that reciprocity in relations between plebeians and patricians of which E. P. Thompson is persuaded. (However, the analysis does give further evidence of the mixed-class character of theatre audiences.) The same commentary wittily depicts the middle class with 'its pocket in the cultural preserves of the traditional elite', but again overlooks the part played by working people in supporting 'English bourgeois sentimental drama'. The spirit or ideology representing humanitarian sensibility in the theatres can, anyway, be distinguished from both the philanthropy of the aristocracy and the liberalism of the middle class, in that the open acknowledgement of class conflict and diversity of class interest appears to have been not only central, but also necessary to it.

Another claim, specifically about theatre, is that any unified or unifying sensibility, or any homogeneity of audience response, arose,

[56] David Brion Davis, 'The Problem of Slavery in the Age of Revolution', in Bender, ibid. argues that there were strong connections between 'domestic suffering' in Britain and a sympathetic recognition of the plight of the slaves—'the cult of sensibility encouraged sympathy for individual misfortune'.
[57] Haskell, ibid. 'Free moral actors' are some of the terms coined in the debate by Haskell in his response to David Brion Davis.
[58] Roy Porter, 'The Enlightenment in England', in Porter and Mikulas Teich (eds.), *The Enlightenment in National Context* (Cambridge University Press, Cambridge, 1981).
[59] Porter, ibid.

not from pure motives, but from a shared commitment to the base forces of a xenophobic nationalism. Although there are many instances of the national anthem and other nationalistic songs being sung in the theatre, this is an inadequate, at best a very partial explanation. It may well be that the language and form of contemporary drama, and politics, relied on a certain kind of Englishness, articulated fairly graphically, and rather gender-exclusively, in the idea of 'the freeborn Englishman', but it appears even more the case that theatrical interaction provided a conflictual arena, in which the language of rights and the advocacy of freedom played across audience, performer, and playwright.[60] In other words, Englishness was a metaphor for constitutional rights and political freedom, maintained against oppressive regimes at home and elsewhere, particularly the *ancien régime* in pre-Revolutionary France, as much as on behalf of xenophobic attitudes in Britain.[61]

This form of nationalism was not necessarily incompatible, either, with criticism of colonialism, although the materiality of colonial domination by England, along with Holland the most successful trading nation in the world and a major colonial power, should not be underestimated. Colonialism, dependent on a colonizing 'us' and a colonized 'them', lends itself to a particular kind of dramatic conception and public performance; and to a process of dialectic exchange as in the case of class politics.[62] Eighteenth-century black culture represented not only the opposite pole to the supposed 'virtues and deficits of British civilisation', but also a stage metaphor, which could capitalize on audience fascination for the unexplained and the undiscovered, or more accurately, the supposedly discovered, but inadequately understood.[63]

---

[60] Baer, *Theatre and Disorder*, documents how the OP riots were led, in some respects, by members of the London Corresponding Society, founded by Thomas Hardy and others to campaign for an extension of the parliamentary franchise (more on this in Ch. 1).

[61] Russell, *The Theatres of War*, in her thesis that previous accounts of the military history of the period have been skewed, argues persuasively that the character of the patriot changed. During most of the time that British rule extended to cover 26 per cent. of the world's population, Britain was at war with France (1793–1815, apart from a brief respite). Russell argues that radical political opposition in Britain was increasingly 'couched in terms of a critique of war'.

[62] Bratton in her introduction to *Acts of Supremacy*.

[63] Michael Pickering, ch. 5, in Bratton (ed.), ibid., makes the case about 'the images of blacks portrayed in song and stage act . . . as conceptual opposites of what whites themselves conceived'.

Both as a visual disturbance, and as a verbal challenge, playwrights like Colman and Morton put this to theatrical use. Melodrama lent itself to the project, as did comedy, with its ability to capitalize on the element of visual and verbal novelty and surprise.[64]

The important argument about colonialism, though, is the one about the extent to which a humanitarian attitude involving fierce opposition to slavery also produced a critique of certain kinds of English nationalism, particularly by highlighting that which should constitute the attitude of the British citizen, as accountable democratic subject, to mercantilism.[65] The merchant and the colonizer, however far they were images of Britain's economic success, were also perceived as the representatives of real and potential exploitation, with Britain being parasitic on the wealth and property of other nations. The ethics of this were not easily accommodated to a spirit of democratic reform and accountability at home. The image of John Bull carried with it this element of moral conscience and political responsibility, as much as the xenophobic attitudes already identified. In the theatre, John Bull was witness and also, increasingly self-critic, with the moral topography of the British citizen explored through him.[66]

## The Moral Actor

It is not only, though, in relation to the constitution of audience and the dialectics of audience response that the issue of humanitarian

---

[64] Heidi J. Holder, ch. 3, in Bratton (ed.), ibid., explores why melodrama was useful to the colonial project.

[65] Drescher, *Capitalism and Antislavery*, addresses this issue (see Ch. 2); for more general reference to questions of race in the Enlightenment, see Peter Hulme and Ludmilla Jordanova (eds.), *The Enlightenment and its Shadows* (Routledge, London, 1990) and Peter Hulme and Neil L. Whitehead (eds.), *Wild Majesty: Encounters with Caribs from Columbus to the Present Day* (Clarendon Press, Oxford, 1992). Edward Kamau Brathwaite, 'A Post-Cautionary Tale of the Helen of Our Wars', *Wasafiri*, 22 (Autumn 1995), engages powerfully and entertainingly (in a number of different typographic styles and fonts!) with Peter Hulme's response to some aspects of Caribbean literature and some criticisms of Brathwaite's work. Brathwaite accuses Hulme of not having read his work, arguing that 'in much/most of this "post-colonial" writing, we hear about the natives but we still don't hear them' (70). This should prompt us to read Brathwaite's extensive range of poetry and prose, perhaps starting with *The Development of Creole Society in Jamaica 1770–1820* (Clarendon Press, Oxford, 1971).

[66] Baer, *Theatre and Disorder*, comments on John Bull as audience, as does the playwright Charles Dibdin. We have seen how other playwrights, namely W. T. Moncrieff and George Colman the Younger, make use of the icon.

sensibility arises. Both class-consciousness and humanitarian sensibility are terms which presuppose a relationship between an individual and a group, with the individual as a member of both a social class and the human species. (Typically, consciousness operates in the rational domain, sensibility in the affective or aesthetic, if one accepts that a distinction between the two domains can be usefully made.[67])

The historiography of 'the crowd' in the eighteenth century frequently encounters a dilemma over the relations between individual and group which has consequences for both class analysis and the aesthetic domain of culture.[68] This revisits the argument about how historians have shaped the category of 'the plebeian' and how far they have been prepared to credit 'the plebeian' as an individual with both a consciousness and an aesthetic ability. As we have seen, there are shades of unwillingness to register aesthetic potential, and even rationality, in the domain of the plebeian consciousness.[69] Moreover, theorizing the case in terms of the concept of 'the crowd' already implies an emphasis on the group which appears to subsume the individual plebeian consciousness to the amorphous mass.

There is an important argument here which relates to that concept

---

[67] There has, of course, been much debate about the Enlightenment duality of sense and sensibility. The other comment worth making, in relation to terminology, is that class-consciousness is nearly always applied to the working class, as distinct from, say, the aristocracy. This conveys a significant betrayal of doubt over whether the workers have a consciousness to bring to bear on class or anything else (i.e. the common élitist assumptions in operation).

[68] Thompson, *Customs in Common*, is again the most useful example in his chapter, 'The Moral Economy of the English Crowd in the Eighteenth Century'.

[69] Ibid. It would be too harsh to say that Thompson suffers from the least 'unwillingness'. It is rather that there is inadvertent slippage over the question of rationality, as in his analysis of 'the moral economy of the crowd'; 'One is confronted by a complex of rational analysis, prejudice, and traditional patterns of response to dearth' (207). There is just a slight suggestion in this that rational analysis is contingent. Something similar happens when he is assessing the contribution of women to food riots: 'It is probable that the women most frequently precipitated the spontaneous actions. But other actions were more carefully prepared' (234). However, in the following chapter, 'The Moral Economy Reviewed', Thompson conducts a lengthy, moving, and extremely powerful analysis of women's contribution to food riots, arguing that 'riot is usually a rational response'. (In the light of this analysis, I seek to align myself with Thompson's feminism as against that of other male commentators, one of whom he accuses of adopting 'the fashionable ploy in the Western academy of offering oneself as more-feminist-than-thou'! (314)). Thompson ventures into the same difficult territory of whether class or political consciousness can be separated from language by referring to a 'plebeian "discourse"' which is 'almost beneath the level of articulacy' (page 350). However, he does so on behalf of 'solidarities so deeply assumed that they were almost nameless'.

identified earlier, via Thomas Haskell, of the moral actor. As with humanitarian sensibility, there has been a tendency to confer any individual ability to act morally, to be a moral actor, on members of the emerging middle class.[70] However, as the plebeian–patrician dialectic was at work in audience, so the concept of the moral actor transcended the imposition of simplistic class categories. The context of theatricality lent to politics not only a dialectical audience process, but also an individual model of enactment, from out of which the role of the moral actor was generated and could be explored. The moral actor as a philosophical concept is thus translated into and produced out of a theatrical role. Part of what produced the intense and generative relationship between politics and theatre was that the concept of the moral actor had the capacity not only to cross the boundary between classes and between political and theatrical performance, but also to offer an exploratory mode of enactment in doing so.[71]

In considering theatricality, there is a danger, as there is in analysing the class system at this time, of imposing inappropriate categories and boundaries on an interpretation of late Georgian performance and performance values, particularly in relation to the role of the actor. One misconception which may arise, for instance, concerns understanding the significance of the actor's prominence. One modern commentator sees the emphasis on the performer in the Georgian period as symptomatic of the demoralized state of theatre at that time.[72] However, eighteenth-century contemporaries, like William Hazlitt, articulated good grounds for giving more significance to the

[70] Dror Wahrman, *Imagining the Middle Class: The Political Representation of Class in Britain, 1780–1840* (Cambridge University Press, Cambridge, 1995) for more on the middle class in this history, to which, some would argue, I give too little attention.

[71] By this, which is a little vaguely formulated, I mean that in the written texts of autobiography and in the dramatic processes of characterization, we can witness new forms of construction of selfhood in process. In relation to slave autobiographies, Sandiford, *Measuring the Moment*, cited in Ch. 2, captures something of what I am trying to say, 'the struggle to preserve the self in the face of repression and denial was dramatized on a different stage and in a different mode' (150). The moral actor was generated out of this struggle and out of the sympathetic witnessing of it. There is much theoretical work on autobiography, too extensive to reference here, which pays testimony to 'the struggle to preserve the self'. The notebooks initiated by Liz Stanley as editor and produced under the auspices of the British Sociological Association Auto/Biography Study Group, form an excellent starting-point; see also my edited collection, *The Uses of Autobiography* (Taylor & Francis, London, 1995), with particular reference to the writing of Sarah Meer.

[72] Kinnaird, *William Hazlitt*, ch. 5.

actor than to the playwright. 'When an author dies, it is no matter, for his works remain. When a great actor dies, there is a void produced in society, a gap which requires to be filled up.'[73] Greater attention to the playwright than the actor came later, in part, with those forces of social and political alienation which resulted in the privileging of some forms of creative act at the expense of others. In an age of massively expanding production of print, it was no accident that the writer should eventually come to seem more important than the performer or the producer of drama.[74]

Georgian theatre appears to have carried a much more fluid understanding of the actor than in the theatre of the later nineteenth century. Moreover, the distinction between a performer and a member of the audience was less marked than in later history. Audiences also acted, and stage actors were often witnesses to audience performance, as were other members of the audience.[75] Enactment was not reified, as an aspect of theatre specialism, but was part of the social process, constitutive of individual sensibility and social relations.

However, whilst Hazlitt and others were able to celebrate the dominance of the actor unproblematically, Denis Diderot, from a previous generation of philosophers and commentators on the stage, had anticipated a difficulty over the role of the moral actor. Usefully for the more general discussion here, Diderot identified the problem in relation to that of sensibility.[76] What appears to trouble him is that those expectations

---

73 William Hazlitt, 'The English Stage', in William Archer and Robert W. Lowe (eds.), *Dramatic Essays* (Walter Scott, London, 1895), 144–54.

74 Williams, *Culture and Society, 1780–1950*, 1961 ed. on the subject of specialism vis-à-vis artistic production, particularly ch. 2, 'The Romantic Artist': 'The emphasis on a general common humanity was evidently necessary in a period in which a new kind of society was coming to think of man as merely a specialized instrument of production.'

75 See Ellen Donkin, 'Mrs. Siddons Looks Back in Anger: Feminist Historiography for Eighteenth-Century British Theater', in Reinelt and Roach (eds.), *Critical Theory and Performance*, for a powerful account of audience: 'Eighteenth-century audiences can in no sense be thought of as passive. They had the power to determine the survival of both plays and performers. They were far more powerful than the press. Based on audience response, a theater manager would decide from night to night whether to run the show or rotate it out of the repertory. These audiences were unconstrained in registering their approval or disapproval of any aspect of performance. I call them "shouting" audiences' (279). Also, Davis, *Actresses as Working Women*, writes about the continuity into the later period of women as spectacle within audience.

76 D. Diderot, 'Paradoxe sur le Comédien', in *Diderot's Writings on the Theatre*, ed. F. C. Green (Cambridge University Press, Cambridge, 1936), 249–317. The article was written in the 1770s, but was not published until 1830. 'Ne prononcez-vous pas nettement que la sensibilité vraie et la sensibilité jouée sont deux choses fort differentes?'

emerging in the Enlightenment, of creating a moral actor in the public sphere characterized by a particular sensibility, were being misapplied to the stage performer. In his article, 'Paradoxe sur le comédien', he urges his readers to distinguish between 'the man of sensibility' who 'obeys natural impulses and expresses nothing but the cry from his heart', and the stage actor, who is playing a part, the skill of which involves learning 'to control or constrain his cry'.[77] In a wry comment on the exhaustions of everyday life, Diderot decries the notion that the business of performance is simply a matter of giving vent to a superior sensibility.

Does an actor not have a father, a mother, a wife, children, brothers, sisters, acquaintances, friends, a mistress? If he were gifted with that exquisite sensibility which is regarded as the chief quality of his calling, given that he's harassed as we are, and affected by a succession of troubles which sometimes dry up our emotions and sometimes tear them apart, how many days would he have left over for our amusement? Very few.[78]

He goes on to discuss how, if the role of the actor were regarded as an art, a skill and an 'honourable one', dramatists would acquire a new method which would be of moral and aesthetic benefit to 'the spirit of our nation'.[79] Diderot's analysis is useful, not only in addressing the techniques of dramatic performance, but also in scrutinizing the term sensibility. In part, his attack on sensibility as affectation is the classic one of the Enlightenment rationalist, like that of Samuel Johnson, who seeks to argue for the forces of reason, as against 'the power of feeling' to which Hazlitt and others are attached.[80] However, it can also be understood as an attempt to distinguish theatrical from other practices in the area of sensibility, and to highlight potential abuses of the role of the moral actor with implications for performance values, stage conventions, and political life.

In the late eighteenth and early nineteenth centuries, politicians

---

[77] Diderot, ibid., in translation, 'The Paradox of the Actor', 98–158.
[78] Ibid.                                                                    [79] Ibid.
[80] Robert W. Uphaus, *William Hazlitt* (Twayne Publishing, Boston, 1985), ch. 7, 'The Dramatic Imagination': 'All those attributes of the dramatic imagination—"truth of nature," emphasis on the particular and local, character as individual expression, passion as spontaneity, and the basically tacit appeal of literature—have at their foundation the conviction that the power of feeling, whose intensity Hazlitt calls "gusto," is the heart of imaginative expression.' See also, David Marshall, *The Surprising Effects of Sympathy: Marivaux, Diderot, Rousseau, and Mary Shelley* (University of Chicago Press, Chicago, 1988), on the relationship between the terms 'sensibility' and 'sympathy'. In his introduction, Marshall writes about 'the interplay of theater and sympathy'.

engaged very directly with questions of performance and performance value, under pressure from the concept of the new, moral actor, just as theatre audiences were expecting some accountability to the idea from stage actors.[81] However far the role of the actor transcended what later became heavily demarcated categories, the ways in which theatrical enactment and its accompanying performance values translated into the political sphere was significantly problematic. What Diderot's concern anticipates is that ethical and political difficulties might arise from conflating performance values across the theatrical and political domains, unless society were to be clear about the different conventions involved in 'playing a part'. There is an important differentiation to be made here over the question of accountability in relation to theatre and politics. In theatre, accountability for the role of the actor is primarily an aesthetic matter, deriving from the quality of the performance. Even where there is too much attention to performance instead of the play's meaning, this is primarily a question of balance or imbalance. In politics, however, attention to performance, to acting, can seriously occlude more significant elements of the political process, such as due representation of either the political issue or the appropriate constituency.

Performance always carries with it the possibility of deception, of mistaking enactment for conviction. Play-acting is, in itself, a suspect term if carried into the wrong domain. Stage actors can mislead an audience into believing, from a convincing performance, that the action is real. Indeed, it may be part of the legitimacy of their art to do so. However, politicians using analogous techniques to produce a convincing performance become culpable if they mislead their audience, or indeed themselves. Diderot was not averse to sensibility *per se*, but had identified the necessary distinctions: that it is not the responsibility of the stage actor or the politician to prove that they are moral actors (men of sensibility, as Diderot puts it[82]), but rather to discover and create the appropriate conventions in which to *represent* the latter faithfully, and to distinguish those conventions accordingly.

Only with a recognition of those distinct conventions can a

---

[81] Although most of his plays were published in the period immediately before the one under consideration here, Richard Brinsley Sheridan (1751–1816) is a striking example of how an attachment to the concept of the moral actor could play across political and theatrical life. Fintan O'Toole, *A Traitor's Kiss, The Life of Richard Brinsley Sheridan* (Granta, London, 1997), illuminates the issues brilliantly.

[82] His gender-exclusivity (the man of sensibility) is, unfortunately, intentional.

conscious assessment be made of what society might realistically expect not only of individuals, as moral actors in society, but also of stage actors and politicians. The implication is that there can be no simple translation of sensibility into ethical, political practice, or theatrical event, without proper and appropriate systems to represent powerful feeling, and without full recognition of the distinguishing conventions in use. In Georgian Britain William Hazlitt as drama critic, William Macready as theatre manager, and others recognized that there were very high expectations of actors, and that this was not just about charismatic individualism, but about this business of what society was expecting of the role of the moral actor, on and off the stage.[83] Actors themselves contributed to the debate, in their attempt to raise the status of their own profession. In the not too distant past, David Garrick, as performer as much as theatre manager, had argued that the stage actor had a social mission.[84] By the time that Sarah Siddons was on the stage, a greater restraint of the kind advocated by Diderot had entered into performance.[85] However, what Diderot had identified was that the invoking of sensibility, via acting, could constitute a dangerous form of misrepresentation, particularly, by implication, if misapplied by politicians.

## A Moral People

It was no doubt in part under the influence of the dramatic polemical language of the London Corresponding Society and the radical press of

---

[83] *The Diaries of William Charles Macready 1833–1851*, ed. William Toynbee (Chapman and Hall, London, 1912). Macready gives much focus to the role of the actor, sometimes inveighing against actors as fools, declaring on 23 March 1833, that he despairs of 'any good result from any combination of actors'. The intensity of his focus can also be seen in his self-criticism: he declares on one occasion that he does not act a part with 'the truth, reality and taste that would satisfy my own judgement'.

[84] Gillian Russell, 'Burke's Dagger: Theatricality, Politics and Print Culture in the 1790s', *British Journal for Eighteenth-Century Studies*, 20 (1997), 1–16, 'Garrick's collaboration with artists such as Zoffany was also designed to elevate the status of acting, which continued to be stigmatised as immoral, as a force for social good'.

[85] West, *The Image of the Actor*, ch. 3, 'Kemble's and Siddons's more restrained classicism resulted from changes not only in the acting profession, but in the very structure of London society'. See Donkin, 'Mrs Siddons Looks Back in Anger', in Reinelt and Roach (eds.), *Critical Theory and Performance*, for a feminist analysis of Siddons's contribution to the stage, particularly her capacity for shifting expectations of the behaviour of women performers: 'The audience now had the experience of being the object of a female gaze in the theater, and it created a shift in power relations . . . That power shift was . . . collectively ratified by audience reception' (285).

the early 1800s that politicians of the subsequent generation involved themselves in accounting for the relationship between the drama and reform politics. Certainly, by the 1830s, some politicians, particularly of the Whig persuasion, as we might expect, have advanced the debate. A notable commentator on the drama in the British context is Edward Bulwer-Lytton, who, as Member of Parliament for Lincoln at this moment in his career, was not only a liberal reformist instrumental in setting up the 1832 Parliamentary Select Committee on Dramatic Literature and involved in more general reforms including lobbying for the repeal of newspaper and stamp duties, but also a social commentator, novelist, and playwright.[86]

In *England and the English*, written contemporaneously with preparations for both the Dramatic Literature Bill and the 1832 Reform Act, Bulwer sets out to account for the state of the British nation, taking the measure of the social and intellectual climate of contemporary culture.[87] The drama is considered alongside political and moral philosophy and is taken very seriously, not only for its artistic dimensions, but as pivotal in engineering the conditions appropriate to a society seeking greater and more effective representation of the people.

Outlining a particular vision of the drama in the context of a more general account of the English nation at the moment of reform, Bulwer is committed to developing an argument about the stage which integrates the political into the process of dramatic performance. An example he gives is that of Athenian theatre, for whose audiences 'theatrical performance . . . was a newspaper as well as a play', arguing that if 'we banish the political from the stage', we 'deprive the stage of the most vivid of its actual sources of interest'. The absence of this integrated model of political theatre concerns him, and he looks to the recent history of the drama to produce the explanations:

In former times, there were reasons which do not exist at present—that rendered the Great the fitting heroes of the tragic stage. Kings do not awaken

---

[86] I introduce Edward Bulwer-Lytton in my Prologue, for his influential role in the Select Committee on Dramatic Literature.

[87] Bulwer-Lytton, *England and the English*. There is a further debate, for which there is not enough space here, about how far Bulwer and Burke share an interest and investment in English nationalism, as against the attempt by Paine and Wollstonecraft to cross national boundaries in the interests of universal human rights. (I refer to Edward Bulwer-Lytton as Bulwer, on the grounds that this is how he is described in Select Committee documents.)

the same awful and mysterious emotions that they once inspired—if not without the theatre, neither will they within its walls. You may go back to the old time, you may present to us an Œdipus or an Agamemnon, a Richard or a Henry; but you will not revive in us the same feelings with which their representatives were once beheld.[88]

We have seen how the death of the French king had taken on an emblematic quality in late Georgian Britain, influencing popular consciousness in terms of how monarchs are perceived and evaluated both on and off the stage.[89] For Bulwer, the monarchy no longer inspires feelings of awe and wonder, and responses to conditions outside the theatre are mirrored within the theatre. If the monarchy fails to inspire 'awful and mysterious emotions', characters representing the monarchy on the stage will also fail to do so. The Court can no longer sustain performance values as indicators of either perfection or perfidy; it has been displaced by the prospect of a moral people. There is still some tension for Bulwer around that classic Enlightenment polarity of reason and emotion, suggesting that the issue is not quite resolved.

Our reason tacitly allows that these names were clothed with associations different from those which surround modern Sovereigns. But our feelings do not obey our reason—we cannot place ourselves in the condition of those who would have felt their blood thrill as the crowned shadows moved across the stage. We cannot fill our bosoms with the emotions that sleep in the dust of our departed fathers. We gaze upon the purple of past kings with the irreverent apathy of modern times. Kings are no longer Destinies.[90]

However, the shift in appropriate sensibility—'our feelings do not obey our reason'—indicates not so much the need to go on killing the king, as the need for a new set of dramatic affiliations and a new system of dramatic representation. Bulwer's proposed alternative to the Court, to kings, queens, and their destinies, is the People, and he recommends that 'the pathos and passion of everyday life' should substitute for representations of the Court. 'And the interest they (kings and queens) excited has departed with their power. Whither?—to the people! Among the people, then, must the tragic author invoke the genius of Modern Tragedy, and learn its springs.'[91] In a hyperbolic flourish, he

---

[88]  Ibid., Book 4, ch. 5.      [89]  In Ch. 1.
[90]  Bulwer-Lytton, *England and the English*.
[91]  Ibid.

addresses his readers as this new audience, arguing that 'the power is in yourselves'. Bulwer thus attempts to address issues related to a demo-cratic theatre, turning our attention to changes in audience interest (and understanding), and to dramatic method itself, neither of which can be sustained on the basis of earlier models of theatre. The model that Bulwer constructs as the target for his challenge to archaic theatre is that of eighteenth-century, adulterated, classical drama, in which the role of the monarch was unquestioningly privileged. In the process of deconstructing this model, he argues that theatrical forms have to be seen in a historical context, and that relations between 'the mob and the king' carry different meanings over time. An unproblematic conception of 'the mob', situated within a hierarchy of rank, had been in the habit of focusing dramatic attention on the figure of the monarch at the level of characterization as well as sensibility.

Originally the personages of tragedy were rightly taken from the great. With a just propriety, Kings stalked the scenic boards; the heroine was a queen, the lover a warrior: for in those days there was no people! Emotions were supposed to be more tragic in proportion as the station of their victims was elevated. This notion was believed in common life and to represent it was therefore natural and decorous to the Stage. But we have now learnt another faith in the actual world, and to that faith, if we desire to interest the spectator, we must appeal upon the stage.[92]

Whatever reservations one might have about Bulwer's reading of history—'for in those days there was no people!'—his commitment to a new 'faith' in the modern age is clear.

How far the term 'the people' can be usefully applied to the eight-eenth century is a question which has attracted much debate, with historians substituting variously the mob, the crowd, the mass, the public, not to mention the rabble and the *hoi polloi*.[93] David Marshall's analysis of the writings of a number of eighteenth- and nineteenth-century authors has bearing on this question of how to define 'the

[92] Ibid.
[93] Thompson, *Customs in Common*, in 'Moral Economy Reviewed'; in a footnote, 'Mark Harrison reprimands me for applying the term "crowd" to what was "a very specific category of mass formation": *Crowds and History: Mass Phenomena in English Towns, 1790–1835* (Cambridge, 1988), p.13. I followed George Rude and Eric Hobsbawm in preferring the term "crowd" to the pejorative "mob" which some previous historians had used. No-one ever supposed that all crowds were riotous, although Harrison's atten-tion to their variety is helpful.'

people', by bringing the issue of theatricality into the definition. Marshall takes a particular view of society as that which is characterized by its theatrical relations, in which 'moral sentiment' (for which we could read 'sensibility') is produced out of the sympathy of the spectator for the actor. It is Marshall's account of Adam Smith which has particular bearing:

In Smith's view, our state is the theater; and an intense concern with theatricality governs both our acts and our reactions. According to Smith we either dread or desire this theatricality, depending upon the point of view of the spectators who represent the eyes of the world. We are not dealing here with an individual spectator who happens to behold our suffering; Smith pictures *a society in which we feel surrounded by an audience.* [94]

Significantly, 'the people' is used confidently by early nineteenth-century commentators, such as Bulwer and other participants in the proceedings of the 1832 Select Committee on Dramatic Literature, to imply this sense of being a member of a society surrounded by audience. [95] 'The people' thus inflects a sense of actors and audience as the characteristic relations of society, the categories operating beyond the physical space of the theatre itself.

When Georg Lukács reflects on the sociology of a later period of nineteenth-century drama, he writes that there has been a transition from a theatre built around received understandings of rank, to the nominal equity of a nineteenth-century theatre of 'the people'. [96] Lukács ranges unproblematically across the lexicon of mob, crowd, mass, and so on, frequently but not exclusively using 'the people', and consistently arguing that the emphasis in nineteenth-century drama falls upon the everyday experience of '*the mass* of humankind'. [97] This contrasts with earlier epochs, particularly that of the Renaissance, where rank, position in the social and political hierarchy, was of primary significance, and questions of personality or individualism were a *function* of that position: 'The old drama, by which we mean here primarily that of the Renaissance, was drama of great individuals, today's is that of individualism. In other

---

[94] David Marshall, *The Figure of Theater* (Columbia University Press, New York, 1986), ch. 7, 'Adam Smith and the Theatricality of Moral Sentiments' (my emphasis).

[95] See Prologue for Bulwer's contribution to the proceedings of the Select Committee.

[96] Lukács, 'The Sociology of Modern Drama' (1909) in Eric Bentley (ed.), *The Theory of the Modern Stage* (Penguin, Harmondsworth, 1968), 425–50.

[97] My own analysis applies Lukács's theories to the slightly earlier period, with the view that challenges offered by 'the new drama' originated there (my emphasis).

words, the realization of personality, its *per se* expression in life, could in no wise become a theme of earlier drama, since personality was not yet problematic.'[98]

This emphasis on individualism occurs at a number of levels, both in relation to the concept of the moral actor, as we have seen, but also very importantly in relation to playwrights' conceptions of dramatic representation, particularly of characterization. What Lukács recognizes is that the later period has to accommodate or explore an unstable conception of the individual, in which rank is under challenge for its social determinacy, and identity is problematic and contested. The people, as audience and as dramatic conception, are requiring the drama, like their political systems, to accommodate and influence a more fluid society, able to reflect and articulate conscious class difference, political conflict and change. That the new drama gives more significance to individualism than the old may appear to represent something of a paradox (the individual as against the people) but, as Lukács registers, the increasing rejection of rank and of received social hierarchy has destabilized fixed notions of identity and personality, requiring new conceptions of dramatic character as well as of the moral actor.[99]

[98] Ibid.

[99] There is then the question of how far understandings of 'the people' carry over from popular theatre to contemporary political populism. Bill Schwarz, ' "The People" in History: The Communist Party Historians' Group, 1946–56' in Centre for Contemporary Cultural Studies, *Making Histories* (1982), 85–92, comments in significant detail on the nature of the relationship between popularity and political radicalism in this history, returning us to E. P. Thompson's claims for a popular libertarian rhetoric: 'Hostility was primarily concentrated against centralized authority from a position made up of a "curious blend of parochial defensiveness, Whig theory and popular resistance".' This, Thompson emphasized, was the tradition articulated by the theorists of the Norman Yoke and, with climactic force, by Tom Paine in his rupturing of constitutional precedent. However, Schwarz airs some useful scepticism about reaching any easy consensus about attributing a radical consciousness to the people *per se*. Agreeing with Bridget Hill's criticism of the gender-specificity of 'the Freeborn Englishman' and 'the Englishman's birthright', Schwarz takes such terms, often taken up uncritically by historians, as instances of the limitations of the attempt to attribute radicalism inclusively. Schwarz's reminders are salutary and need to be accommodated in critique without rejecting what is described as Thompson's 'qualitative' commentary on the lives of the people in this history. We should also applaud Schwarz for his inclusion of reference to women historians, not only in relation to Bridget Hill, but also for the intriguing account he gives of Dona Torr earlier in this piece: 'The central personality of the Group (Communist Party Historians' Group) and instigator of its collective project appears to have been the enigmatic figure of Dona Torr, a founder member of the Communist

It is a crucial emphasis, though, that Bulwer's criticisms on behalf of 'the people' are directed as much at the political domain as they are at the drama. It is not only that 'the English' fail to find 'politics on the stage', it is also that they 'find their stage in politics'. For Bulwer, as for the manager-actor William Charles Macready, this is a problem. As Macready puts it, 'What a theatre is the House of Commons; what wretched actors and what vile parts they play!'[100] Macready and Bulwer carry over criticisms of play-acting from the British drama to the British government, and particularly the Houses of Parliament. Macready in particular articulates this as a question of poor performance, but the issue is fundamentally the same—that the body politic uses play-acting for the purposes of deception and abuse of its accountability to the people. Politics and theatre are intimately related, but we must consider, as Diderot's analysis of the actor had prompted us to do, that the performance conventions of politics and theatre need to be distinguished, both from historical ones and from each other, if their separate processes of accountability in representing the people are to operate in the interests of the social good.

## Celebratory Naturalism, with a Concluding Word on French Connections

There remains a need to account for why, however appropriate late Georgian drama was to its time, it became inappropriate to subsequent generations of theatre managers and producers. To say that the plays were topical is not so much a way of explaining the dilemma, as an invitation to explore what the character of that topicality was, what its particularities and peculiarities were. The first move, in reassessing the theatre of the period, beyond those questions of audience and critical criteria already addressed, is to register the radicalism of much of its birth and context.

It was no accident that melodrama, for instance, was born in the 1770s in a France approaching revolution ('le mélodrame' means literally a play with music). In 1775, Rousseau coined the modern usage, in relation to his *Pygmalion*, whereas earlier writers, including Diderot,

---

Party. It is difficult to find out much about her except for the over-riding fact that she was universally admired by the younger historians who gathered round her' (67).

[100] Macready, *The Diaries of William Charles Macready*, p. 11, 10 Feb. 1833.

had continued to use the term primarily to connote opera, with little distinction from that form.[101] The origins of the French melodrama run parallel with Napoleon's dislike of Parisian theatre, which forced the drama of the period on to the boulevards. A new passion for theatre had emerged in 1790s France, across all classes of society, with commentators speaking of melodrama taking the place of the pulpit, and sharing in the oratory of political associations, law courts, and the press.[102] Significantly, as a more literate drama gave way to spectacle, Guilbert Pixérécourt, in many ways the primary proponent of melodrama in France, had claimed that he was writing melodrama for those who could not read. In other words, playwrights were aware of the educational and political context in which the form was emerging, and of their social mission with it.

The first British playwright identified with the form is Thomas Holcroft, whose *Tale of Mystery*, performed at Covent Garden in 1802, following a year that Holcroft had spent in France, clearly draws on French influence.[103] The first fully Anglicized melodrama, though, is held to be J. B. Buckstone's *Luke the Labourer*, analysed earlier.[104] The latter play's political associations are clear, as is their derivation from the British context. There remains, though, an assumption that melodrama was less politically driven in Britain than in France (possibly one more instance of slippage in historical hermeneutic.[105] It may well be that it is *Victorian* Britain which witnesses the dispersal or defusing of melodrama's radical tendencies). However, early nineteenth-century melodrama in Britain

[101] Willie G. Hartog, *Guilbert de Pixérécourt* (Honoré Champion, Paris, 1913), ch. viii. Hartog traces the influence of Pixerecourt on the origins of the melodrama in France.

[102] W. D. Howarth, 'Word and Image in Pixérécourt's Melodramas: The Dramaturgy of the Strip-Cartoon' in Bradby, James, and Sharratt (eds.), *Performance and Politics in Popular Drama*, records Charles Nodier's observation about the pulpit.

[103] Hartog, *Guilbert de Pixérécourt*, whilst recording the acclaim given to *Tale of Mystery* by Genest in his *History of the English Stage*, argues that Holcroft could have been 'un peu plus franc', in acknowledging that the play was not merely under the influence of the French melodrama, but a direct translation from a play by Pixérécourt.

[104] Ch. 4. See Louis James, 'Was Jerrold's Black Ey'd Susan More Popular than Wordsworth's Lucy?' in Bradby, James, and Sharratt (eds.), *Performance and Politics in Popular Drama*, for reference to Buckstone.

[105] Kruger, *The National Stage*, does argue, despite rejecting the possibility that Georgian theatre might have disrupted the old order in Britain, that British, French, and American drama shared something of a common legacy: 'collective significance can be derived . . . from their common attempts to appropriate the political and cultural authority of the Enlightenment inheritance of national enfranchisement along with its contradictory but compelling transformation into national spectatorship' (185–7).

*does* emerge in a subversive, political context, the significant contrast with contemporary France being in relation to the more educated character of the British audience.[106] (It seems, perversely, that melodrama is more likely to be credited with radical potential if its audience is thought to be entirely illiterate.)

Michael Booth is one writer who does identify the origins of melodrama in terms of a radical, political context, arguing that it was in part inspired by such theories as those of William Godwin about the perfectability of man.[107] Booth also argues, significantly, that melodrama was created by a legislature insisting on the inclusion of music in the drama, in an attempt to disrupt political meaning, again suggesting that melodrama carried with it latent, if not palpable, political associations.[108] Early German and French melodrama, he writes, are informed by a 'fervent libertarian spirit and stress on the rights of the individual'. Interestingly, though, despite having invoked Godwin, a *British* political philosopher, even Booth seems reluctant to acknowledge the forces of libertarianism in early British melodrama.[109] This is somewhat symptomatic of the historical difficulty in registering the radicalism of British theatre at this time, even where credit to origins in libertarian thought is given.

It is only very recently that any radical potential in the genre or mode of early British melodrama has been recognized. Highly notable here is Elaine Hadley's account of melodrama in terms of 'theatricalized

---

[106] It is possible that British audiences were more literate than their French counterparts. Leigh Hunt and Edward Bulwer-Lytton concur in their testimony to the educated state of the British people. There is a discussion, touched on earlier, about how far reform movements are also committed to education, in the British context at least. The London Corresponding Society, for instance, makes explicit reference to education as part of the process of producing the right conditions for reform of the parliamentary franchise. There are, of course, further questions about how far the commitment was to autodidactism rather than formal education, and perhaps in opposition to formal education, and how far self-education can be equated with literacy.

[107] Booth, *English Melodrama*, ch. 2: melodrama was 'inspired by a view of man that regarded him as innately virtuous, endowed with a strong moral sense, and capable of perfectibility through an appeal to his emotions'.

[108] David Mayer, 'The Music of Melodrama', in Bradby, James, and Sharratt (eds.), *Performance and Politics in Popular Drama*, argues, though, that that particular strategy did not succeed, not least because music has the power to intensify rather than disrupt the meaning of the spoken word. There is more in earlier chapters about legal requirements as to the inclusion of music, etc.

[109] Booth, *English Melodrama*, ch. 2.

dissent' and the 'radical restructuring of hierarchical England'.[110] Early melodrama in Britain, she argues, helped to unite audiences of diverse rank, producing an 'inclusive public'.[111] Melodrama should not be interpreted as a 'bastard' genre, but 'as rightful heir to tragedy and comedy'.[112] It is also the mode which gives a public and exploratory form to the social context of selfhood, in a history where Romanticism, under pressure from the forces of alienation, threatens to privatize the self.[113] Theatre has this particular capacity for registering an exploration of the changing social self; as David Marshall argues, 'Theater . . . represents, creates, and responds to uncertainties about how to constitute, maintain, and represent a stable and authentic self . . . and epistemological dilemmas about knowing or being known by other people'.[114]

The retrieval of melodrama as a form worthy of serious critical consideration also connects with another argument about theatrical realism or naturalism. Realism was in part a consequence of 'the crisis in sympathetic recognition' that performances of melodrama set out to alleviate.[115] This contributes to a debate about how far realism is properly theorized in the period, and about how far late Georgian theatre is

---

[110] Hadley, *Melodramatic Tactics*, introduction, also raises important questions in relation to 'prejudicial assumptions about audience' in reviewing melodrama. Other recent commentators on melodrama include Hays and Nikolopoulou, *Melodrama*; McConachie, *Melodramatic Formations*; Jeffrey D. Mason, *Melodrama and the Myth of America* (Indiana University Press, Bloomington, 1993).

[111] Hadley, *English Melodrama*, ch. 2, 'The Old Price Wars: Melodramatizing the Public Sphere in Early-Nineteenth-Century England'.

[112] Ibid. Hadley's analysis of the Old Price riots corroborates my theory of cross-class exchange, claiming that theatre at this time was one of the few places where 'a broad cross section . . . might congregate to join in the same endeavour'. 'Words were acts of riot' in a situation where 'the public was asserting its right to political participation'. She makes direct and explicit connections between the OP riots and the 1806 Westminster election in terms of political radicals as 'critical spectators' and critical spectators as political radicals, issues mentioned earlier in my account. I agree with Hadley's analysis of melodrama as an heir to more honourable genres than it is usually credited with, although would wish to put the emphasis on comedy rather than tragedy. It is possible that what was subsequently lost from the era is a relationship between melodrama and comedy which integrated what later became two very distinct and perhaps incompatible genres.

[113] Ibid., ch. 1, 'Magyars and Michaels, Unromantic Melodrama'. Hadley puts my own formulation rather more judiciously, arguing that the romantic subject looks different when viewed via melodrama.

[114] Marshall, *The Figure of Theater*, introduction.

[115] Hadley, *English Melodrama*, ch. 1.

a precursor to late nineteenth-century naturalism.[116] Some of the most crucial definitions of naturalism, most of which derive from the later history towards the end of the nineteenth century, could be applied to the earlier period, particularly with an adjustment to the possibility that naturalism and melodrama are not incompatible. What is commonly understood as theatrical naturalism, particularly with the Lukacsian emphasis on identity in flux as against character created out of the determinants of rank, might be said to develop at least a century earlier than has been generally supposed. Raymond Williams's capacity for wide definitions is helpful here:

Naturalism . . . in its widest sense, . . . is an absorbed interest in the contemporary everyday world, and a corresponding rejection or exclusion of any supposed external design or system of values . . . The insistence on the drama of ordinary life, on the dramatic importance of people without formal rank, altered action and character in a single movement.[117]

Critical snobbery about spectacle (not literate enough) and audience (too much messy class business) has distracted critics from seeing that many late eighteenth- and early nineteenth-century playwrights were committed to this search for adequate ways of representing 'ordinary life'. The discussion of theatrical naturalism has inevitably been situated in the wider context of late nineteenth-century Europe, in relation to such proponents of *naturalisme* as Emile Zola, who gave the name to a particular set of ideas which he could apply in his pioneering, lifetime's project with the novel.[118] Zola drew forcefully on contemporary, post-Darwinian philosophies about science, about determinism, environment, and heredity, not available in the same form, of course, in the earlier history. It is interesting, though, that Zola was much more committed to depicting a range of classes and class attitudes in his fiction, than is available in that

[116] McConachie in Reinelt and Roach (eds.), *Critical Theory and Performance*, comments on the problem of 'presentism' in terms of 'unthinkingly reading current practices into the past' and over the question of how far the association of the category of production with the rise of realism is properly theorized.

[117] Raymond Williams, *Drama from Ibsen to Brecht* (1952; 1976 edn. Penguin, Harmondsworth), conclusion.

[118] See Lilian R. Furst and Peter N. Skrine, *Naturalism* (Methuen, London, 1971), particularly ch. 3, 'Groups and Theories', for a lucid, introductory account of the *naturalisme* of Zola, whose contribution to the theory, spanning some thirty years, 'comprises the 1867 preface to the second edition of *Thérèse Raquin*, *Le Roman expérimental* (1879), *Le Naturalisme au théâtre* and *Les Romanciers naturalistes*, both of 1881, and finally the 1897 *Lettre à la jeunesse*' (28).

late nineteenth-century *theatre* which has continued to be acclaimed. However far he has been criticized for his bourgeois bias, his literary project with naturalism is graphically inclusive of working-class characters and their imagined perspectives.[119] In this sense, it could be that the sort of project Zola was committed to with the novel had been foreshadowed, in some aspects, in the drama of the earlier history.

Another problem with definitions of naturalism has been the insistence on genre purity, which has produced a failure to see that naturalistic representation is compatible with other forms. The assumption, long since subjected to question by Williams and others, has been that naturalism must be imitative of life, must depend on the convincing deception that what happens on the stage is indistinguishable from what happens off it. That a naturalistic theatre could have emerged out of, or at the very least coterminously with a particular attachment to spectacle, even outrageous spectacle, is a disturbance to such critical thinking. One commentator perceives this when writing about critical responses to popular drama and the mummers' play, arguing that such theatre has been disparaged in part because it is 'imagistic' rather than naturalistic in the terms that have come to be valued.[120]

In confining the debate about theatrical naturalism to the later history, in taking critical bearings from the theatre of the 1880s forwards, to a time when the focus of dramatic action *was* on the middle classes rather exclusively, there has been a problem about the extent to which theatrical naturalism has become conflated with the bourgeoisie.

The inner history of naturalism is really this: that it developed *as a style*—a characteristic way of handling the world—in bourgeois society, but that it developed *as a form*, capable of major dramatic importance, in a period in which bourgeois society was being fundamentally criticized and rejected, mainly by people who nevertheless belonged in its world. There is then a contradiction in naturalism, but also a tension out of which the great drama of Ibsen directly came. The style assumed an understandable, recognizable, manageable everyday world; the form, while linked to this, discovered a humanity which this same world was frustrating or destroying.[121]

---

[119] Emile Zola, *L'Assommoir* (1876) is perhaps the most graphic example of Zola's attempts to write about the everyday world of the French working class, and to imagine the action from the perspective of members of that class.

[120] Green, 'Popular Drama and the Mummers' Play' in Centre for Contemporary Cultural Studies, *Performance and Politics*.

[121] Williams, *Drama from Ibsen to Brecht*, his emphasis.

Williams recognizes that the definition of the term is circumscribed by a particular kind of critique, that it is not only that the everyday world is the subject of scrutiny, but also that the dramatic perspective on that world is an adversarial one. Ordinary life is defined according to the hermetic of bourgeois self-criticism, the middle class examining itself. However, what we are seeing with the earlier history explored here is the emergence of theatrical naturalism, in some of its central tenets, before that hostile or beleaguered emphasis of the late nineteenth century. Late eighteenth- and early nineteenth-century British theatre is a theatre of celebratory naturalism, not uncritical, but before the advent of that more alienated bourgeois self-criticism, identified by Williams as dating from the 1860s. It would, perhaps be inadvisable to attempt any claim that the earlier model was as searching or as successful as the later in its modes of characterization. Rather, its virtue lies in the vitality of its discovery *of* something to celebrate, an ordinary life worthy of more dramatic consideration than the lives, ranks, and destinies of kings.

The fundamental, dramatic interest of George Colman, Elizabeth Inchbald, John Walker, Douglas Jerrold, is in this everyday world of ordinary people, not kings and queens, not the nobility (except for their vices), but the lives and perspectives of factory workers, oppressed wives and daughters, cottagers, farmers and farm labourers, domestic servants, and other representatives of daily life in Britain. This was what the British theatre world of 1789 to 1833 took as its focus, and this is what audiences constituted out of members from all classes flocked to see and share. It was not only that large parts of the audience were politically informed, it was also that they were able to take away with them from the theatre the effects of a reciprocal process; the moral audience was able to translate theatre experience into acting on behalf of the parliamentary reform movement, the abolition movement, agrarian reform, the factory movement, and the early women's movement. Strong elements of that political education and debate crucial to the glorious causes of the Georgian era had been forged in the crucible of the theatre; and the theatre was protected against intervention by the State, despite intermittent efforts at legislative control, by the internal dynamic of its own relationships between audience, actor, and writer, together with its ability to generate and question those performance conventions and values central to the project of political change.

# Epilogue

## Profane Plays and Immoral Oratorios; Or, Caprice and Plum Puddings in the Lord Chamberlain's Office

What follows is a dramatized version of the testimony given by George Colman the Younger to the 1832 Select Committee on Dramatic Literature, elements of which are analysed in my Prologue. Colman's testimony is almost entirely based on the transcript of the proceedings, the difference between this version and the original being that the questions posed by interviewers are here attributed to named persons. It is certain, however, that Sir Thomas Slingsby Duncombe was in the chair on this occasion and that all persons to which this dramatized version refers were members of the committee. The dramatic licence involved is that of allocating actual questions to named participants, attempting in the process a certain consistency of characterization, on the basis of modest biographical research into the political and professional lives of committee members. For instance, most of the questions aimed directly at clarification about legislative practices are allocated to Lord John Russell, one of the key parliamentary reformers of the era. One of the most significant participants, as I have observed on a number of occasions, is Edward Bulwer-Lytton, to whom I have attributed a range of questions about financial arrangements *vis-à-vis* the Examiner's relationship to playwrights and theatre managers. Mr Alderman Waithman claims those questions particularly directed at eliciting information about theatrical practices in the city of London, the Earl of Belfast is left the residue of questions about morality and the drama, Colonel De Lacy Evans offers cryptic comments on any reference to riot or hubbub in the theatres, and so on (with apologies for any elements of stereotype).

An abbreviated form of what follows was performed, in a rehearsed reading, in the lunchtime of a conference on the subject of theatre and politics in the age of reform, held at Homerton College, Cambridge, in

April 1997. Homerton colleagues performed as follows: John Murrell as George Colman, David Whitley as Slingsby Duncombe, Mike Bonnett as Bulwer, Peter Warner as the Earl of Belfast, John Hammond as Waithman, Philip Rundall as De Lacy Evans, and John Gray as Lord John Russell. I here offer my version of the script before it was edited for performance, itself a shortened version of the original testimony.

## A licensed version of Mr George Colman's testimony to the:

## 1832 SELECT COMMITTEE ON DRAMATIC LITERATURE

*Dramatis Personae*

Members of the Select Committee present:
Mr Thomas Slingsby Duncombe, Chair
Mr Edward Bulwer-Lytton
Earl of Belfast
Mr Alderman Waithman
Colonel De Lacy Evans
Lord John Russell
Lord Viscount Mahon: speechless

Witness:
Mr George Colman, Examiner of Plays

> DUNCOMBE *walks on without taking the chair for the moment—more of a master of ceremonies than a narrator.*

DUNCOMBE.  On the 31st May, 1832, the House of Commons ordered that a select committee be appointed to inquire into the state of the laws affecting dramatic literature. Part of the committee's brief was to examine the condition of what were commonly known as the patent theatres, Drury Lane, Covent Garden and the Haymarket, the only spaces licensed for the performance of serious drama. A committee of twenty-four members was appointed, of which five had to be present to constitute a quorum. On this occasion, there were seven members present. [*Taking Mahon from the audience*] Lord Viscount Mahon, reputed for his quiet tact and inclined to persuade committees to his view without much intervention and without provoking opposition.

WAITHMAN. Mr Alderman Waithman, self-taught man of letters, successful linen draper and one-time Lord Mayor of London.

DE LACY EVANS. Colonel De Lacy Evans, rumoured to have ordered the cavalry charge at Waterloo and to have had two horses killed beneath him; radical reformer as Member of Parliament for Rye.

RUSSELL. Lord John Russell, Whig and radical, prime mover of many leading reforms to legislation, most particularly to the suffrage, and consistently opposed to political corruption.

BELFAST. The Earl of Belfast, noted by Lord Greville, the memoirist, to have attempted, on the very day that he was sworn in as a Privy Councillor in 1830, to protect the new king, William IV, against a street mob and his own indiscretion in having strolled unchaperoned in the streets of London.

BULWER-LYTTON. Mr Edward Bulwer-Lytton, one of the younger generation of playwrights with a particular investment in questioning George Colman. Bulwer had been established as a key figure in opening the chairing of the Select Committee's proceedings.

DUNCOMBE. And, delegated to take the chair on this occasion, Mr Thomas Slingsby Duncombe, Whig and radical, active in championing the unfortunate, most particularly political prisoners, and universally acknowledged to be the best dressed man in the House of Commons. [*He takes the chair after this, and then continues*] On 20th June, the committee called as witness, Mr George Colman [*Colman takes the witness seat, clutching a paper he has written; he hesitates very slightly on seeing Bulwer; the narrator continues commentary while this is happening*] particularly famous as a playwright for his *John Bull* and *Inkle and Yarico,* two of the most popular plays of the era. By this time in his career, it was Colman's official function to act as Examiner of Plays, that is as right-hand man to the Lord Chamberlain, who had the sole privilege, conferred by Royal decree, of deciding which plays should be licensed for public performance.

[*Throughout the action, members of the Select Committee should gesture to Duncombe when they wish to speak, except on occasions of inadvertent interruption*]

DUNCOMBE. Will you have the goodness to state to the Committee what situation you hold in the Lord Chamberlain's office?

COLMAN. I hold under the Lord Chamberlain the office of Examiner of all theatrical entertainments.

DUNCOMBE. How were you appointed?

COLMAN. I was regularly sworn in. My appointment was made out in the Treasury and went through the Privy Seal, and then through the Lord Chamberlain's office.

DUNCOMBE. In what year?

COLMAN. In the year of 1824, in February 1824.

DUNCOMBE. What is the form of the oath that was administered to you?

COLMAN. The oath that is administered, or a great part of it, is the oath that is generally administered to persons holding situations in His Majesty's household. Then I am particularly sworn (after fidelity to His Majesty, as usual), to serve His Majesty faithfully as the Examiner of Plays, and to be obedient to the Lord Chamberlain.

DUNCOMBE. What do you conceive to be serving His Majesty faithfully as to the examining of plays?

COLMAN [*looking at his paper for a prompt*]. Making reference to my paper on the subject, a copy of which you should all have received . . . If I were to read that it would save the Committee a vast deal of trouble?

DUNCOMBE [*looking somewhat bemused*]. Please have the goodness to give the information *viva voce*.

COLMAN [*slightly rattled*]. The Examiner of Plays takes care that nothing should be introduced into plays which is profane or indecent, or morally or politically improper for the stage.

*Pause*

DUNCOMBE. What composition or production upon the stage do you conceive, as Examiner, you are empowered to license or empowered to prohibit?

COLMAN. I have not the power to license or to prohibit anything. I am the Examiner of Plays.

DUNCOMBE. Deputy to the Lord Chamberlain, you mean?

COLMAN. Deputy, as far as the reading of plays goes, but not as to the power of licensing or rejecting. I have no power over the theatres as reflected from him.

DUNCOMBE. But when a play is submitted to you for examination how do you proceed upon it?

COLMAN [*doggedly*]. Making reference to my paper, 'The Examiner is a very subordinate person [*a fractional pause in his reading allows Bulwer and Duncombe to exchange a raised eyebrow*], and no further interferes directly from himself with the managers than by recommending them to omit any passage palpably exceptionable, and all oaths, as well as all religious expressions and allusions too sacred for the stage. The Lord Chamberlain is the licenser, to whom the Examiner forwards an outline, and sends his opinion of the entertainment which he has officially perused, and then the Lord Chamberlain signs, or does not sign the form of licence, as he may think proper.'

DUNCOMBE. What do you consider palpably exceptionable, that is at your own discretion?

COLMAN. It must be very palpable to everybody before I should interfere. I allude to political and personal allusions, downright grossness and indecency, or anything that would be profane, which any candid man could not but say was improper, about which there could be two opinions.

*Pause*

EARL OF BELFAST. The committee have heard of your cutting out of a play the epithet 'angel' as applied to a woman?

COLMAN. Yes, because it is a woman, I grant, but it is a celestial woman. It is an allusion to the scriptural angels, which are but celestial bodies. Every man who has read his Bible understands what these are, or if he has not, I will refer him to Milton.

RUSSELL. Do you recollect the passage in which that was struck out?

COLMAN. No, I cannot charge my memory with it. I do not recollect that I struck out an angel or two, but most probably I have at some time or other.

RUSSELL. Milton's angels are not ladies?

COLMAN. No, but some scriptural angels are ladies I believe. If you will look at Johnson's *Dictionary*, he will tell you they are celestial persons, commanded by God in terrestrial business.

RUSSELL. Supposing you were to leave the word 'angel' in a play or a farce, will you state your opinion as to what effect it would have on the public mind?

COLMAN. It is impossible for me to say what effect it would have; I am not able to enter into the breasts of every body who might be in the gallery, pit, or boxes.

RUSSELL. But you must have some reason for erasing it?

COLMAN. Yes, because it alludes to a scriptural personage.

RUSSELL. Must an allusion to Scripture have an immoral effect?

COLMAN. I conceive all Scripture is much too sacred for the stage,

except in very solemn scenes indeed, and that to bring things so
sacred upon the stage becomes profane.

DE LACY EVANS (*with relish*). What would be the result of using ordinary oaths, such as Damme or anything of that sort?

COLMAN. I think it is immoral and improper, to say nothing of the
vulgarity of it in assemblies where high characters and females
congregate; I certainly think it is improper, and beyond that, I
believe you will find there are Acts of Parliament where swearing is
restrained under penalty. I think nobody has gone away from the
theatre the better for hearing a great deal of cursing and swearing.

DE LACY EVANS. How do you reconcile the opinion that you have
just given with your making of those terms, such as Damme or any
of those small oaths which you say are immoral and improper, to say
nothing of their vulgarity, in some of your own composition which
have met with great success on the stage?

COLMAN. If I had been the Examiner I should have scratched them
out, and would do so now; I was in a different position at that time,
I was a careless immoral author, I am now the Examiner of Plays. I
did my business as an author at that time, and I do my business as
an Examiner now.

RUSSELL. Do you suppose that those plays of yours which were so
pleasing to the public...

EVANS [*interrupting*] . . . and are acted still with great success, and from
which you have not the power of erasing those small oaths . . .

RUSSELL. Do you suppose that those plays of yours have done much
mischief to the morals of the town?

COLMAN. They have certainly done no good, and I am sorry I inserted
the oaths. As a moral man, one gets a little wiser as one goes on, and
I should be very happy to relieve my mind from the recollection of
having written those oaths.

*Pause*

BULWER [*after a mild gesture of frustration*]. Did you regret being the
author of *John Bull?*

COLMAN. No, that is a different thing: I might not be sorry to have
made a good pudding, but if there are any bad plums in it, I should
be glad to have them out.

BULWER. But do you not think that what you call the bad plums
contributed to the success of the piece?

COLMAN. No, certainly not; it is from habit, the actors think it harnesses the thing stronger if they use 'damme' for which they are liable 40 shillings penalty. I will give you an instance in one of my own plays. Habit has made it forcible and strong to say 'damme', but if 'hang me' were generally adopted, it would not be as strong; that is perfectly harmless to me, though not to the person hanged, and it would be quite as forcible to the audience. Sir Stephen Rochdale, in *John Bull*, says, 'Damme me, if it isn't the brazier!' Now, putting a gentleman in that position is wrong; [*De Lacey looks as if he might beg to differ*] in the first instance, morally so; if he happened to make a mistake, and it was not the brazier, he would be damned. Now, if he said, 'Hang me, if it wasn't the brazier!' would not that do as well? [*Momentary pause—Waithman might want to support Colman, Bulwer might be yawning, Russell might be wondering where it's all leading* . . .]

WAITHMAN. In that play also you talk of Eve, there is a very good joke about Eve; one of the characters has no more idea of something, than Eve had of pin-money. Do you call that improper?

COLMAN. Yes, that had better be omitted.

WAITHMAN. But the audience is always struck with that?

COLMAN. Yes; but I think all allusions to the Scriptures had better be avoided; and recollect [*turning his attention to addressing Bulwer and Duncombe*] I only recommend to the management to leave it out: if they do not choose to leave it out I say nothing further about it. My directions to them, if directions they can be called, begin, 'Please to omit the following underlined passages', and they do omit them, or not as they please.

*Pause*

BULWER [*after a nod to Duncombe*]. On the question of fees?

COLMAN. Yes. [*Rattled*] I believe questions have been asked relative to fees . . . questions which may cast doubt on my office?

BULWER. Yes?

COLMAN. Yes.

DUNCOMBE [*diplomatically*]. You will have the goodness to answer questions on the matter?

COLMAN. Certainly.

*Pause*

BULWER. On the manager of a theatre receiving back the play or the piece that has been submitted to your inspection, you compel him to pay two guineas?

COLMAN. I do not compel him, I demand it as a prescriptive claim.

BULWER. Under what authority do you exact the two guineas?

COLMAN. A fee of two guineas for each licence has been paid time out
of mind to the Examiner, who is regularly and legally sworn into
office, and his appointment is signed and sealed by the Lord Chamberlain; so that the fees paid to Examiners by authors are very mate-
rially less in the present day than they were in former times,
according to the comparative value of the pound at different periods.

BULWER. But what proof have you that previous Examiners of Plays
received two guineas for their inspection?

COLMAN. I cannot conjure the dead from their graves, but I believe it
is perfectly well understood from tradition that it has been so since
the Act of 1737.

BULWER. Suppose a poor author should bring you a very excellent
work, and he should represent that this fee was more than he could
conveniently pay?

COLMAN. I hope I should not be deficient in charitable feelings on
such an occasion, besides my *esprit de corps* is in favour of dramatists.

BULWER. But you certainly would not in such a case impede the grant-
ing of a licence on account of not receiving the fee?

COLMAN. No, surely not; God forbid that I should!

BULWER. Yes?

COLMAN. Certainly. If I met with any person to whom two guineas
was an object, I should certainly withhold the claim, but in general
I ought to have my fees. I think Dr Johnson did mention somewhere
in his life of Addison, that Addison was very scrupulous as to his fees;
he would not give them up to his friends, and the reason was that
two guineas were very little to them individually but made a great
difference to him in the aggregate.

BULWER. What kind of difference do they make in your case? [*Colman
is confused for a moment*] How much do you earn annually from your
role as Examiner?

COLMAN. Between 300 and 400 pounds a year.

BULWER. Yes?

COLMAN. Yes.

*Pause*

RUSSELL. Could we return to the question of that which the Lord
Chamberlain's office is empowered to license or to prohibit? For
instance, are lectures in astronomy subject to your examination?

COLMAN. I think that every thing on the stage ought to be. The Duke of Montrose thought so, and astronomical lectures were licensed at that time.

RUSSELL. Have they been licensed since?

COLMAN. I do not believe that anybody has been talking to us about the stars lately.

RUSSELL. Are Mr Charles Mathew's entertainments licensed at the Adelphi?

COLMAN. Yes, certainly. The last, the Monopolylogue, as he calls it, is a farce, or, I beg your pardon, a comedy. It is a regular dramatic piece, but he acts all the characters himself.

RUSSELL. That is licensed?

COLMAN. Yes.

RUSSELL [*dogged*]. It is submitted to your examination?

COLMAN. Yes.

RUSSELL. Are oratorios licensed?

COLMAN. Yes, in the Duke of Montrose's time they were, and I think they ought to be now, but *not* for the sake of the fees.

RUSSELL. Why then?

COLMAN. Because I think they may be immoral things.

RUSSELL [*bemused*]. Immoral oratorios?

COLMAN. Yes; it sounds like a contradiction, but it is so. If you read the *Biographia Dramatica*, you will find there is one mentioned as scandalously immoral.

RUSSELL. Did not Mr Hawes resist the Lord Chamberlain recently in the case of an oratorio?

COLMAN [*blushing*]. Yes; a licence was granted to him but he would not pay for it, and he placarded me in his advertisements.

RUSSELL. Was the licence refused or granted?

COLMAN [*rattled*]. The licence was granted, and he would not pay the fee, but he placarded me and blackguarded me, and that set me, at the five minutes' leisure I had, to calculating the amount. He said if the precedent were admitted, God knows what expense future oratorio-makers and undertakers would be subjected to . . . but, by my calculation, I believe it amounted to no more than four guineas in two or three years.

RUSSELL. Did you prohibit him playing it?

COLMAN. No, he played it and chuckled at his triumph, and sung and roared away. His oratorio went on, he had his licence and I had not my two guineas.

RUSSELL. Was the performance withdrawn?

COLMAN. No, it took place.

BULWER. Then it appears that dramatic performances do take place without paying the fees?

COLMAN. Highway robberies do take place, but they are contrary to the law.

BULWER. Where is the law for your taking fees? Do you find it in the Act of Parliament? [*dogged*] Is it a written law?

COLMAN. No; they are the fees prescriptively claimed for ninety-five years.

*Pause*

RUSSELL [*deliberate and dogged reiteration of his previous question*]. Could we return to the question of that which the Lord Chamberlain's office is empowered to license or to prohibit? Is it your opinion that no play can be acted without having previously received the licence of the Lord Chamberlain?

COLMAN. Yes. [*Pause*] But as to those theatres over the water, on the other side of the Thames, they are perfectly lawless; they only act under the London magistrates' licence, which is to license music and dancing; for the legislature when it passed the Act of 1737, did not contemplate that the town of London would get so overgrown as it is. They never thought of those people that have since struck up, who get the common magistrate's licence for music and dancing, and abuse it to the extent you have seen.

WAITHMAN. Do they bring pieces to you to be licensed, or not?

COLMAN. No; they set us at defiance; they are outlawed, or at least lawless.

WAITHMAN. Then you have no remedy?

COLMAN. There is a remedy, and I believe they have tried it by informing, but the expense is so great that those whom it concerns do not like to inform any further. As I have enough to do as an Examiner, I do not choose to turn common informer.

WAITHMAN. What is the penalty?

COLMAN. The penalty, if you act anything unlicensed in a regular theatre is very heavy indeed, fifty pounds for each time the offence is repeated, upon every person engaged in it, and a forfeiture of the grant by which they have the right of opening the theatre.

*Pause*

EARL OF BELFAST [*referring to his copy of Colman's paper*]. You say, in the paper which you have given in, that a piece was brought forward at Paris, in which incest, adultery, murder, and parricide formed the groundwork; do you consider you would be perfectly justified in refusing to license a piece in which those crimes were introduced?

COLMAN. No; not precisely that; let me see how the plot thickens. I should not refuse to license the murders of Richard III and so on, but when it comes to such things as human nature and morality shudder at and revolt against . . .

BELFAST. Does not human nature and morality shudder at Macbeth, if we can suppose morality to shudder?

COLMAN. Yes; but it is a matter of history.

BELFAST. Do you mean to say in those cases you would only withhold the licence to those plays which seem to have justified such acts, or do you mean from the mere introduction of the thing?

COLMAN [*with stupendous confidence*]. Exactly.

BELFAST. Which?

COLMAN. Things that seem to any reflecting or dispassionate mind to really justify murder.

BELFAST. Either to justify it or encourage it?

COLMAN. Yes. We have murders upon the modern stage more frequently than the ancients had.

BELFAST. You mention incest, murder, adultery, parricide, but are not those crimes the results of passions upon which the interest of great dramatic performance is founded?

COLMAN. Yes; in some instances.

BELFAST. Would you wholly exclude them?

COLMAN. No; nor are they excluded in general. It is only where there is something so shocking as to justify exclusion.

*Pause*

RUSSELL. Have you any idea of what you should consider *politically* wrong?

COLMAN. Yes, certainly; anything that may be so allusive to the times as to be applied to the existing moment, and which is likely to be inflammatory.

RUSSELL. You would think under a Tory administration, anything against the Tories would be wrong, and under a Whig administration, anything against the Whigs?

COLMAN. I should say to the manager, 'I do not pretend to interfere, but you had better not allow it for the sake of your theatre or you will have a row in your theatre.' I heard but the other day that the word reform was mentioned, and I understand there was a hubbub.

DE LACY EVANS  [*roused*]. Where was that?

COLMAN. At all the theatres.

EVANS. Hm.

RUSSELL. In the exercise of your censorship at the present moment, if the word reform should occur, you would strike it out?

COLMAN. No; I should say, 'I think you had better omit it; I advise you to do so for your own sakes, or you will have a hubbub.'

BULWER. There was a play of Charles the First that you refused to license?

COLMAN. Yes.

BULWER. Authored by Miss Mitford?

COLMAN. Yes.

BULWER. Why did you refuse to license that?

COLMAN. Because it amounted to everything but cutting off the King's head upon the stage.

BULWER. So does *Julius Caesar*?

COLMAN. Yes; but not in that way. If you take the trouble of reading the two plays, you would see the difference. [*Bulwer raises an eyebrow at the suggestion that he might not take the trouble*] There is a discretionary power in the Lord Chamberlain.

BULWER. Is it all a matter of discretion or caprice?

COLMAN. It is the discretion of the Lord Chamberlain.

BULWER. Or a caprice?

COLMAN. You call it so.

*Pause*

DUNCOMBE. The committee will only trouble you with two further questions. First, could you tell the committee whether or not the Lord Chamberlain has the power to remove you from your office of Examiner?

COLMAN. I do not know how far the Lord Chamberlain's power extends, but it has always been considered the next thing to a patent place; it is not a patent place certainly.

DUNCOMBE. Finally, is your appointment for life or at will?

COLMAN. I understand for life, unless I misbehave myself.

DUNCOMBE. . . . . although as it turned out, George Colman's life was not destined to last much longer. He was already sick when the Select Committee met, and he died shortly afterwards, in 1836. [*They each leave the stage in turn*] [*Taking responsibility for Mahon*] Lord Viscount Mahon went on to help found the British Museum and National Gallery; he died in 1875.

WAITHMAN. Mr Alderman Waithman, like Colman, barely survived the Select Committee, dying a year later.

DE LACY EVANS. Colonel De Lacy Evans went on to have a long and distinguished military career, and was promoted to Major General; he fought and was wounded in the Crimea, but survived the battle-field to die after retirement in 1870.

RUSSELL. Lord John Russell went on, in the 1840s, to become Home Secretary and then Prime Minister, remaining one of the country's leading reformers; he lived until he was 86.

BELFAST. The Earl of Belfast went on to inherit the title of the Marquis of Donegal, became Vice-Chamberlain of the royal house-hold, was Captain of the Yeomen of the Guard from 1848 to 1852, and completed his distinguished career as Lord Lieutenant of County Antrim.

DUNCOMBE [*but he does not leave*]. Mr Thomas Slingsby Duncombe went on to plead the cause of imprisoned Chartists and to play a part in the unification of Italy, honoured by the Italians for his services to them; he died in 1861.

BULWER. Mr Edward Bulwer-Lytton whilst never aspiring, as far as history tells, to become an Examiner to the Lord Chamberlain himself, did, before changing his political allegiance from Whig to Tory [*slightly nervous cough*], become both a prominent legislator and a leading playwright.

DUNCOMBE. Bulwer's radical hopes for the Select Committee were not fully realized until 1843, when a further piece of legislation broke the monopoly system of the patent theatres, allowing the serious drama to be performed freely beyond Covent Garden, Drury Lane and the Haymarket. However, it was not until the second half of the *twentieth* century, that the control of the Lord Chamberlain's office over censorship was finally lifted.

# Bibliography

## PLAYS

Baillie, Joanna, *A series of plays in which it is attempted to delineate the stronger passions of the mind. Each passion being the subject of a tragedy and a comedy* (Cadell and Davies, London, 1798).

Behn, Aphra, *Oroonoko, or The History of the Royal Slave*, ed. K. A. Sey (Ghana Publishing Corporation, Tema, Ghana, 1977).

Bickerstaff, Isaac, *The Padlock* (Garrick's Head, London, 1768).

Buckstone, J. B., *The Forgery! or the Reading of the Will*, British Museum Manuscripts, additional manuscipts 42915, folios 1–59, 1832.

—— *Luke the Labourer* (Cumberland, London, 1826).

Burney, Frances, *The Complete Plays of Frances Burney* (Pickering, London, 1995).

Colman the Younger, George, *Inkle and Yarico* (Robinson, London, 1787).

—— *John Bull; or, The Englishman's Fireside* (Longman, London, 1806).

Inchbald, Mrs Elizabeth, *Every one has his fault* (Wogan, Dublin, 1793).

—— *Wives as they were, and maids as they are* (Robinson, London, 1797).

—— *To marry, or not to marry* (Longman, London, 1805).

Jerrold, Douglas, *The Rent Day* (Chapple, London, 1832).

—— *The Factory Girl* (British Museum, Lord Chamberlain's Office, 42,918, 1832) folios 410 to 791.

McReady, William, *The Irishman in London; or, the happy African* (Longman, London, 1793).

Mitford, Mary Russell, *The Dramatic Works of Mary Russell Mitford* (Hurst and Blackett, London, 1854).

Moncrieff, W. T., *Reform; or, John Bull Triumphant* (Richardson, London, 1831).

Morton, Thomas, *Speed the Plough* (Longman, London, 1800).

—— *Education* (Longman, London, 1813).

—— *The Slave; a Musical Drama* (Miller, London, 1816).

Murrey, W. H., *Obi; Or, Three-Fingered Jack* (Dicks, London, 1800).

Robinson, Mary, *The Sicilian Lover* (Hookham and Carpenter, London, 1796).

Southerne, Thomas, *Oroonoko* (Wenham, London, 1778); adapted from the novel by Aphra Behn.

Walker, John, *The Factory Lad* (1832; Dent, London, 1976).

## AUTOBIOGRAPHICAL WRITINGS

Clare, John, *John Clare's Autobiographical Writings*, ed. Eric Robinson (Oxford University Press, Oxford and New York, 1983).

Equiano, Olaudah, *The Interesting Narrative of the Life of Olaudah Equiano or Gustavus Vassa, The African* (printed for and sold by the author, Union Street, Middlesex Hospital, 1789; 1969 and 1989 editions, ed. Paul Edwards (Dawsons, London); 1995 edition, ed. Vincent Carretta (Penguin, Harmondsworth).

Hardy, Thomas, *Memoir, in Testaments of Radicalism*, ed. David Vincent (Europa Publications, London, 1997).

Macready, William, *The Diaries of William Charles Macready 1833–1851* (Chapman and Hall, London, 1912).

Prince, Mary, *The history of Mary Prince, A West Indian Slave* (Westley and Davids, London, 1831).

Robinson, Mary Darby, *Memoirs of the late Mrs Robinson* (Hunt and Clarke, London, 1826).

—— *Perdita: The Memoirs of Mary Robinson*, ed. M. J. Levy (Peter Owen, London and Chester Springs, 1994).

Somerville, Mary, *Personal Recollections, from early life to old age, with selections from her correspondence by her daughter, Martha Somerville* (Murray, London, 1873).

Wedderburn, Robert, *Robert Wedderburn, The Horrors of Slavery and Other Writings*, ed. Iain McCalman (Edinburgh University Press, Edinburgh, 1991).

Whiteley, Henry, *Three months in Jamaica in 1832* (Hatchard, London, 1833).

Wordsworth, William, *Preface to the Lyrical Ballads* (1800 and 1802; Methuen, London, 1963).

—— *The Prelude, or Growth of a Poet's Mind* (1805; Oxford University Press, Oxford, 1970).

## THEATRE HISTORY, POLITICAL HISTORY, AND OTHER

Archer, William, and Lowe, Robert W. (eds.), *Dramatic Essays* (Scott, London, 1895).

Baer, Marc, *Theatre and Disorder in Late Georgian London* (Clarendon Press, Oxford, 1992).

Bagster-Collins, Jeremy F. *George Colman the Younger (1762–1836)* (Bentley, London, 1946).

Bailey, Peter, *Leisure and Class in Victorian England: Rational Recreation and the Quest for Control* (Routledge, London and University of Toronto, 1978).

Barrell, John, *The Dark Side of the Landscape: The Rural Poor in English Painting 1730–1840* (Cambridge University Press, Cambridge, 1980).

—— The Political Theory of Painting from Reynolds to Hazlitt (Yale University Press, New Haven, 1986).

Bender, Thomas (ed.), *The Antislavery Debate: Capitalism and Abolitionism as a Problem in Historical Interpretation* (University of California Press, Berkeley, Los Angeles, and Oxford, 1992).

Bentley, Eric (ed.) *The Theory of the Modern Stage* (Penguin, Harmondsworth, 1968).

Bermingham, Ann, *Landscape and Ideology: The English Rustic Tradition, 1740–1860* (Thames and Hudson, London, 1987).

Blackburn, Robin, *The Overthrow of Colonial Slavery, 1776–1848* (Verso, London and New York, 1988).

Blakemore, Steven, *Burke and the Fall of Language* (University Press of New England, Hanover, NH, and London, 1988).

Bolt, Christine, *Victorian Attitudes to Race* (Routledge, London, 1971).

Booth, Michael R., *English Melodrama* (Jenkins, London, 1965).

Boulton, J. T., *The Language of Politics in the Age of Wilkes and Burke* (Routledge and Kegan Paul, London, 1963).

Bradby, David, James, Louis, and Sharratt, Bernard (eds.) *Performance and Politics in Popular Drama* (Cambridge University Press, 1980).

Brathwaite, Edward Kamau, *The Development of Creole Society in Jamaica 1770–1820* (Clarendon Press, Oxford, 1971).

Bratton, J. S., *Acts of Supremacy: The British Empire and the Stage, 1790–1930* (Manchester University Press, Manchester, 1991).

Brewer, John, *The Pleasures of the Imagination: English Culture in the Eighteenth Century* (HarperCollins, London, 1997).

*British Labour Struggles, Contemporary Pamphlets, 1727–1850* (Arno Press, New York, 1972).

Bulwer-Lytton, Edward, *England and the English*, ed. Standish Meacham (University of Chicago Press, 1970).

Burke, Edmund, *Reflections on the Revolution in France* (Dodsley, London, 1790).

Burroughs, Catherine B., *Closet Stages: Joanna Baillie and the Theater Theory of British Romantic Women Writers* (University of Pennsylvania, Philadelphia, 1997).

Carlson, Julie A. *In the Theatre of Romanticism: Coleridge, Nationalism, Women* (Cambridge University Press, Cambridge, 1994).

Centre for Contemporary Cultural Studies, *Making Histories, Studies in History-Writing and Politics* (Hutchinson, London, 1982).

Clarke, John, Critcher, Chas, and Johnson, Richard (eds.), *Working Class Culture* (Hutchinson, London, 1979).

Colley, Linda, Britons, *Forging the Nation 1707–1837* (Yale University Press, New Haven and London, 1992).

Conger, Syndy McMillen, *Mary Wollstonecraft and the Language of Sensibility* (Fairleigh Dickinson University Press, London and Toronto, 1994).

Conolly, L. W., *The Censorship of English Drama 1737–1824* (Huntingdon Library, San Marino, Calif., 1976).

Costanzo, Angelo, *Surprizing Narrative: Olaudah Equiano and the Beginnings of Black Autobiography* (Greenwood Press, New York and London, 1987).

Crosby, Christina, *The Ends of History* (Routledge, New York and London, 1991).

Cunningham, Alan, *The life of Sir David Wilkie* (Murray, London, 1843).

Davis, Tracy C., *Actresses as Working Women: Their Social Identity in Victorian Culture* (Routledge, London, 1991).

De Bolla, Peter, *The Discourse of the Sublime* (Blackwell, Oxford, 1989).

Diderot, D., *Diderot's Writings on the Theatre*, ed. F. C. Green (Cambridge University Press, Cambridge, 1936).

Donkin, Ellen, *Getting into the Act:Women Playwrights in London 1776–1829* (Routledge, London and New York, 1995).

Donohue, Joseph, *Theatre in the Age of Kean* (Blackwell, Oxford, 1975).

Drescher, Seymour, *Capitalism and Antislavery: British Mobilization in Comparative Perspective* (Macmillan, London, 1986).

Ellis, F., *Sentimental Comedy: Theory and Practice* (Cambridge University Press, Cambridge 1991).

Evans, Eric J., *Britain Before the Reform Act* (Longman, London and New York, 1989).

Ferguson, Moira, *Subject to Others* (Routledge, London and New York, 1992).

Findlater, Richard, *A Review of Theatrical Censorship in Britain* (Macgibbon and Kee, London and Letchworth, 1967).

Fladeland, Betty, *Abolitionists and Working-Class Problems in the Age of Industrialization* (Louisiana State University Press, Baton Rouge, La., 1984).

Foreman, Amanda, *Georgiana, Duchess of Devonshire* (HarperCollins, London, 1998).

Fowell, F. and Palmer, F., *Censorship in England* (London, 1913).

Franklin, Caroline, *Mary Robinson, the Poetical Works* (Routledge, London, 1996).

Frow, Ruth and Edmund (eds.), *Political Women 1800–1850* (Pluto, London, 1989).

Furniss, Tom, *Edmund Burke's Aesthetic Ideology: Language, Gender, and Political Economy in Revolution* (Cambridge University Press, Cambridge, 1993).

Furst, Lilian R., and Skrine, Peter N., *Naturalism* (Methuen, London, 1971).

Fussell, G. E., *Landscape Painting and the Agricultural Revolution* (Pinter Press, London, 1984).

Hadley, Elaine, *Melodramatic Tactics: Theatricalized Dissent in the English Marketplace, 1800–1885* (Stanford University Press, Calif., 1995).

Hartog, Willie G., *Guilbert de Pixérécourt* (Honoré Champion, Paris, 1913).

Hays, Michael, and Nikolopoulou, Anastasia, *Melodrama: The Cultural Emergence of a Genre* (Macmillan, London, 1996).

Heaton, Mrs Charles, *The great works of Sir David Wilkie* (Bell, London and Cambridge, 1868).

Hemingway, Andrew, and Vaughan, William (eds.), *Art in Bourgeois Society* (Cambridge University Press, Cambridge, 1998).

Hilton, Boyd, *The Age of Atonement: The Influence of Evangelicalism on Social and Economic Thought, 1795–1865* (Clarendon Press, Oxford, 1988).

Hindson, Paul, and Gray, Tim, *Burke's Dramatic Theory of Politics* (Avebury, Aldershot, 1988).

Hobsbawm, E. J., and Rudé, George, *Captain Swing* (Pimlico, London, 1993).

hooks, bell, *Yearning, Race, Gender, and Cultural Politics* (Turnaround, London, 1991).

—— *Talking Back: Thinking Feminist, Thinking Black* (Sheba, London, 1989).

Hulme, Peter, and Whitehead, Neil L. (eds.), *Wild Majesty: Encounters with Caribs from Columbus to the Present Day* (Clarendon Press, Oxford, 1992).

Hunt, Leigh, *Selected Dramatic Criticism*, ed. Lawrence H. Houtchens and Carolyn W. Houtchens (Columbia University Press, New York, 1949).

Hunt, Lynn, *Eroticism and the Body Politic* (Johns Hopkins University Press, Baltimore, 1990).

Jerrold, W. Blanchard, *The work of Douglas Jerrold* (Bradbury and Evans, London, 1863).

Jones, Chris, *Radical Sensibility: Literature and Ideas in the 1790s* (Routledge, London, 1993).

Kaye, Harvey J., and McClelland, Keith, (eds.), *E. P. Thompson, Critical Perspectives* (Polity Press, Cambridge, 1990).

Kelly, Linda, *The Kemble Era: John Philip Kemble, Sarah Siddons, and the London Stage* (Random House, New York, 1980).

Kinnaird, J., *William Hazlitt* (Columbia University Press, New York, 1978).

Klonk, Charlotte, *Science and the Perception of Nature: British Landscape Art in the Late Eighteenth and Early Nineteenth Centuries* (Yale University Press, New Haven and London, 1996).

Kruger, Loren, *The National Stage, Theatre and Cultural Legitimation: in England, France, and America* (University of Chicago Press, Chicago, 1992).

McCann, Gerard, *Theory and History: The Political Thought of E. P. Thompson* (Ashgate, Aldershot, 1997).

McConachie, Bruce A., *Melodramatic Formations* (University of Iowa, Ames, Ia., 1992).

Marshall, David, *The Figure of Theater* (Columbia University Press, New York, 1986).

—— *The Surprising Effects of Sympathy: Marivaux, Diderot, Rousseau and Mary Shelley* (University of Chicago Press, Chicago, 1988).

Marshall, Herbert, and Stock, Mildred, *Ira Aldridge—The Negro Tragedian* (Rockliff, London, 1958).

Mason, Jeffrey D., *Melodrama and the Myth of America* (Indiana University Press, Bloomington, 1993).

Mayhew, Henry, *The Morning Chronicle Survey of Labour and the Poor* (1850; Caliban Books, Sussex, 1981).

Meisel, Martin, *Realizations: Narrative, Pictorial and Theatrical Arts in Nineteenth-Century England* (Princeton University Press, Princeton, 1983).

Midgley, Clare, *Women Against Slavery* (Routledge, London and New York, 1992).

Moraga, Cherrie, and Anzaldua, Gloria (eds.), *This Bridge Called My Back* (Kitchen Table: Women of Color Press, New York, 1981).

Mullan, John, *Sentiment and Sociability: The Language of Feeling in the Eighteenth Century* (Clarendon Press, Oxford, 1988).

Murphy, Arthur, *The Life of David Garrick* (1801), cited in *The Georgian Playhouse*, catalogue of the exhibition devised by Iain Mackintosh and Geoffrey Ashton, Hayward Gallery, London, 1975.

Ngugi Wa Thiong'o, *Moving the Centre: The Struggle for Cultural Freedoms* (James Currey, London, East African Educational Publishers, Nairobi, Heinemann Educational Books, Portsmouth, NH, 1993).

Nicoll, Allardyce, *A History of English Drama, 1660–1900*, 6 vols. (Cambridge University Press, Cambridge, 1952).

Nicholson, Watson, *The Struggle for a Free Stage in London* (Constable, London, 1906).

O'Gorman, Frank, *The Long Eighteenth Century* (Arnold, London and New York, 1997).

Oldfield, J. R., *Popular Politics and British Anti-Slavery: The Mobilisation of Public Opinion against the Slave Trade 1787–1801* (Manchester University Press, Manchester, 1995).

Orr, Clarissa Campbell (ed.), *Wollstonecraft's Daughters* (Manchester University Press, 1996).

O'Toole, Fintan, *A Traitor's Kiss: The Life of Richard Brinsley Sheridan* (Granta, London, 1997).

Paine, Thomas, *The Rights of Man* (Johnson, London, 1791).

Palmer, Bryan D., *E. P. Thompson: Objections and Oppositions* (Verso, London, 1994).

Pascoe, Judith, *Romantic Theatricality: Gender, Poetry and Spectatorship* (Cornell University Press, Ithaca, NY, and London, 1997).

Plasa, Carl, and Ring, Betty, *The Discourse of Slavery* (Routledge, London, 1994).

Porter, Roy, and Teich, Mikulas, (eds.), *The Enlightenment in National Context* (Cambridge University Press, Cambridge, 1981).

Potkay, Adam, and Burr, Sandra, (eds.), *Black Atlantic Writers of the Eighteenth Century* (Macmillan, Basingstoke, 1995).

Price, Lawrence Marsden, *Inkle and Yarico Album* (University of California Press, Berkeley, 1937).

Reinelt, Janelle G., and Roach, Joseph R., *Critical Theory and Performance* (University of Michigan Press, Ann Arbor, 1992).

Rendall, Jane (ed.), *Equal or Different: Women's Politics 1800–1914* (Blackwell, Oxford, 1987).

Richards, Kenneth, and Thomson, Peter (eds.), *Nineteenth Century British Theatre* (Methuen, London, 1971).

Russell, Gillian, *The Theatres of War: Performance, Politics, and Society 1793–1815* (Clarendon Press, Oxford, 1995).

Sandiford, Keith A., *Measuring the Moment: Strategies of Protest in Eighteenth-Century Afro-English Writing* (Susquehanna University Press, Selinsgrove, Pa., 1988).

*Spectator*, for Steele's entry about the *Inkle and Yarico* story (1711; Routledge, London, 1888).

Stedman, John Gabriel, *Narrative of a Five Years' Expedition against the Revolted Negroes of Surinam*, ed. Richard and Sally Price (1790; John Hopkins University Press, Baltimore, 1988).

Stephens, John Russell, *The Censorship of English Drama 1824–1901* (Cambridge University Press, Cambridge, 1980).

Stevenson, Nick, *Culture, Ideology and Socialism: Raymond Williams and E. P. Thompson* (Avebury, Aldershot, 1995).

Swindells, Julia, *The Uses of Autobiography* (Taylor & Francis, London, 1995).

—— and Jardine, Lisa, *What's Left? Women in Culture and the Labour Movement* (Routledge, London, 1990).

Taylor, Barbara, *Eve and the New Jerusalem: Socialism and Feminism in the Nineteenth Century* (Virago, London, 1983).

Thompson, E. P., *The Making of the English Working Class* (Penguin, Harmondsworth, 1963).

—— *Whigs and Hunters: The Origin of the Black Act* (Allen Lane, London, 1975).

—— *Customs in Common* (Merlin Press, London, 1991).

Thompson, William, and Wheeler, Anna, *Appeal of One Half the Human Race, Women, Against the Pretensions of the Other Half, Men, To Retain Them is*

*Political, and Thence in Civil and Domestic, Slavery*, ed. Michael Foot and Mary Mulvey Roberts (1825; Thoemmes Press, London, 1994).

Uphaus, Robert W., *William Hazlitt* (Twayne Publishing, Boston, 1985).

Wahrman, Dror, *Imagining the Middle Class: The Political Representation of Class in Britain, 1780–1840* (Cambridge University Press, Cambridge, 1995).

Waites, Bernard, Bennett, Tony, and Martin, Graham (eds.), *Popular Culture: Past and Present* (Open University, Croom Helm, London, 1982).

Walker, Alice, *Living by the Word: Selected Writings 1973–1987* (The Women's Press, London, 1988).

Walvin, James, *An African's Life: The Life and Times of Olaudah Equiano, 1745–1797* (Cassell, London, 1998).

West, Shearer, *The Image of the Actor: Verbal and Visual Representation in the Age of Garrick and Kemble* (Pinter Publishers, London, 1991).

Williams, Raymond, *Drama from Ibsen to Brecht* (1952; Penguin, Harmondsworth, 1976).

—— *Culture and Society 1780–1950* (Penguin, Harmondsworth 1958).

—— *The Long Revolution* (Chatto & Windus, London, 1961).

Wilson, Ellen Gibson, *Thomas Clarkson* (William Sessions, York, 1989).

Wilson, Kathleen, *The Sense of the People: Politics, Culture and Imperialism in England, 1715–1785* (Cambridge University Press, Cambridge, 1995).

Wollstonecraft, Mary, *The Female Reader* (Johnson, London, 1789).

—— *A Vindication of the Rights of Men* (Johnson, London, 1790).

—— *An Historical and Moral View of the Origin and Progress of the French Revolution* (1794), in *The Works of Mary Wollstonecraft*, ed. Janet Todd and Marilyn Butler (Pickering, London, 1989).

—— *The Wrongs of Woman* (1798; Oxford University Press, Oxford, 1976).

Zerilli, Linda, *Signifying Woman: Culture and Chaos in Rousseau, Burke, and Mill* (Cornell University Press, Ithaca, NY, 1994).

## REPORTS AND CORRESPONDENCE

Report from the Select Committee on Dramatic Literature in *Reports from the Committees*, 1831-2, vol. vii, 1832 (House of Commons, London).

*Parliamentary Reports of Special Assistant Poor Law Commisioners on the Employment of Women and Children in Agriculture* (Hansard, London, 1843).

George Colman to the Duke of Montrose, 29 September, 1825, British Library Add MS 42, 873, vol. ix.

Richard Oastler to the Duke of Wellington, eight letters in *Richard Oastler, King of Factory Children* (Cochrane, London, 1972).

Thomas Macaulay to Thomas Flower Ellis, 30 March, 1831. http://www.spartacus.schoolnet.co.uk/PRI832.htm

# Index